SHADOW WARRIOR

血
と
汗
と

SHADOW WARRIOR

Secrets of Invisibility, Mind Reading, and Thought Control

Jōtarō

CITADEL PRESS
Kensington Publishing Corp.
www.kensingtonbooks.com

CITADEL PRESS BOOKS are published by

Kensington Publishing Corp.
119 West 40th Street
New York, NY 10018

First printing: November 2009

10 9 8 7 6 5 4 3 2 1

Printed in the United States of America

Library of Congress Control Number: 2009930445

ISBN-13: 978-0-8065-3124-3
ISBN-10: 0-8065-3124-X

For S~

血と汗と血と汗と血と汗と血と汗と血と汗と血と汗と血と汗と血と汗と血と汗と

Prologue

Here is a man.

He stands motionless on the curb of a road.

It is a scene like any of a thousand others, in any of a thousand other cities, on any of a thousand other days.

On this particular occasion, however, the entire course of human history may hang in the balance. Perhaps a closer look is warranted.

It is evening. The city's new electric lighting system has not yet been perfected. A light mist hangs in the air, making halos around the streetlamps. Visibility is poor. It is the end of the workweek, so the road, or more accurately, the avenue, as well as the sidewalks flanking it, is even busier than usual. It is winter. People are dressed in overcoats and moving briskly. Surfaces are slippery.

The city is gray. So is the man. One must look closely to pick him out against this background. His appearance is unremarkable. He might be in his mid-fifties; he stands about five feet eight; he is somewhat pale and seems to be gaining in girth what he is losing in hair. His face is strong, but not striking. As is so often the case, its strength resides principally in the eyes. He is clean-shaven, and, judging from his laugh lines, of generally good humor, although at this particular moment his wide brow is furrowed in indecision.

Our concerned man wears a dark, heavy overcoat with a thick lining. It is expensive, but tasteful and unobtrusive. Above its lapels a bowtie can be seen, perched slightly askew between the wings of a freshly starched collar. Below, the cuffs of well-tailored suit trousers are evident; below them, a pair of old but well-polished, lace-up dress shoes. It is not quite in keeping with the style of the day in this place, but it is unmistakably the uniform of a gentleman. On a day like today, such a man might very well be wearing overshoes—but this man is not.

The concerned gentleman stands slightly stooped, and yet something about his bearing suggests he is no stranger to the parade square. His gaze snaps from side to side, with mild annoyance, as if seeking some elusive target. He seems slightly embarrassed to be obstructing this little corner of the sidewalk and takes pains to be as inconspicuous as possible. One hand pats a pocket absently, while the other hangs at his side, fingertips rubbing together as if rolling a cigar.

The concerned gentleman soldier, then, is muttering to himself. "God's teeth," he curses under his breath.

It is a British expression. This may explain a great many things, including the slight sartorial incongruity, the absence of galoshes, and the look of consternation. He is a visitor to the city of New York, and has, most likely, lost his way. He is perhaps late for a formal dinner appointment. His left hand is searching yet again for the forgotten

directions. His eyes are sweeping from street to street, seeking some familiar landmark or sign. The other hand wishes it had a cigar to calm its owner's nerves. At length, there is a flash of recognition.

The British gentleman soldier is accustomed to doing things by the numbers. He therefore looks to his right, not his left, before crossing. He is also used to the streets of London where traffic signals have not yet been introduced, for it is December 1931. Thus, the glowing red light at the intersection means nothing to him. Impatiently, he steps into the middle of Fifth Avenue. What happens next? Will there be an accident? Will he survive? We shall see. Of somewhat greater impact in the grand scheme of things, however, is the question of whether it will matter. In this regard, the answer is perhaps. And for present purposes, a "maybe" is enough, for we are now entering the realm of the butterfly.

The idea of chaos is hardly new. Perhaps the earliest use of the term was in Hesiod's *Theogeny* in seventh century B.C. To the ancient Greeks, chaos and cosmos were regarded as the fundamental and interdependent aspects of existence.[1] Like many terms, its meaning has been modified slightly over the centuries to suit particular purposes. Latterly, the word has been used to define a mathematical theory popularized by the French scientist Henri Poincaré, whose research into the stability of the solar system during the nineteenth century set the world of Newtonian physics on its ear. To many, Poincaré is considered the father of chaos theory.

During the 1960s, an American meteorologist named Edward Lorenz was working at MIT to develop a computerized model of a

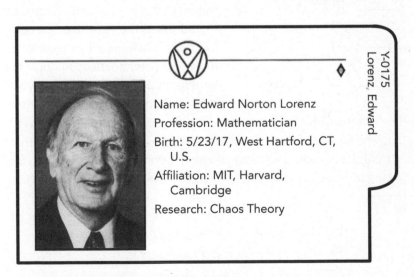

Name: Edward Norton Lorenz
Profession: Mathematician
Birth: 5/23/17, West Hartford, CT, U.S.
Affiliation: MIT, Harvard, Cambridge
Research: Chaos Theory

Y-0175
Lorenz, Edward

1. The Greek idea is similar but not quite as symmetrical as the Chinese concept of yin and yang.

simplified weather system. To save time on one particular occasion, he decided to start the program from the midpoint by entering previously obtained data rather than waiting for his relatively slow computer to calculate its way to the same point. Within an hour, the results had begun to deviate wildly from those produced in earlier iterations predicated on the same initial conditions. Lorenz pondered the problem and eventually realized that the numbers he had entered manually in the most recent run of the program had only been complete to three decimal places, whereas the computer could and had been calculating all the way to six.

The anomaly was thus accounted for, but it was not fully explained. Scientific theories of the day held that initial deviations of such minor proportions should nevertheless have produced sub-stantially similar outcomes. The extraordinary sensitivity of this, and many other complex systems, to slight changes in initial conditions, forms the basis of chaos theory. In an address to the American Association for the Advancement of Science in 1972, Lorenz encapsulated his findings in a more poetic and vivid fashion: "Does the flap of a butterfly's wings in Brazil," he asked, "set off a tornado in Texas?" With that, the term "the Butterfly Effect" made its way into our lexicon.

Centuries before the birth of either Lorenz or Poincaré, the following popular verse served to illustrate exactly this aspect of chaos theory:

> *For want of a nail, the shoe was lost,*
> *For want of the shoe, the horse was lost,*
> *For want of the horse, the rider was lost,*
> *For want of the rider, the battle was lost,*

For want of the battle, the kingdom was lost,
And all for the want of a horseshoe nail.

Continuing the analysis within the confines of this metaphor, one might well ask what the chances are that the particular nail (or the absence thereof) described at the outset of the verse actually causes the fall of the kingdom in the penultimate line.

A better understanding of the principles involved can be achieved by examining the proposition in reverse order. It seems unlikely, although not impossible, that an entire kingdom would fall as the result of a single battle. The battle in question may have been the pivotal one, but let us assume for the sake of argument that, at a minimum, more than one battle is at issue. Clearly, each battle would involve more than a single rider; in addition to the number of men required to field a kingdom's cavalry, there are also the scouts, the messengers, and the various other mounted personnel. Furthermore, it is likely that the number of horses involved in the campaign would actually exceed the number of riders, for horses are also needed to transport the massive quantity of supplies required to equip an army in the field. Each horse, of course, would be shod with four shoes. Each shoe, in turn, would require seven nails. When one thus considers the number of nails in all the shoes of all the horses of all the riders in all the battles for the survival of the kingdom, the chances of a significant problem arising because of a horseshoe malfunction suddenly seem rather less remote.

Next, suppose that rather than the ultimate undoing of the defensive campaign residing wholly in the province of chance, there is an intelligence at work. What if, even before the onset of hostilities, a trained observer had been watching the military machinery of the kingdom as it geared up for battle? From a well-concealed position, perhaps under the very nose of the palace guard, this saboteur may have been studying the command structure, intercepting deployment orders and battle plans, and searching for chinks in the armor—

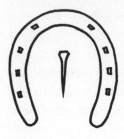

points at which a seemingly meaningless deviation on an order of magnitude undetectable in the first three decimal places—might make all the difference over time. The intruder would not undertake any action substantial enough to draw scrutiny. He would not have to. All it takes is a slight nudge in one direction, a gentle prod in another, or the removal of a nail from the shoe of a horse destined to carry a rider on a critical mission, for example. These tiny waves will wash against the rock. Over time, the rhythm of the tide will swell. Eventually, the entire kingdom may be swept away. This is *kochojutsu*—the art of the butterfly.

A Master of the Japanese martial arts first coined the term "kochojutsu" to describe the way in which a minor expenditure of energy at the right place or time in a process could be equivalent to or greater than a much larger effort at a later or less carefully selected point. But this term simply identified an idea, or rather a collection of ideas, which had already existed for millennia. Included in this discipline are skills as diverse as camouflage, concealment, and deception (CCD); lie detection and deductive reasoning; statistical analysis and scientific experimentation; and techniques of disinformation, persuasion, and manipulation.

Almost every art, martial or otherwise, encourages practitioners to refine their abilities, to strive to do more and more with less and less, until they are able to do virtually anything with almost nothing. This is especially true in the martial realm where the student strives to attain a level of expertise said to reside only in the void. Mastery of the skills just described can, under the right conditions, allow practitioners to produce results that seem to defy common experience, logic, and the laws of physics. And all of this is ideally achieved with such minimal effort that the result is fairly character-ized as a work of art.

The legends of almost every culture contain references to classes of people whose powers appear supernatural. *Ninja*, Japanese as-sassins known for their stealth, were said to be able to walk through walls, appearing and disappearing at will. Among the gypsy clans of Eastern Europe there are those who, it is claimed, can read minds and look into the future using cards, crystals, or even tea leaves. During Britain's Dark Ages, as detailed in the *Malleus Maleficarum*, some people believed that witches had among their powers the abil-ity to control the minds of others with spells and potions. And leg-end has it that the monks of the Shaolin temple in China's Henan Province could render themselves invulnerable to attack by control-ling the flow of *chi* in their bodies.

Magic? Perhaps, but sufficient scrutiny will reveal that each of these seemingly mystical abilities has at least some grounding in re-ality. Does invisibility require actual transparency, or is one simply able to pass unnoticed? If future events can be forecast and people's inner thoughts divined through observation, investigation, and analysis, is it any less powerful a gift? Is invincibility really a matter of winning every battle, or is it simply having the wisdom to fight only battles that can be won?

These skills are real. They have been taught in select circles for centuries. They are the tradecraft of the interrogator and the fortune-teller; the mercenary and the woodsman; and the thief and the assassin. They can be learned, but the knowledge does not come easily. Their elements are sensitivity, awareness, nuance, and patience. They can be as delicate and ephemeral as the wings of the butterfly from which their collective designation takes its name. But they also have the power to change the course of history.

Before embarking on our studies in the art of the butterfly, a degree of orientation is required. Unlike certain theoretical disciplines, this art from is based on observable and reliable principles applied over centuries in the most practical of contexts. Its effects resonate all around us, wherever human interaction is taking place. The corner café, therefore, becomes our classroom; the sidewalk our study hall; the hotel lobby our homeroom; and the public house our proving ground. Viewed in this way, life itself becomes both a lecture hall and a grand laboratory.

The first step in the process of studying this art—and herein lies the real secret—is an awakening, a conscious decision to open wide the senses to the world around us, the birth of a new awareness. For only by opening our eyes to detail and our ears to nuance can we transcend the ordinary and the everyday and travel into the shadow realm of insight and illusion. Unlike those who move through life passively, aware only of such information as is presented to them in a direct and obvious fashion, practitioners of the butterfly art will learn to take an active and intelligent role in gathering and analyzing data, as well as in deciding how to use it to best effect. This journey is not a rapid one; it will take time. Travelers on this path must be willing to slow their pace enough to allow for introspection, observation, and careful consideration, well beyond the imperative of satisfying life's pressing necessities.

Sitting at an outdoor café for a few hours, watching the world go by, is as good a place as any to begin. For how long can you sit still before becoming restless and uncomfortable? Do others seem to notice your discomfort? How quickly and how often does the waiter come by to move you along? Where are other patrons looking? What are they doing? Close your eyes for a moment, and try to recreate the image of the people and the place in your mind? How much do you remember? What can you tell just by looking at someone? What can you surmise? Try this process with a partner, and compare your conclusions. If you are bold enough to follow up on your analysis, how accurate was it?

Exercise One: Situational Awareness

Notes—Identify and memorize key tactical points: Entrances and exits; windows and reflective surfaces; tables, chairs, counters, and other obstacles.

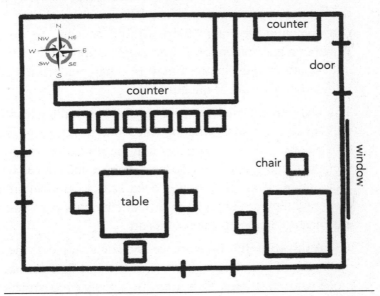

This process can teach you many things. In the realm of the butterfly, it can teach you almost everything. Everywhere there are people of all shapes and sizes, pursuing wildly different agendas. They each have different approaches and different sets of techniques and skills, but whether they are successful or not, each interaction can be instructive and enlightening. One last thing: in the process of making your observations—of people watching—notice how few of them are watching you back.

Whatever our reasons for taking up this discipline, we are not alone in the endeavor. Our colleagues, while relatively few in number, live and work among us. And while virtually everyone, whether he knows it or not, has cause to call on certain of the abilities discussed herein on occasion, it may be helpful to identify five archetypes, professionals for whom such skills are more than mere conveniences or curiosities; they are tools of the trade.

1. **The Operative:** There are those among us whose jobs require that they be able to come and go without being detected; that they can observe events without being seen; and that they can communicate information without seeming to do so. Whether a government or private organization employs them and whatever their motives may be, their tradecraft is the foundation of the art of the butterfly.

2. **The Detective:** Here we refer to those whose calling involves making observations, gathering clues, and assembling pieces of a puzzle. These investigators may be asked to examine a scene to identify a potential suspect or to examine a person to ascertain his level of knowledge, complicity, or motivation. Either way, they are engaged in a deductive process that is a critical stage in the practice of this art.

3. **The Analyst:** In this category we find such people as the actuary, the financial consultant, and the intelligence officer: those who must keep close track of activity on a variety of fronts in an effort to stay one step ahead of emerging situations. We also encounter the social scientist, who seeks to predict and explain the behavior of specific groups of people, and the mental health specialist, who focuses on the conduct of given individuals. Their abilities in this regard are powerful

tools for any practitioner of the butterfly art.

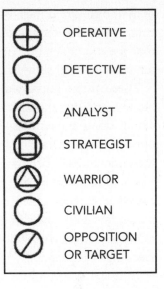

⊕	OPERATIVE
♀	DETECTIVE
◎	ANALYST
⊡	STRATEGIST
△	WARRIOR
◯	CIVILIAN
⦸	OPPOSITION OR TARGET

4. **The Strategist:** Regardless of profession, having the ability and willingness to plan, prepare, and deploy assets to maximum effect is of paramount importance. This process is commonly observed and analyzed in the political arena, whether engagements are played out in the corridors of power, on the floor of the legislature, or, as Carl von Clausewitz observed, by other means; for in each of these environments, a seemingly minor consideration like a horseshoe nail or the beat of a butterfly's wing can make the difference between victory and defeat.

5. **The Warrior:** Whether or not we wear a uniform, we are all eventually called to one kind of battlefield or another. For the trial attorney, the theater of engagement is the courtroom. For the politician, the campaign is of the electoral variety. For the sportsman, the operational field is bounded by a white line. It is in this context—the realm of the butterfly—that the constituent abilities just discussed combine, coalesce, and resolve eventually into their ultimate form of expression.

The study and application of these skills require the exercise of a modicum of discretion. By virtue of legal mandate, ethical consideration, and practical reality, certain abilities discussed herein should be applied only by a select few practitioners or by those confronted with a very specific and unusual state of affairs. Most people, for example, will never have a reason to infiltrate an enemy stronghold or the need to make an object disappear into thin air, during the course of their ordinary duties, but it is wise to learn to recognize the application of these techniques by others. One should also recognize that the principles that apply to such specialized situations can often shed light on somewhat more common circumstances as well.

There are no firm dividing lines in this text: it is written in shades of gray, and the applicability of its lessons depends in large part on who is doing the reading. What of the reader, the student, the practitioner, then? Whatever his (which term is intended to embrace the feminine as well throughout this text) actual profession may be, in this field of study he will be by turns "gray man," investigator, forecaster, "eminence grise," and master tactician. In the pursuit of each particular ability, he will learn to emulate the example most helpful to his objective. He will look to the laboratory and listen to the wise teachings of the faculty. He will adapt.

Innumerable volumes have been written on such subjects as warfare, espionage, forecasting, and police work individually, but a vast majority of these treatments have quite naturally approached their subject matter in a direct and exclusive fashion. While the art of the butterfly runs through these various disciplines like a golden thread, it often comprises only a tiny and unseen portion of their makeup. In order to focus on this common strand specifically, then, we must position ourselves at a somewhat more oblique angle. In so doing, of course, we risk sacrificing a degree of precision with regard to certain collateral matters, but the primary and overarching objective remains clear.

Notwithstanding this cross-disciplinary approach, our inquiry may be informed from time to time by the writings of certain experts in a given field—our faculty if you will. The present-day training of intelligence operatives often parallels, and even draws on ancient techniques detailed in the treatises of such past masters as Sun Tzu and Clausewitz. Modern efforts to understand human behavior may be assisted by the writings of such pioneers as Abraham Maslow and Sigmund Freud, whereas attempts to control human behavior are perhaps better served by the examples of Niccolò Machiavelli

Name: Niccolò di Bernardo dei
Machiavelli

Profession: Diplomat

Birth: 5/3/1469, Florence, Italy

Affiliation: Florentine Militia

Notes: Chancellor of the Rebublic
of Florence; Author of *The
Prince*; Political realist

S-0022
Machiavelli, Niccolò

and François Leclerc du Tremblay. Harmonizing all these components in a viable and effective fashion has been the goal of strategists throughout history, from the time of Miyamoto Musashi to the battlefields of tomorrow, and the application of these theories has changed the course of history on more than one occasion, for the art of the butterfly is as old as humanity itself.[2]

2. Various military and intelligence agencies teach their operatives that the intelligence-gathering process can be traced back at least as far as biblical times. ("And Moses sent them to spy out the land of Canaan, and said unto them, Get you up this way southward, and go up into the mountain: And see the land, what it is, and the people that dwelleth therein, whether they be strong or weak, few or many; And what the land is that they dwell in, whether it be good or bad; and what cities they be that they dwell in, whether in tents, or in strong holds; And what the land is, whether it be fat or lean, whether there be wood therein, or not. And be ye of good courage, and bring of the fruit of the land. Now the time was the time of the firstripe grapes."—Num. 13:1–3, 17–20.)

SECTION ONE

Invisibility

It is rumored that within the secured perimeter of a government laboratory in a certain southwestern American state, there is a stadium-sized observation area. Gauges monitor pressure and temperature in the enormous room, and banks of cameras are fixed to the walls. All this attention is directed toward the center of the structure where a thin sheet of alloy hangs suspended by a web of wires and cables. What makes this slice of metal so extraordinary is that

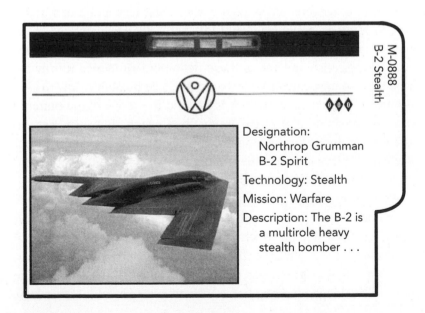

M-0888
B-2 Stealth

Designation:
 Northrop Grumman
 B-2 Spirit

Technology: Stealth

Mission: Warfare

Description: The B-2 is
 a multirole heavy
 stealth bomber . . .

when conditions are just right, its skin reflects, or rather projects, whatever image or item is placed behind it, with near-perfect precision. It becomes, in effect, invisible to the eye.

Whether or not such a material actually exists, it is undeniable that modern stealth technology and electronic countermeasures have the ability to render aircraft and other military vehicles virtually invisible to electronic detection. In an unguarded moment, a pilot of a bomber so equipped admitted that he had, at the request of the tower controller in a sleepy hamlet along his flight path, engaged his jamming equipment for about thirty seconds, "just to see what would happen." When he lifted the blackout, he reported that pandemonium ensued. The controller indicated that rather than experiencing some degree of electronic interference as he had anticipated, his entire network shut down. The scope, he admitted, had simply gone blank.

The *American Heritage Dictionary* offers four separate definitions of the word, "invisible." Only one of these speaks to the technological effects described in the preceding: "Invisible: (1) impossible to see." The other three versions are somewhat less ambitious in nature: "(2) not accessible to view, hidden; (3) not easily noticed or detected; (4) not published (in financial statements)." The technology required to satisfy the first of these definitions (if indeed it truly exists) is so sophisticated that it would likely be available only to governmental agencies. As such, it is beyond the scope of the butterfly art. The ability to realize the latter three effects, however, has existed for centuries, and anyone with sufficient training and preparation can achieve it. It is to these more realistic, more attainable, and more practical interpretations that we now turn.

The power to appear only to the extent or in the manner of one's choosing is perhaps the most essential aspect of the art of the butterfly, for it is a skill on which many others depend. The behavior of others is governed almost entirely by what they perceive rather than by what truly is. Control perception and you will have acquired the keys to the kingdom. Long before the advent of stealth technology, individuals and organizations studied and employed techniques of CCD. This has, of course, been especially true in time of war.

During World War II specialized units, sometimes assisted by professional magicians, were tasked with concealing troops, stores, vehicles, bases, and on a few occasions, entire towns from detection by the enemy. In the Cold War era that followed, individual intelligence operatives engaged in infiltrating or exfiltrating in hostile territory employed many of the same principles. A review of these techniques, drawn from a variety of sources, suggests that this subject can be conveniently divided into five parts: appearance, position, movement, activity and spirit, or mood.

The Master—for he was more than a teacher—of the art of the butterfly invited three volunteers to attack him. Faced with a class of fresh recruits, he needed to establish the power of his principles, as well as his person, without unnecessary delay. He succeeded. As the fit young fighters converged on his position, each hoping to be the first to land a blow, he simply disappeared. It was not that he ducked, dodged, or sidestepped. He just vanished. One moment, his black robe was obscured by a tightening noose of arms and legs clad in rough white cloth; the next, he was standing several feet behind the throng, idly twirling a bladed weapon that he had retrieved from the nearby wall rack.

APPEARANCE

O divine art of subtlety and secrecy! Through you we
learn to be invisible, through you inaudible; and hence we
can hold the enemy's fate in our hands.

—Sun Tzu, *The Art of War*

Initial perceptions of people are governed largely by outward appearances. Learning to control appearance, therefore, is an important step in managing perception. Let us begin with the immutable,
the aspects of appearance that cannot be changed, at least not without resorting to extreme measures. For the average person, more or
less by definition, this presents no substantial difficulty. The appearance of a man standing five feet ten with a moderate build and
sandy brown hair will generally attract little attention. But what of
the exceptionally tall, short, or wide individual?

It is said that, over the years, certain otherwise promising candidates have been turned away form the clandestine services on the
grounds of appearance—not necessarily good or bad, but simply
striking in some way and, therefore, far too memorable for this type
of work. In this regard, of course, we are not talking of applicants for
any of the army of administrative, technological, legal, analytical, or
consular positions that comprise the bulk of the intelligence work-
force. We are speaking of a select few individuals with the peculiar
temperament and particular abilities required to serve in an operational capacity. Paramount among the weapons in such an operative's armamentarium is the ability to pass unseen. The color of the
cold warrior is gray. In certain circles, this type of operative is even
referred to as the gray man.[1]

What is to be done, then, with natural, physical challenges? To
the extent possible, they must be neutralized. According to various,

---

1. As just discussed, any gender-specific terminology employed herein is a function of
idiom and grammatical convention; the skills described are equally applicable to and
practiced by both men and women unless otherwise specified.

now declassified, training manuals, height can be effectively obscured in several ways. Operatives can remain seated for a variety of plausible reasons, wear lifts or high-heeled shoes, or modify their posture. One specific agency's training materials discuss the effect that the type of hat, height of trousers, length of coat, and type of accessories carried (e.g., umbrella or cane) can have on the perception of height.

Weight may also be problematic, but it can be augmented by wearing padded garments or overstuffing pockets in combination with a carefully managed posture, and can be mitigated by wearing concealing clothing; an overcoat under appropriate circumstances or a well-cut suit perhaps. Selective use of horizontal and vertical patterns can also serve to mislead with respect to this characteristic. One can easily achieve the modification of jaw or jowl lines—highly distinctive characteristics for the purposes of identification—by the insertion of some minimal padding.

As demonstrated by the optical illusion diagrams above and be-

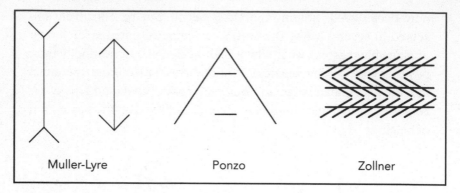

| Muller-Lyre | Ponzo | Zollner |

low, what sits atop, below, and beside a figure can clearly alter the perception of its dimensions. Similarly, the position of one object relative to another can trick the eye, as can the pattern of the material being viewed. Such trompe l'oeils are the gray man's stock in trade.

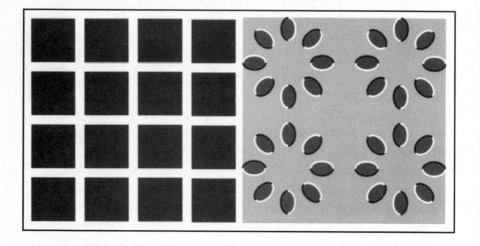

On a finer level, features like piercing blue eyes, bright blond hair, or sculpted cheekbones will tend to attract attention. Such notable attributes can nevertheless be masked, in these cases by dark glasses or colored contact lenses, hats, and beards, respectively. Celebrities employ these techniques all the time to avoid attracting unwanted attention. One should take care, however, that the disguise is not more obvious than that which it seeks to conceal. The heavy-rimmed sunglasses, dark homburg, and ill-fitting beard in combination advertise ineptitude of Clouseauesque proportions.

Skin tone and hair color are also memorable features. Fortunately, both are easily modified. One particular operational manual details methods of improvising a disguise by applying rust, soot, or burned cork to freshly washed skin, and ash, flour, or talcum powder to wet hair to change its apparent pigmentation. Stubble can be simulated by applying grease with a rough sponge, and artificial wrinkles or blemishes can be added with a pencil or the end of a burned match. In this regard, another treatise on clandestine methods discusses the exploitation of the "look away" reflex; a useful instinctive behavior observed in people who encounter those with deformities or unsightly conditions. This same document goes on to caution, however, that such temporary measures may only withstand a cursory inspection.

In certain circles, entire classes or chapters are dedicated to a single, albeit vital, aspect of this process: attention to the hands. In addition to the importance of ensuring that the appearance of the hands is consistent with any general disguise, the condition of these extremities alone can telegraph a great deal about the person to whom they are connected. Soft skin and well-manicured nails protruding from French cuffs will appear to belong to a different social stratum than the rough, scarred instruments that dangle at the ends of rolled-up flannel sleeves.

For some, their physical distinctiveness may simply be too pronounced to allow them to pass unnoticed, but for the vast majority of people, their immutable attributes, with perhaps a modicum of artful camouflage, are easily addressed. It is in the realm of the discretionary aspects of one's presentation that the real challenges, as well as opportunities, emerge. This is so because, unlike the gray man, a vast majority of people spend inordinate amounts of time and energy trying to achieve the opposite result. They want to be noticed. By simply reversing such efforts, we can achieve a contrary effect.

Of primary importance is the matter of grooming. Those men and women who take time to achieve elaborate hairstyling, either cranial or facial, or who apply striking makeup are trying to send a message. Whether or not the message has the desired effect on an intended recipient is quite beside the point. The bouffant hair, the goatee, and the bright red lips and nails are all akin to waving a flag. They are saying, "Look at me." Whether or not others like what they see, they will be looking.

This is not to suggest that the only danger lies in trying to improve one's appearance. The goal here is merely plainness and not unattractiveness. Seriously unkempt or uncut hair or a pale and washed-out complexion may be just as memorable as any of the aforementioned embellishments. The idea is simply that no message of any kind should be sent or received. The choice of style, if any, should appear unstudied and unremarkable.

Sometimes, operatives may wish to project an appearance that falls toward one or other end of the spectrum of memorability so as to allow them to "disappear" at will by shedding the disguise and replacing it with another or just reverting to their natural appearance. The OSS,[2] for example, in teaching field agents the art of the "quick change" stressed that quite simple and easy alterations of hairstyle, makeup, clothing, and profile will allow the same operative to manufacture a range of different personas at will.

With the rare exception of the person whose appearance is not only striking but immutably so, following the guidelines just presented will create a gray template over which any number of layers may then be superimposed with ease. Of these, perhaps the most important is clothing. Clothes may not make the man, but they certainly control the initial perception of him. And if the practitioner is skilled in the art of the butterfly, an initial perception is all there will be.

---

2. The Office of Strategic Services, the wartime precursor to the CIA.

Just as with grooming choices, there are several guiding principles with respect to dress. Naturally bright colors and bold styles usually draw the eye. Conservative cuts in shades of gray do not. But in this regard, appropriateness of place and time are critical variables. The navy jacket and khakis that are de rigueur at the yacht club may as well be a police uniform at a rave. Conversely, not only would the young man in jeans and a T-shirt stand out in a fine restaurant or hotel, but he would probably stand outside. And of course when moving in circles where such things matter, the lady wearing a fashion as outdated as last year's may as well be dressed in a burlap sack. What is the same is inconspicuous. And what is the same varies by location and circumstance.

In some arenas—in hospitals, in the military, and in many parts of the service industry uniforms are required. This convention provides the gray man with a veritable passport to those places. In other circles the dress code is so circumscribed that it *almost* constitutes a uniform. For lawyers and high financiers, it is the dark suit; for medical or scientific personnel, it is the white lab coat; for repairmen of all sorts, it may be overalls; and for the manual laborer, it has evolved into a flannel shirt over jeans and work boots. One may, from time to time, encounter a casually dressed doctor or a smartly dressed plumber, but we are talking here of norms. We are talking of what is typical, what is expected, and what is therefore unremarkable.

Even an approximation of any of the modes of attire described in the preceding will typically survive an initial inspection, but additional care must be taken when a more thorough examination is anticipated. Such seemingly insignificant matters as a clothing label, the wrong choice of tie, or inconsistent footwear can sabotage the intended effect. The devil, as they say, is in the details, and the keen observer of the human condition will take note of such things as a matter of course.

Shifting our analytical point of view on this subject for a moment, among the principle weapons available to the interrogator is *cross-*

checking: comparing answers with one another and looking for internal inconsistency. Anyone can lie. It takes a well-trained professional to maintain a deception, in plausible detail, over the course of a lengthy interview. Seemingly inconsequential incongruities begin to emerge until the subject is caught in an outright contradiction. So it is with appearance. A blazer does not usually go with jeans and a T-shirt, a pair of cheap shoes puts the lie to the Armani suit, and a doctor with cracked and dirty fingernails will invite a second look. Again, this is not to imply that a roughneck should not want to dress himself up a little, that a studio executive cannot save a few dollars on footwear, or that a doctor might not want to do a spot of gardening before his rounds. It is just that each of these people will likely attract a little attention. They will be noticed.

The key to passing undetected, as with so many other aspects of the butterfly art, is giving people what they want or, to be strictly accurate, what they *think* they want. People expect professors of European literature to wear faded tweed jackets with patches on the elbows. They assume that the lady in the white skirt and sweater is off to a tennis match. They detect, at least at a subliminal level, that the burly fellow with the close-cropped hair is probably a cop or a soldier. Deviating from these stereotypes will cause them to think. It will cause them to notice. It will cause them to remember.

Props are another powerful tool in the art of blending. The term "prop," as used in theater, is short for the word "property." But there is another meaning, one that is equally apt in the present context, which speaks to supporting or buttressing something. People will usually simply assume that the man walking along the street jingling his keys is on the way to his car; that the woman in the lab coat holding a clipboard belongs in this office and is probably in the process of an official evaluation of some sort; and that the fellow with the homburg and cane is old or foreign and might be balding, disabled, or both. These, and many other impressions, can be easily created by the adoption of assorted simple and readily obtainable personal effects.

Starting from the top, hats, especially for men, are currently out of style. There was a time when a hat was a necessary part of any well-put-together ensemble, but these days it is typically a sign of age, occasion, occupation, individuality, or a receding hairline. There are two exceptions: One is the ubiquitous baseball cap. As much a part of American culture as the sport from which it takes its name, it provides a convenient way to disguise hair and even the upper part of the face under appropriate circumstances. The other is the sweatshirt hood, but it should be noted that this particular garment is frequently featured in the composite sketches of police departments throughout the world for this very reason. Setting aside these two particular examples, then, the hat, even in women's fashions, is an unusual, and therefore memorable, accessory.

Glasses come in as wide a variety of shapes and sizes as any article of clothing, and can serve many purposes over and above the mere correction of vision. Sunglasses have the dual advantage of concealing both the appearance of one's eyes as well as the direction in which those eyes are looking. On a sunny day, therefore, they are valuable tools, but in situations where it is clear that there is no need for them—indoors or in inclement weather—they single out the wearer by their very purpose.

From early childhood on, we are taught, however unfairly, that prescription lenses betoken both intelligence and lack of physical ability. As we grow, the importance and relevance of the former consideration may begin to obscure the latter, but this misperception remains firmly entrenched and can be exploited to advantage. Furthermore, glasses can be used in a number of expressive ways: pulled down onto the bridge of the nose to indicate skepticism; taken off as a prelude to a more frank or intimate discussion; or waved to make a point. Lawyers with perfect vision have been known to wear and use glasses with clear lenses at trial for exactly these reasons.

Like hats, earrings (for men) are not in vogue at present. As a result and notwithstanding the "earring code" of the seventies and eighties, the man who wears rings in either ear risks having others make assumptions about his lifestyle or at least his personality. For women, small and unobtrusive stud earrings are fairly common fashion accessories, but those of the larger, hoop variety will draw more attention. And as with tongue piercing, such accessories will tend to attract the attention of people in general but single men in particular. The number and variety of additional piercing possibilities now available to those with an interest in such things is truly shocking and is thankfully well beyond the scope of this treatment. Suffice it to say that pierced noses, chins, eyebrows, and the like, are still unusual enough sights to leave a strong impression in the memories of any who see them.

Like glasses, cigarettes and smoking implements are tremendously telling and expressive accessories. Smoking has, of course, fallen out of favor in recent years. Its role in the art of the operative, however, deserves further discussion if only for historical purposes. As a threshold matter, the habit of smoking cigarettes generally indicates youth, age, or ignorance. The smoking of cigars, by contrast, continues to be associated with wealth and power. Furthermore, the smoking of either item can explain otherwise conspicuous loitering behavior and has the additional effect of keeping most other people at bay. In the past, smoking has been used to initiate contact, to signal, and to flirt at times. Certain brands are associated with specific groups or types of people. Lighters and matches can attract attention or can be a distraction. They can also provide light or fire when needed. Finally, for those who do smoke, the provision or withholding of a cigarette can be a tremendously powerful tool.

The wearing of neckties, originally a kind of Elizabethan bib, has since evolved into an elaborate and complex societal convention. Ties indicate that the wearer is at least attempting to make himself presentable for a particular purpose. For police officers, bartenders, store clerks, and the like, the tie is issued as part of a uniform and, as a result, provides little information. For others, a tie is a necessary part of their working wardrobe, but the material, style, and color are discretionary matters. Accordingly, it can provide clues to the interested observer. Is it expensive or cheap? Silk? Imported? Brightly colored? Dated? Dimpled? What knot is used? Each of these choices sends a message.

Certain color and style combinations are associated with a given political persuasion. Others, the so-called "power ties," are supposed to indicate that their owners are "players" in the business world. But if the medium-wide, yellow, silk Versace, tied with a carefully dimpled Windsor knot, may be said to speak to its owner's status, then the crested tie fairly shouts. No message could be clearer than hanging the coat of arms of a given institution about one's neck. On a much more subtle level are the secret designs and knots known only to the membership of certain select groups, as diverse as university social clubs and organized crime syndicates.

Associated with the necktie are several additional items, among them the pin, the clip, and the pocket handkerchief. In an era when the jacket and tie are no longer exclusively worn with a white collar, the use of these accessories tends to indicate a slightly more sophisticated sartorial sensibility, or a least a pretension thereto. Like anything else however, these otherwise sublime accents can be, and often are, overdone to ridiculous proportions. Either way, these se lections speak to any who choose to listen.

Jewelry of almost any kind will catch the eye; that is, after all, what it is intended to do. The simple rule here is, if you wish to blend, do not wear any. In this category, brief mention should be made of wristwatches and wedding rings. An accurate timepiece is a valuable instrument for the achievement of many of the operational objectives under discussion. Watches are commonplace enough that the right selection will rarely attract attention. The type of timepiece should be neither noticeably cheap nor very expensive, and for blending purposes, it must be worn in the conventional fashion, that is, face on the outside of the wrist. Often, people expect to see wedding rings on the fingers of men and women of a certain age, and in these cases, it is the absence, rather than the presence, of this particular piece of jewelry that may be considered remarkable.

In the realm of clothing, there are a multitude of other accessories or stylistic variations to be considered: suspenders, belts, vests, double-breasted jackets, cuffs, and hemlines, to name just a few. When the practitioner's goal is the analysis of others—a subject taken up at length in one of the following sections—such details may provide significant insight into the personality of the target. For the purposes of blending, however, anything out of the ordinary is to be avoided.

In addition to clothing and accessories, there is a wide assortment of other items, the carrying of which reliably creates a given impression. A camera worn around the neck, especially in combination with the right clothing and a wandering gait, suggests tourism. It also allows the "tourist" to observe other people and things without appearing to be actively engaged in conducting surveillance. Already touched on earlier was the power of the clipboard. The sense of authority and belonging that this prop conveys can apply equally to a briefcase, a file folder, or a steno pad. Moreover, others will tend to avoid contact with the person in the room who reminds them most of a hall monitor or other petty official.

More specific messages can also be telegraphed using props. Entering a room while shaking an umbrella suggests that it is raining or that, at a minimum, the weather is inclement. Try this, even on a day when the sky and the forecast are clear, and see how many people simply assume that you know something they don't. Scanning a room and glancing at one's watch periodically says, "I am expecting to meet someone here," as clearly as holding up a sign would. And simply looking up at a tall building with an expression of concern can cause a virtual traffic jam of rubbernecking on the sidewalks of any city street in the land.

All the factors discussed thus far relate to visual stimuli, but perception is informed by all five senses. A pungent odor, a familiar taste, or the sensation created by an artful touch; these things can be every bit as evocative as a visual image under the right circumstances. The fragrance, food, and massage industries take full advantage of this feature of the human condition on a daily basis. In the environment of the relatively impersonal, everyday encounter *en passant*, however, the auditory faculty is perhaps the next most important consideration.

It might seem obvious that an unnecessarily loud, abrasive, or grating tone of voice will draw the attention, not to mention the annoyance, of those standing nearby. But a quick trip to the classroom café will demonstrate that a significant proportion of the population either doesn't understand this idea or doesn't care. The volume at which people send and receive information, whether in person, by cell phone, or from the television, often exceeds the necessary level significantly. For the gray man, such conduct is the equivalent of setting off an alarm.

As we are beginning to see, however, in the realm of the butterfly, neither is the polar opposite to be embraced. Where shrillness will arrest, a conspiratorial demeanor will intrigue. Furthermore, as a tactical matter, both the nature and content of a whisper are easier to detect than a message simply conveyed in a low tone and an unassuming manner. In fact, people are so used to eye contact, enunciation, and physical engagement accompanying conversation that if these conventions are dispensed with, a brief statement may pass unnoticed right next to the ear of the enemy as it were.

As well as tone and volume, conversation also has direction and timing, or at least it should have. Observe, or better yet, experience the dynamic of four people sitting together at a table. If only one person talks at a time, it is easy to maintain concentration. When the discussion breaks down into pairs, it is still possible to remain focused as long as each party is engaged with an adjacent party. But when the lines of communication cross, it produces a highly distracting level of dissonance for both the participants and any interested bystander.

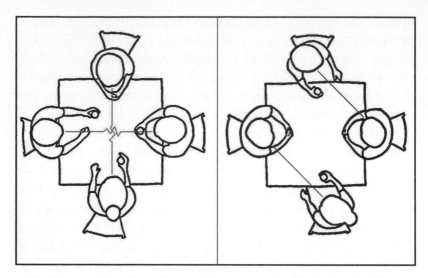

In this way, the flow of conversation can be likened to the flow of traffic. As long as everything moves in a steady, moderate, and parallel fashion, other "drivers" will proceed along the way more or less on autopilot. But an aggressive move, linguistic tailgating, speeding, or cutting across an existing line of flow, for example, will consistently draw attention. As touched on above, so will the conversational equivalent of driving in the center lane at thirty miles per hour or, worse still, crawling along the shoulder.

As well as paying close attention to voice modulation, care should be taken to avoid both national and regional accents. As we have come to understand, that which is unusual is also remarkable. A Canadian accent is as out of place in Texas as a Texan drawl would be in New York. Subtler distinctions can be observed among such close cousins as the British, South Africans, Australians, and New Zealanders. And in some cultures, one's accent points the way to both social and geographic points of origin. While there may be little that one can do to mask a strong accent on short notice, it is worth taking note of the famous observation that it is possible to get by in the United States with just a few words of slang. As long as the speaker's efforts to convey his meaning with a minimum of verbiage are not obvious, this can be a surprisingly effective concealment technique.

Infinite details are taken into consideration with regard to voice, but the same fundamental principles just articulated govern each one. There are also many other sounds, conscious or otherwise, that tend to draw attention and should therefore be monitored. Return to the classroom and witness for yourself the myriad coughs, sneezes, snorts, yawns, and the like, that serve as physical punctuation in many people's conversations. In this regard, reviewing a videotape of oneself can be an instructive if somewhat surprising experience.

No discussion of appearance would be complete without at least a cursory examination of the effect of body language on perception. There are many types of nonverbal communication and almost as many ways of interpreting them. While this ability may be more critical to the art of analyzing others than it is to the art of blending, these twin endeavors are in many ways two faces of the same coin. There is agreement among experts that the way in which we hold ourselves can invite or deter the attention of others. Which one of these effects is achieved is largely a matter of physical openness. All other things being equal, the people whose body language suggests that they are preoccupied or pensive are more likely to be dismissed as potential participants in the proceedings by those around them. They are off in a world of their own and, therefore, play no part in this one.

This effect can be achieved in a variety of ways: Where someone chooses to "aim" himself, his face, torso, or his feet speaks to his area of interest and therefore involvement. The man who stands at a bar, drink in hand, and looks straight ahead is far less approachable than the one who turns sideways on his stool, leaning on the rail and surveying the crowd. The lady who sits alone at a table, facing inward with her chair drawn up close appears to be less interested in company or attention than the one who positions herself a little farther back, tilted slightly to the side.

At the next level of magnification, crossed arms, legs, or ankles are thought to be subconscious barriers. Likewise, hunched shoulders, clasped hands, pursed lips, and furrowed brows contribute to a perception of hostility or tension. Even the adoption of a slightly strained facial expression can serve to deter contact. Taken together, these cues say "keep away," and if employed judiciously, they merely whisper it.

Generally speaking, a rigid and tightly focused bearing telegraphs inflexibility and therefore inapproachability, whereas a fluid carriage is more inviting. A square or open-legged stance with feet pointed toward observers, by contrast, tends to have a welcoming effect. Likewise, leaning forward, employing "mirroring behavior," and adopting an open expression encourages others to approach. But remember that excessive rigidity and extreme relaxation both violate the normality rule in equal measure.

Crossed arms or legs (hostility)	Direct eye contact (interest)
Fully facing the speaker (openness)	Tilted head, unfocused eyes (boredom)
Arms/legs wide open (receptiveness)	Hand to cheek (evaluating)
Leaning closer (seduction)	Steepled fingers (considering)
Hands on hips (readiness)	Open hands (sincerity)
Slouching, hands in pockets (dejected)	Pinching bridge of nose (evaluation)
Hands behind back (formality)	Drumming fingers (impatience)
Sitting up straight (anticipation)	Pulling ear (indecision)

Finally, in an effort to manage these myriad conscious concerns, the gray man must take care to guard against the naturally resulting tendency to exhibit unintended physical signs of stress: rapid breathing, studied movements, surreptitious glances, and constant fidgeting of all kinds. These "tells" are among the primary targets of the interrogator and the countersurveillance expert and can damage the gray man's mission irreparably.

In summary, the cumulative impact of one's appearance depends on many, interrelated factors. The preferred path—the middle course—is a nebulous concept at best and is further dependent on ever-evolving circumstances. Moreover, appearance is just one of several components in the art of blending. Overemphasizing this particular piece of the puzzle can have the opposite effect to that which is intended. The answer, as simple as it sounds, and as hard as it is to achieve, lies in behaving as naturally as possible under the circumstances.

> *In pondering the Master's disappearing act, could it have been his flowing outer robe, the sleeves of which sometimes concealed his wiry forearms and at other times hung loosely from his shoulders, allowing his hard hands to dart out unexpectedly from the place where the wide lapels converged? Perhaps . . .*

LOCATION

That the defensive in an especial manner enjoys the
assistance which ground affords is plain in itself; as to
what concerns the advantage which the defensive has in
surprising by the force and form of his attacks, that results
from the offensive being obliged to approach by roads
and paths where he may be easily observed, whilst the
defensive conceals his position, and, until almost the
decisive moment, remains invisible to his opponent.

—Carl von Clausewitz, *On War*

Returning for a moment to the laboratory of everyday life, how
many times do we go to retrieve some item—keys, wallet, a remote
control, perhaps—only to find that it has simply vanished. Every
sense and recollection at our disposal tells us that it was right there
a moment ago, and we can conceive of no logical explanation for its
disappearance. In truth, of course, the thing we seek is probably no
more than a few feet from where we are standing, but at that exact

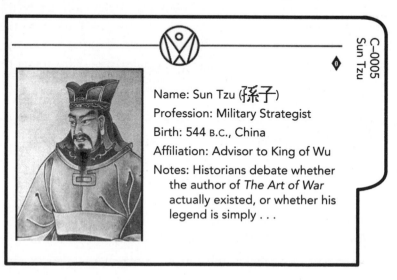

C-0005
Sun Tzu

◆ 0

Name: Sun Tzu (孫子)
Profession: Military Strategist
Birth: 544 B.C., China
Affiliation: Advisor to King of Wu
Notes: Historians debate whether
    the author of *The Art of War*
    actually existed, or whether his
    legend is simply . . .

moment, it may as well be completely invisible. And all of this is simply the result of a slight misperception as to location.

In a broader sense, the seminal treatises of Sun Tzu and Clausewitz discuss the strategic importance of knowing one's geographic location. In *The Art of War* in the chapter entitled "Armed Struggle," the Chinese general says, "One who does not know the mountains and forests, gorges and valleys, swamps and wetlands cannot advance the army." Likewise, the German strategist writes, "[I]t is self-evident that in every country there are points of commanding importance, where several roads meet, where our means of subsistence may be conveniently collected, which have the advantage of being centrally situated with reference to other important points, the possession of which in short meets many requirements and affords many advantages."

Name: Carl Philipp Gottlieb von Clausewitz

Profession: Military Strategist

Birth: 7/1/1780, Burg bei Madeburg, Prussia

Affiliation: Prussian Army

Notes: Served in Rhine campaigns and later Napoleonic Wars; Author of *Vom Kriege (On War)*

M-0127
Clausewitz, Carl

In virtually every type of endeavor, be it fighting a battle, trying a case, or doing the shopping, a thorough knowledge of the location at issue is of enormous value. Being able to switch to an alternate path when the more direct way is blocked or knowing a few convenient escape routes can be critical abilities in many situations. Even simply having a passing familiarity with one's surroundings and enjoying the confidence that this level of comfort naturally engenders can have a dramatic effect on one's ability to perform under pressure. The last thing anyone needs to be doing under stress is desperately trying to locate a landmark, an exit, or a bathroom.

Over and above the general importance of geographical familiarity, one finds many additional tactical considerations that may be specific to a given location. There are times, for example, when practitioners wish to meet in a public place to provide cover, protection, or company. A usually bustling city street in the business district may become rapidly deserted as soon as the last rush hour train has departed. Conversely, when looking for privacy, it is important to know that an otherwise secluded parking garage becomes the site of a veritable stampede at 4:30 P.M. when the government office next door closes for the day. Such critical information is easily obtained but is just as easily overlooked with disastrous consequences.

As with much of the butterfly art, using location to best advantage requires a modest investment of time. To reap the maximum reward from this perspective, it is helpful to complete a thorough reconnoiter of the theater of engagement. It is also important for the operative to ensure that his level of familiarity with the territory at issue is greater than that of the opponent. For this reason, field agents of all kinds are taught to get to the rendezvous point long before the other party's arrival. Not only can a location thus be scouted, but it can sometimes even be adapted slightly to suit particular purposes. Chairs can be added or removed from a table. Windows can be opened, closed, or angled. Obstacles can be removed or repositioned.

In this treatment, the term "location" speaks not only to the stage on which the action takes place, be it a living room or a park, but also to the positioning of the players and objects on that stage: what cinematographers often call the "mise-en-scène." For an "actor" to pass undetected, this latter consideration can be of even greater import than the former. In an operational setting, matters of both place and placement are critical to the implementation of perhaps the most powerful weapons in the operative's tactical arsenal: techniques of CCD.

At the most fundamental level, determining the location of a given person or object (or "asset" in the language of the operative) is accomplished almost entirely by visual means. People do not typically register what they do not see. Psychologists believe that during an early stage of infancy, babies do not even understand that people and things continue to exist when they are removed from immediate view. Even into adulthood, "out of sight," as they say, "is out of mind." Thus, developing and maintaining an awareness of lines of sight is one of the most critical aspects of concealing location.

For an operative seeking to avoid detection in a public place, choosing a position that is out of the visual "line of fire" is a relatively straightforward matter. In the classroom café, for example, certain tables are clearly far more prominently positioned than others. The two-top table situated in the middle of the restaurant, beneath a chandelier, next to an aisle, and exposed on all sides presents a far more prominent target than does the corner booth with its high back and subdued lighting.

Also, remember that fields of engagement, both visual and tactical, are three-dimensional. Even those people with sufficient common sense or training to sweep a room from side to side on entering will rarely look down and almost never look up. For this reason, many close quarters battle (CQB) instructors teach their students to come around the corner in a crouch when clearing a room. It is also one of the many reasons that snipers tend to prefer an elevated firing point.

As several army manuals on urban warfare point out, an appreciation of elevation can be useful in a range of combat environments. Most urban and even suburban locations are multitiered; that is to say, the shops, buildings, and other structures tend to have more

Exercise Two:
Lines of Sight and Escape Routes

Notes: Locate the best seat in the house to observe the opposition without being observed; for reflections, angle of incidence equals angle of reflection; proximity to alternate escape route also a consideration.

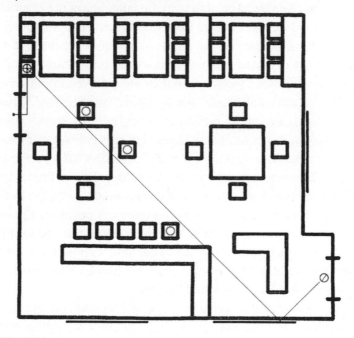

than one level. For purposes of surveillance, these structures provide elevated vantage points, ideal for seeing without being seen. In the same way, a table on the upstairs level of a restaurant or a chair on the mezzanine level will be subjected to far less scrutiny than will its eye-level counterpart. Next time you find yourself in such a position, take a moment to look down and notice how few others ever look up.

In combination with direction and elevation, any thorough analysis of location will consider proximity. The distance between the observer and the subject, especially under poor weather conditions, affects visibility significantly. It is difficult to overlook the presence of someone in our intimate or personal space, however artfully disguised he may be.[3] At this range, conscious recognition is assisted by instinct and amplified by senses other than the visual. As the subject moves farther away, he is more easily overlooked. This is especially so once the target has moved beyond the range of easy facial recognition—say about a hundred yards.

In the matter of positioning oneself to avoid detection, there is a second and often competing imperative to be considered—the operative's own ability to observe matters. Adopting a vantage point so remote and oblique that one can neither see nor be seen is rarely of any use. The art lies in manipulating the situation so that one's strength is both absolute and relative. Making use of reflections is one way that this result can be achieved in the context of surveillance. Unless squarely confronted by a mirror, people seldom pay much attention to reflections when going about their daily business. Keeping an eye on shop windows, polished metal surfaces, and reflective materials of all kinds, at a variety of angles, makes it possible to monitor positions to the front, side, and even behind, without ever exposing oneself to direct observation. It is equally important to take note of others employing this same technique.

Lines of sight can not only be manipulated but they can also be obscured or obstructed. In its simplest form, this technique involves positioning oneself behind an obstacle. In an open area, a tree, a vehicle, or the corner of a building will often suffice. Indoors, an alcove, a doorway, or a leafy plant perhaps will do the trick. By concealing his position immediately behind an obstacle, the operative

---

3. Opinions vary, but the intimate zone is generally thought to be located within about eighteen inches of the body. The personal zone is said to be between about one and a half feet and four feet from the body. As with many other aspects of the butterfly art, however, this rule is not absolute. When the surrounding circumstances are just right, it is even possible to pass unseen within an inch or two of another person.

can ensure that he enjoys a wide field of view with minimal and brief exposure, whereas the reverse is not true for anyone else who may be watching.

The obstruction need be neither large nor total to be effective. By way of example, the story is told at universities throughout the land of the inventive young co-ed who emerged from the shower to find herself the victim of a fraternity prank that deprived her of her clothing leaving her with only a small washcloth. Forced to make her way from the bathroom to the dorm room, she chose to cover her face with the only item available, thereby exposing her body but concealing her identity. This effect can be achieved, albeit in a much less spectacular fashion, with an open newspaper, book, or magazine. When it is raining or inclement, the same technique can be employed by using an umbrella held at a right angle.

Also, subtler ways of applying the principle of obstruction are available. While light may not exactly block lines of sight, too much or too little can at least obscure them. Many ancient treatises on military tactics speak to the importance of the position of forces relative to the sun. Anyone who has had to walk or drive due east at dawn can confirm that it is virtually impossible to make out anything or anyone in an arc of about thirty degrees around the sunrise. In fact, sun glare accounts for a significant proportion of automobile accidents, especially during the winter months when the snow contributes to this effect. When conditions are right, this time-tested technique can still be employed to advantage.

Conversely, shadow can also be used to conceal. This circumstance is more effective than mere darkness because of the power of contrast. The human eye can adjust to low light conditions generally; the process takes about thirty minutes, but the eyes have a much harder time detecting objects in darkness juxtaposed with light. This is so because the rods responsible for night vision can be "bleached out" for several minutes by exposure to white light. For this reason, nighttime operatives of all kinds use red lenses on their flashlights. Consistent with this principle, an alley, the lee of a building, or a position that is simply far enough to the side of a streetlight can provide a safe haven for the gray man.

According to a number of tactical manuals, after terrain, weather is the next most important CCD consideration. Heavy rain and thick fog, for example, can obscure visibility in the space of a few yards. In an urban environment, people's umbrellas also tend to limit their fields of vision. Pedestrains usually walk directly toward or away from a strong wind, rarely facing the perpendicular. Snow produces glare and focuses attention on conditions underfoot as opposed to alongside. And concealing clothing of all kinds attracts little attention when the weather justifies it. The person who wishes to advance without being recognized can exploit all these factors.

Learning the art of the butterfly is a process of gradual refinement. Of necessity, therefore, its principles progress from the obvious to the sublime. Granted, the more attenuated the connection between the cause and the intended effect, the greater the probability that intervening forces will alter the eventual outcome, but therein lies the artistry. As the number of variables increases and the interplay among them becomes ever more complex, the result becomes less certain. But when the desired effect is eventually achieved, it is a wondrous thing indeed: much like Lorenz's tornado over Texas.

Concealment by obstruction or impediment is a relatively straightforward proposition. Of significantly greater complexity is the ability to hide in plain view. As with our earlier studies in shadow and light, this too is often a matter of contrast. Certain trained observers of detail, fingerprint analysts, for example, are capable of picking out a tiny deviation in a seemingly homogenous group of samples. For most people, however, this is an impossible or at least an improbable feat. As a result, so long as he takes care that nothing he does makes him stand out in any significant way, the gray man can melt into a crowd with relative ease. He can simply disappear into a mass of humanity when the conditions are right.

Another means of avoiding detection while in plain view is the

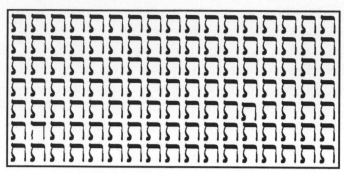

Which letter is different?

EEEEEEEEEEEEEEEEEEEEEEEEE
EEEEEEEEEEEEEEEEEEEEEEEEE
EEEEEEEEEEEEEEEEEEFEEEEEE
EEEEEEEEEEEEEEEEEEEEEEEEE
EEEEEEEEEEEEEEEEEEEEEEEEE
EEEEEEEEEEEEEEEEEEEEEEEEE
EEEEEEEEEEEEEEEEEEEEEEEEE
EEEEEEEEEEEEEEEEEEEEEEEEE

Is it easier in English?

use of distraction techniques. For instance, how many of us have been sitting in a bar or some other establishment and noticed that it appears we are being watched by one or several of the other patrons, only to discover that we have inadvertently positioned ourselves next to or underneath the television set? The irony here is that despite our proximity to the principle object of the other people's attention, such is the hypnotic effect of this device that we have still probably not been noticed. How much more invisible would we have been, then, had we selected a table at the opposite end of the establishment?

Despite increasing appearances to the contrary, the television set is not the only thing that can hold others spellbound. Any type of spectator event—a sporting contest, the giving of a speech, or a street performance—will typically have the same effect. With their attention focused on the matter before them, people are usually oblivious to what is going on behind or beside them. On a slightly darker note, the general public's curiosity, and therefore its susceptibility to distraction, is perhaps more pronounced when it is morbid. As with the phenomenon of rubbernecking at the scene of an automobile accident, the distracting event need not be a pleasant one.

The event also need not be coincidental. There are many ways to create a distraction, either with or without the aid of an accomplice. With the assistance of a confederate, the matter is simplicity itself. The making of virtually any kind of scene in public by one person will have and hold the attention of others, thereby eliminating scrutiny with respect to anyone or anything else. Something as innocuous as a shout emanating from one end of a shop, for example, will reliably divert attention from the other.

When acting alone, the process is a little more involved. Training programs teach field operatives ways to arrange an item or group of items so that they will create just such a diversion on the happening of a triggering event or after a period of time. An empty bottle balanced upside down on a door handle will crash to the ground at the slightest attempt to turn the knob from the other side. Similarly, a cigarette tucked into a book of matches by the filter end will burn down in a matter of minutes, eventually igniting this improvised flare and anything else nearby. Something as simple as surreptitiously tossing a noisy item far away from one's position, a coin perhaps, will give rise to a brief auditory distraction. Tiny packets of flash powder marketed as toys are dramatically reliable, and even the tired, old "hey, look over there" ploy can still work on occasion.

Continuing in the vein of distraction techniques, one should note that the appearance of a beautiful woman has a magnetic effect on all the men and a fair number of ladies in any given location. This is true of celebrities as well and of attractive men to a slightly lesser degree. In such matters, it is also true that increased numbers tend to have an exponential impact on the effect. As illustrated in the cinematic version of the extraordinary exploits of world-class con-man Frank Abagnale, for example, a wanted felon might just get past a cordon of FBI agents if dressed as an airline pilot (blending) in the company of several attractive stewardesses (distraction).

While we are in the way of drawing on popular culture for examples, a few words are in order regarding that most improbable of gadgets, the Somebody Else's Problem (SEP) device. According to the science fiction author Douglas Adams:

> An SEP . . . is something that we can't see, or don't see, or our brain doesn't let us see, because we think that it's somebody else's problem. That's what SEP means. Somebody Else's Problem. The brain just edits it out, it's like a blind spot.
>
> —*The Hitchhiker's Guide to the Galaxy*

While the technology may be far-fetched, the idea is very real. In the modern world, people are constantly being bombarded by stimuli from a variety of sources: telephone, television, radio, faxes, and live interactions as well. In order to preserve their sanity, they have evolved certain conscious and subconscious filters. Of necessity they dismiss masses of information as irrelevant, uninteresting, or unimportant on an hourly basis. Falling squarely in this category are issues they identify as being SEP.

"Somebody else's problem" is to be distinguished from "somebody else's business," a subject that tends to have exactly the opposite effect on observers. The technique works precisely because it is a *problem*, and people therefore have a natural aversion to paying attention for fear of getting involved. What type of problem will work best depends largely on the type of target, but a few common examples include litter, homelessness, messes and spills, and tedious matters of all kinds. For example, few things will compel a pedestrian to cross the street as surely as a group of earnest looking people with clipboards stopping passers-by on the sidewalk ahead to ask them to complete a survey.

How, then, do we apply this principle in an operational sense? In combination with the factors already discussed, the person seeking to avoid attention should create the appearance of some activity that is clearly SEP. Drawing our data from the laboratory of life once again, there was once a group of cadets at a certain military academy who had a tradition of pulling annual pranks on the unfortunate residents of the town in which they were based. One year, they obtained several mannequins from a shop owned by one of their parents, dressed them in workman's clothes complete with orange safety vests and yellow hard hats, and positioned them in and around an open manhole cover in the center of town. In order to perfect the illusion, they placed detour signs around the location and made sure that drivers would only have a brief and obstructed view of the scene before having to turn down another street. It took over a week for anyone to notice.

Such elaborate measures are not always necessary in creating the impression that the matter at hand is SEP. Janitors, repairmen, and inspectors of all sorts move around us, equipped with mops, tool belts, and theodolites, attending to matters that most people view as not their problem. These workers are seldom noticed unless it is our area, utility, or property that requires their attention. Even then, some among us rarely take the time to pay any attention to the type of people they typically think of as "support staff." Secretaries, waiters, and service people of all types are, to them, virtually invisible. Not only does this leave such potential marks blind to an entire segment of the society in which they live, but it also makes them all the more attractive as targets.

In China, the art of *feng shui* lays down principles for the auspicious location of every object relative to every other. In the United

States, the business of real estate is said to depend on three main points: location, location, location. In the realm of the butterfly, this factor is likewise critical. It merely serves a different purpose.

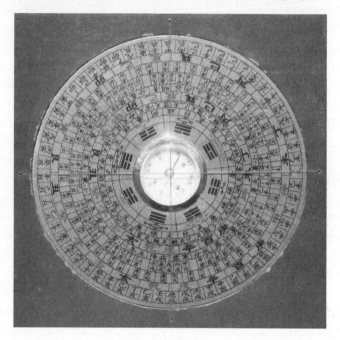

Could his vanishing be attributed to the way he orchestrated the movements of the multiple attackers so that they fairly tripped over one another in their haste to be the first to get a piece of him and, therefore, momentarily obscured his position with their own bodies? Perhaps . . .

MOTION

Movement amongst the trees of a forest shows that the
enemy is advancing. The appearance of a number of
screens in the midst of thick grass means that the enemy
wants to make us suspicious. The rising of birds in their
flight is the sign of an ambuscade. Startled beasts indicate
that a sudden attack is coming. When there is dust rising
in a high column, it is the sign of chariots advancing;
when the dust is low, but spread over a wide area, it
betokens the approach of infantry. When it branches out
in different directions, it shows that parties have been
sent to collect firewood. A few clouds of dust moving to
and fro signify that the army is encamping. Humble words
and increased preparations are signs that the enemy is
about to advance. Violent language and driving forward
as if to the attack are signs that he will retreat.

—Sun Tzu, *The Art of War*

Apart from manning a stationary observation post, very few of the
operative's objectives can be achieved from a fixed position. Typical
missions such as infiltrating a location, delivering or retrieving an
item, exfiltrating an asset, and conducting roving surveillance at
times all involve a degree of motion. Yet in both animal and human
kingdoms, motion tends to catch the attention of predators of all
sorts. How then can the operative best neutralize this natural tendency?

This question has occupied intelligence agents for as long as the
art of espionage has been practiced, and defensive measures continue to be taught and tested to this day in secure training facilities
as well as on the streets of capital cities around the world. The level
of scrutiny to which the operative is subjected increases during time
of war, whether of the hot or cold variety, and from these historical
examples, much of modern methodology has evolved.

Common to most schools of countersurveillance is the idea that an initial distinction must be drawn between "man on man" and "zone" surveillance. When the operative is already being watched by others, he, as "the rabbit," must attempt to lose "the hounds," at least for a period of time, if he is to complete his mission. The art of evading detection while passing through a specific zone, by contrast, requires the operative to avoid being "made" in the first place. By virtue of the diminished level of individual attention implicit in the latter category, we often consider zone infiltration the easier operational objective. So it is to this subject that we turn first.

Perhaps the most straightforward way to avoid detection is to employ the masking principles discussed earlier in this book, but in a dynamic fashion. Ensuring that there is some constant obstruction or impediment to surveillance is clearly more difficult to achieve when the operative is in motion, as opposed to occupying a fixed position, but with sufficient training and experience, it is an obtainable objective.

It is a fact of the modern world that one can travel great distances without ever stepping outdoors. The labyrinth of subways, indoor malls, and pedestrian walkways found in most cities and quite a few towns can provide sheltered passage to most places, exposing the traveler only to the scrutiny of those in the immediate vicinity. Such passageways can be used to provide cover for the operative who intends to enter a potentially hostile zone.

When fixed, contiguous cover is unavailable, a more creative approach must be adopted. One of the most challenging aspects of remaining concealed while underway is that the operative is not the only thing in motion. But where there is adversity, there is also opportunity. In this type of situation, for instance, there is the challenge to dealing with many types of motion: the operative's own, the surveillance team's, and other things and people as well. Thus, the complexity of the analytical process is increased exponentially. The operative must keep track of several dynamic factors that are themselves in a state of constant change relative to his own position. It is

---

Exercise Three:
Moving Under Cover (Elevated Observation Post)

Notes: Find the best route from the operative's point of origin to the destination*; opposition surveillance located on rooftop adjacent to origin; awning provides cover from elevated surveillance point . . .

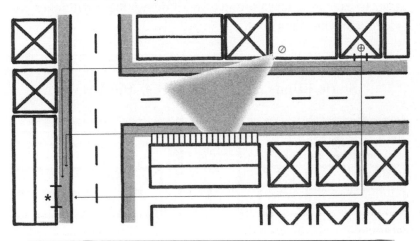

---

a little like trying to catch a fly ball while running instead of standing still and, at the same time, keeping an eye on the runner on base, the umpire, and the crowd.

Rather than letting this make the job twice as hard, the skilled practitioner can try to use one element of this motion to mask or offset another. But before he can have any chance of making this work, a little time must be invested in further study. There is a natural rhythm to life, whether it be the call of the wild animals or the stop and go of traffic at an intersection. These things can be used to advantage. Specific patterns can be used to cover others directly. The sound of footfalls on autumn leaves if timed to coincide with the chirping of the cicadas will not give away one's position. Likewise, the quick dash from one doorway to another can be concealed entirely from onlookers if it takes place behind a slowly moving bus.

This fairly straightforward tactic can be employed under more complicated conditions as well. It is possible, for example, to use a steadily moving object, like a car, as a blind between two changing positions—the operative's own and that of the watcher most probably. This inexact art may require increasing or decreasing the pace or making use of additional barriers at times, but it is actually far easier to execute than it sounds. In so doing, the practitioner can hide in a moving blind spot.

Exercise Four:
Static Blinds, Moving Screens, and Draws

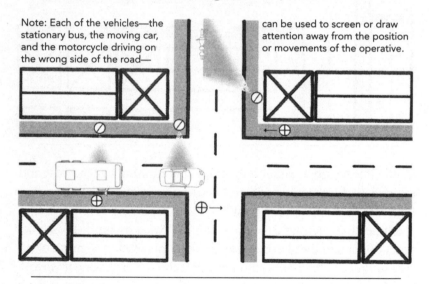

Note: Each of the vehicles—the stationary bus, the moving car, and the motorcycle driving on the wrong side of the road— can be used to screen or draw attention away from the position or movements of the operative.

This is so, at least in part, because human instincts permit us to accomplish certain tasks automatically, which, if intellectualized, would likely elude us. What is the differential in frequency and pitch between your child's sleepy cry and her angry cry? How many turns are there between your work and home? What exact moves are required to tie your shoe? These are things we may not be able to articulate, but nevertheless, we just know them. And this instinctive ability, colloquially known as "op sense," may be the most important asset in the gray man's operational portfolio.

Sometimes the number of variables at issue is simply too great to be analyzed with logic. In preparing to cross a street, for instance, there are the vehicles on both sides, the pedestrians at each corner, the vendors, the people exiting the stores, the noises emanating from the stores, the aircraft overhead, the steam grates underfoot, and a thousand other factors to be considered. Sit still for a few minutes. Observe the pattern. Absorb the pattern. You will know when the time is right to make your move. It is a little like the moment your body at last agrees to follow your brain's earlier command to take that first plunge of spring from the diving board into the chilly waters below.

Another way to defeat surveillance is simply to avoid it. Having a working knowledge of the back alleys and side exits found in all metropolitan and some suburban locations allows the operative to select a route that is unlikely to be heavily trafficked or closely watched. In places where the lack of construction removes these options, nature provides alternatives. In rural locales and more sparsely populated suburbs, there are almost certainly several large tracts of undeveloped land. Uninhabited, untraveled, unlit, and frequently forested, these green belts, easily identified with a topographical map, can provide the gray man with virtual invisibility in his travels.[4] It is important to recognize and accept that these approaches will frequently require the

4. Availing oneself of such unbroken trails, especially if the great outdoors is the actual theater of engagement, requires at least a rudimentary knowledge of field craft. As a threshold matter, without having the ability to navigate in some fashion, these alternate routes are of virtually no value at all and can in fact be quite hazardous. Navigation over short distances can be easily accomplished using a map and compass, the point-to-point method, or dead reckoning. Knowing which dangerous plants and animals populate the area, how to traverse a small creek or rock fall, and what to do if injured will suffice for most limited trips into the bush. For more ambitious undertakings, a wider array of skills is required. A serious cross-country trek or an outing lasting more than a day or so can require competence in such areas as shelter building and camouflage, food procurement, and preparation, and specialized skills relating to water, snow, or mountainous terrain.

taking of a somewhat indirect or winding path to one's destination. This is simply the cost of passing undetected.

When surveillance cannot be obstructed or avoided altogether, it can at least be impeded. Whether traveling within or outside of town, remember the forces of nature can be powerful allies or vicious opponents, depending on the nature of the operational environment. For example, heavy weather conditions that might provide ideal cover in an urban setting can slow or halt one's progress altogether in the field. Knowing what conditions to expect and the way they will affect different tactical scenarios are, therefore, of paramount importance.

Moving in the shadow of something else works to conceal the operative's presence in much the same way that the beat of a song can cover the tick of the synchronous metronome. But this is not the only such approach that can be employed to pass undetected. Sound-canceling machines work by projecting mirror images of the target frequency, thus, in effect, canceling it out. In a similar sense, a sufficiently pronounced motion in one direction can distract the attention of onlookers from a move in the opposite direction. An emergency vehicle, sirens blaring as it speeds eastbound through an intersection, for example, will likely offset any attention directed at the westbound lane.

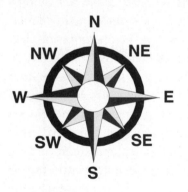

When it is impossible to provide direct cover for the operative's movement, there are still ways in which his motion, like his location, can be controlled to blend with the background so that any who may be looking will not truly see. In this regard there are three major components to be considered: route, rhythm, and rate. These related and sometimes overlapping factors must work in concert if they are to be deployed to best effect.

As has already been discussed in some detail, the goal of fading into the background sometimes demands the taking of an indirect route so as to avoid the most common and convenient positions for hostile surveillance. It may also require studying and conforming motion to the general rhythm of a situation. With respect to rate, the rule is "More haste, less speed." In the realm of the butterfly, infinite care must be taken to control this aspect of one's conduct, for rushing tends to reduce the operative's ability to perform well. It causes him to fumble, to trip, and to overlook things. It also attracts unwanted attention.

A person who is clearly in a hurry tends to be noticed. People get out of the way. They may also wonder what the source of the urgency is. This is especially true when driving to one's destination. Motorists usually assume that anyone who is going faster than they are is a maniac, and anyone who is going slower is an idiot. Idiots and maniacs are noticed. And in the end, jockeying for position in a long line of traffic will usually only shave a few seconds off arrival times. Test this proposition by picking out a few easily recognized vehicles in your travels; then, stop at a rest area and see how long it takes them to catch up with you after you have fought so hard for pole position.

Rapid motion also tends to be noisier and messier than a measured pace. Particularly in the field, the cracking and disturbance of undergrowth that result from a mad dash is easy to detect and track even long after its occurrence. In the city too, the sound of rapid footfalls at one's back is one of the most reliable attention getters, especially after dark. Finally, there is the matter of one's gait. Much can be detected by the trained observer from the way in which someone walks. The slouch of the chronically depressed and the rigidity of the soldier are equally conspicuous characteristics. Watch yourself in this regard, on videotape if at all possible, and strive for a nondescript result.

While the principles discussed in the preceding are commonly taught for the purposes of zone infiltration, we may apply many of them to counter man-on-man coverage as well. There are, however, certain issues specific to the art of one-on-one observation. Understanding these operational considerations depends in large part on whether one approaches the matter from the point of view of the watcher or the watched and whether the goal is pursuit or evasion. The latter skill, of course, depends to a large degree on the level and nature of the former, so we shall begin this part of our analysis with the hunter, and not the hunted. We shall further assume that the hunter's goal is merely to track his prey, for anything beyond this is for an altogether different book.

The first commandment of surveillance is "Thou shalt not get caught." The successful completion of a single surveillance operation, while often extremely important, is rarely mission critical in a strategic sense. Alerting the target to the presence of that surveillance, however, can be. This is to say, in light of the first commandment, we must make a determination even before any active steps are taken as to whether the operation should be postponed or abandoned at the first sign of recognition by the target. As frustrating as this can be, hard experience has taught field operatives that once established, the so-called "bailout" protocol must be scrupulously observed.

The scope of any pursuit or surveillance operation depends in large part on the resources at one's command. When executed by government or affluent private entities, such endeavors are quite large and may include literally dozens of agents, several vehicles, homing devices, and aerial or satellite reconnaissance. Such resources are beyond the means of most people and even some organizations. They also take much of the challenge and most of the art out of the equation and, thus, have no place in the realm of the butterfly. We shall therefore proceed with a more modest approach in mind.

Intelligence agencies have long experimented with ways of "tagging" a target using electronic transponders, invisible paints, and even pheromones. This allows for a buffer of sorts, in that a momentary loss of visual contact does not necessarily doom the operation to failure. But even without the assistance of high-tech gadgetry, it is still possible, and quite helpful, to mark the target. Police officers manning drunk driving checkpoints, for example, have been known to clean off one of the headlights of every car in the parking lot of the local bar so as to be able to identify them on the road at some later point by the differential in brightness. Surveillance professionals without access to assistance or technology may engage in similar practices, marking the bumpers of the target's vehicle with a small piece of reflective tape or painting a drop of Wite-Out on an umbrella so as to allow for easy identification from an elevated vantage point in poor weather.

Before heading into the field, the operative-as-hunter must take a moment to consider his appearance. Drawing on the principles discussed in the preceding and making sure that he is properly attired for the physical demands of the pursuit, he must ensure that nothing about his physical presentation will draw the attention of the target. When traveling by car, the same rules should inform the choice of vehicle: nothing too flashy, clunky, bright, faded, or exotic. At the same time, adequate power and maneuverability must be available. If the circumstances permit it, a motorcycle can be an excellent choice for these purposes.

The next step in the process is, naturally, to tail the target without being detected. We have already discussed the subject of blending with the environment in detail. Keeping these foundation principles in mind, we now apply them to this bilateral undertaking. In this regard, range to target is a critical factor. Trainers teach surveillance operatives to maximize their distance from the object of their attention up to the point that maintaining visual contact becomes questionable and then to close the range by about a third to provide a margin of error.

They are also taught to ensure that the path of pursuit is not one-dimensional. Rather than moving directly behind the target, they will position themselves to one side, and if at all possible, at a different elevation. For example, if the target's course takes him down a street, they may cross to the other side. If the target is going through a mall, they might watch from an upper floor. Practiced at its highest level, this technique even makes it possible to follow from in front, making good use of peripheral vision, reflection, and blending. Whether traveling by car, by bike, or on foot, the experienced practitioner makes use of blind spots, both static and dynamic, to ensure that he is never directly exposed to the target's view, even peripherally.

Inevitably, the question of being made will arise: what do you do when it appears that the target has noticed something out of the ordinary? As just discussed, if the stakes are not high and the opportunity for another attempt is readily available, it may be best to abort the operation. If this is not an acceptable or desirable option, it may be possible to brazen it out. Almost anywhere the target leads, there will be other people walking and driving all around, for all kinds of purposes. They may stop, start, turn, and reverse course, for any of several, perfectly innocent reasons: they may notice an attractive item in a shop window; they may choose a different destination midcourse; they may realize that they have forgotten some essential item back at their departure point. All these rationales could equally apply to the operative. He must simply play the part.

In the category of brazen responses to potential identification, the story is told of the attractive, young, female operative who when confronted with that moment of eye contact that unmistakably denotes recognition marched right up to her target and said, "I saw you watching me on the corner back there, and wondered if you'd like to get a cup of coffee." Bold, certainly, and at least in some situations, perhaps the best means of keeping the subject in view and under control.

There is an American Indian saying to the effect that the hunter can make many mistakes, but the hunted, only one. With respect to surveillance and countersurveillance, this paradigm is reversed. Unless the ultimate goal is apprehension, then the subject can fail to evade his pursuers all day long and succeed just once, whereas the watcher cannot afford to be made at all. Turning then to the subject of evasion, then, we find several tactical imperatives can be addressed here as well.

While the employment of blending skills and the use of "cutouts" or intermediaries for passing material and information can help the gray man avoid detection in the first place, the art of evasion presupposes that the target has already been identified. The first requirement, therefore, is that the operative be aware that he is under surveillance at all. In all manner of professions and circumstances, both malignant and benign, people may have reason to believe that they are the subject of someone else's attention. While this can trigger a useful, general awareness of the possibility of being watched, the most powerful countermeasure to surveillance is, of course, direct identification of the watchers.

Awareness is essential in the realm of the butterfly. Maintaining an active appreciation of the world around us in its infinite complexity is both the way to this place as well as the destination itself. Keeping a running inventory of people, vehicles, and other objects in the immediate vicinity, even at a semiconscious level, will assist the operative in many ways, not least in recognizing that someone may be watching.

The process of conducting surveillance requires that there be a known starting point for the target, and the tailing is much easier for the "hounds" if the destination and even the probable route are also ascertainable. To eliminate these liabilities when operating as the "rabbit," operatives will avoid following regular patterns, either in time or in place. They will depart given locations at different times, from different points of egress. They may use the loading bay door. They might take the service elevator on occasion or the stairs at times. They will make use of the back alleys and green belts discussed previously.

Once in motion, the well-trained field agent will pause from time to time to take a look behind, as well as beside and overhead. If this can be achieved subtly, perhaps making use of reflection, peripheral vision, and hearing, so much the better. The less concerned the pursuer is about being made, the more careless he will become in this regard. Thus, when it is necessary to stop and turn, the skilled practitioner will try not to do so obviously. Coming to an abrupt halt midstride and peering at the street behind advertises one's concern to everyone. Pausing ostensibly to pick up a curio from a street vendor, to read a sign, or to look at one's watch simply says nothing at all.

Should the practitioner find himself pursued on foot in an outdoor or wilderness setting, different rules and principles apply, borrowed this time from the woodsman. Where the sounds, sights, and smells of the city serve to cover a trail to some degree, the same is not true in the wild. Noises and odors may carry for many miles, and unobstructed and unpopulated lines of sight increase potential following distances considerably. Furthermore, the relatively untraveled character of these surroundings can assist the hunter in tracking his prey.

Those who wish to pass undetected in the forest move slowly. Unlike a sidewalk or a grassy patch, the leafy floor may conceal broken branches, sinkholes, and wildlife, the disturbance of which will leave a trail. The sight of two ends of a broken spiderweb fluttering in the breeze while the spider herself is in the process of responding

to the kinesthetic damage report can alert the observant pursuer that something has recently passed this way. Both webs and tripwires are easier to spot in bright sun and after the rain.

The wilderness can also provide assistance in the effort to disappear. Crossing flowing water will break the trail of scent detectable to various animals. The movement of wildlife can create helpful distractions. And storms of all kinds may serve to cover tracks.

What is of paramount importance in moving through the bush is that the operative adapts himself to this environment. Unlike urban areas, the outdoors is not designed for our convenience. We must therefore be sensitive to its particular patterns and conventions, if we are to exploit it to best advantage. Those who wish to evade or pursue silently in the wild, for example, tend to wear soft, rubber-soled shoes rather than heavy boots. The thin layer separating foot from floor allows for greater sensitivity, sensation, and silence and leaves less of a track.

The process of "shaking a tail," whether in an urban or a rural environment, is greatly assisted by employing choke points or channels: places that by virtue of their dimensions, limited number of entrances, or other features make it difficult for people to slip by unnoticed. Inside, virtually any doorway can serve this purpose, as can a tunnel or enclosed walkway. Outside, narrow sidewalks, alleys, or corners can have the same effect. In a rural or wilderness setting, a narrow trail through treacherous ground or a bridge or stream can be employed in a similar fashion. Whatever the choke point, it is important to stop on the other side, preferably in a concealed position, and wait for a few minutes to see who might be following. This process can be assisted by paying close attention to any reaction the pursuers may have when they recognize that their target has come to an unexpected halt.

Whether operating in an urban or a rural environment, remember that it is far easier for the target to identify and elude those in pursuit by entering an environment where he blends and they stand out. For the young, casually dressed practitioner, a college campus might work; for the older, better-dressed operative, a fine dining restaurant or upscale club may be the right choice.

When driving, the process of pausing to check for pursuers is assisted by the constant flow of traffic. Pulling over to the side of the

Exercise Five: Choke Points and Channels

Notes: The road cones and the two desks inside the building's entrance form choke points; the passage between the two buildings, the stairs, and the single-lane road are channels.

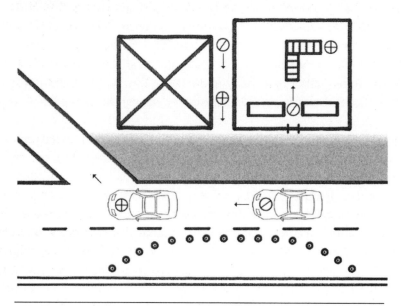

road, into a rest area or a gas station, will force anyone behind you to do the same, or he will risk losing track of the target. Anyone in front will be long gone, and a quick check overhead will reveal whether there is an airborne component to be addressed. If surveillance is being assisted by satellite, there is little to be done other than to remain indoors, and even this affords little protection from modern imaging systems.

The British eloquently employed many of these principles of evasion to effect perhaps the most daring exfiltration of the Cold War: the escape of former KGB Colonel Oleg Gordievsky from under the watchful eye of his surveillance team. Gordievsky, the most senior KGB official at the Soviet Embassy in London, had for some time been a double agent for British Intelligence. Unfortunately for him and his family, an American traitor named Aldrich Ames betrayed this secret to his Soviet masters. Consistent with standard KGB practices, Gordievsky was recalled to Moscow, confronted with the evidence against him, and then released, with a team of watchers tailing him to see where he would go and whom he might contact.

Relying on the power of patterns, his British handlers instructed Gordievsky to continue his daily practice of jogging in a nearby park. After a few uneventful days, he brought with him a concealed change of clothing and, using a convenient choke point to buy a few moments of privacy, engaged in a quick change of appearance. Using the principle of the path less traveled, he made his way out of an unguarded exit, then used another channel to reach the subway to St. Petersburg, and finally took a bus to the country where he met up with his exfiltration team.

During the second phase of the operation, at least the parts that can now be told, Gordievsky was to be taken across the border in the trunk of a diplomatic vehicle, masked with a thermal blanket to avoid detection by high-tech means. Unfortunately, at the border a canine sentry began to alert in the area of the trunk. One of the team members, who was evidently well versed in the art of the butterfly, had the presence of mind to counter this threat with a hastily improvised distraction technique—a half-eaten ham sandwich. A few miles later, when Gordievsky heard a specific song being played on the radio, he knew it was safe to emerge, and one of the greatest intelligence coups of the Cold War had been achieved.

Could it have been the way he turned almost imperceptibly in one direction, inviting the opponents to follow the path of a circle around his position only to reverse the turn suddenly when the time was right, and thereby spring the trap? Perhaps . . .

ACTION

But it is necessary to know well how to disguise this characteristic, and to be a great pretender and dissembler; and men are so simple, and so subject to present necessities, that he who seeks to deceive will always find someone who will allow himself to be deceived.

—Niccolò Machiavelli, *The Prince*

When the goal is simply to get from one destination to another without being identified, then the principles discussed in the preceding section should be sufficient. But more often than not, the operative is also tasked with achieving some specific objective while passing unnoticed: picking up a package perhaps or making contact with a source. If the operative is already under surveillance, these actions will be difficult to conceal; even if he has not yet been identified, such activities will tend to attract unwanted attention. When there is such an additional component to the mission, an entirely new set of skills is implicated. Thus, having acquired the ability to move from place to place largely undetected, we must now turn to what can be accomplished along the way or once we have arrived.

The proving ground for this new skill set was the world of the so-called "pipeliners." During the height of the Cold War a kind of uneasy stalemate, sometimes referred to as a balance of terror, developed between the two global superpowers. The intelligence agencies of each nation were fully aware that operatives of the other lived and worked on their soil, frequently under the cloak of diplomatic immunity, but wielding the dagger of espionage in the shadows. In many cases, therefore, counterintelligence officers knew the identities of virtually every foreign covert operative at a given consular station, but could do nothing but watch them, so watch them they did.

In response to the unprecedented intensity of this type of surveillance, exacerbated by the home-court advantage, Western intelligence agencies developed a new set of countermeasures known collectively as "the Moscow Rules." Implicit in these protocols was the assumption that the adversary had already identified the operative and that he would be at all times subjected to extensive and professional surveillance. No longer could he hope to evade detection simply by trying to avoid drawing attention in the first place, and his chances of getting "out of the loop" for any length of time were slim to none. Thus, the actions that needed to be taken would have to be executed right under the nose of the enemy.

The most common operational goals relate to the manipulation of items: picking them up, leaving them behind, moving them from place to place, and the like, all without anyone noticing. In the parlance of the pipeliners, these objectives include such activities as the "dead letter drop," the depositing of a message in a prearranged location for retrieval by a colleague at a later time, and the "brush by," a live exchange of items by two agents whose paths converge for only a moment, without any apparent acknowledgment of one another.

The preferred method for executing these exchanges without detection is the creation of a moment "in obscura" (or I.O.): a brief interval in which any possible surveillance is momentarily interrupted. This effect can be achieved by the use of channels and choke points, but it can also be created by timing the action to coincide with the passing of an obstacle of sufficient size or even rapid acceleration or a sudden change of direction sufficient to throw off the ever-present surveillance team by just a few seconds.

In one particularly notorious example, a double agent who knew he was under FBI surveillance disconnected the brake lights on his vehicle and then had his wife lead the watchers down a dark and winding road while he sat in the passenger seat. At just the right moment, the wife increased speed to put some distance between the vehicles and then slowed rapidly enough (without the telltale glare of brake lights) for the husband to bail out without being detected. The deception was complete when the wife activated the "jack-in-the-box," a dummy silhouette rigged to pop up in the passenger seat to cover the husband's departure.

Exercise Six: The *In Obscura* Moment

Notes: A moment *in obscura* can be created using the building's contours, doorways or stairwells, or the people and objects within it and without. The I.O. moment allows many actions, among them the brush-by below.

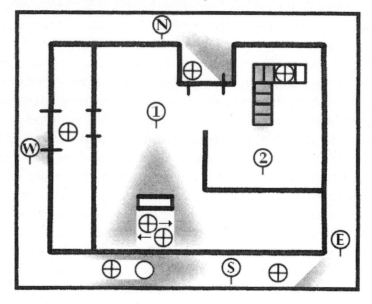

When conditions conspire to make it impossible to procure an I.O. moment, then the operative must move his game to yet another level. Under the constant scrutiny of his unwelcome audience, he must now draw on the art of the magician: a professional who is an occasional visiting member of the faculty. The magician makes his living executing seemingly impossible actions, ideally without the truth ever being detected. His abilities take an extraordinary amount of time to develop and maintain. Fortunately, those who would borrow from his box of tricks are usually under a little less scrutiny and can, therefore, get by with a somewhat less polished performance.

The type of tricks at issue in this regard must first be distinguished from the psychological and emotional techniques employed by mentalists, psychics, fortune-tellers and the like, in their efforts to read minds and predict or control behavior. There is still something of value to be learned from such professions, but these latter abilities are more appropriately addressed in subsequent sections of this material. For present purposes, we confine our attention to the type of magic that involves manipulating physical items.

In this regard, there are three principle categories to be considered: concealment, illusion, and misdirection. These approaches permit the practitioner to achieve an objective without anyone else noticing, but each does so in a different way. The first is based on the now familiar practice of obstructing or obscuring people's ability to see, this time at extremely close proximity. The second involves making people think that they are seeing something that is not really so. The third depends on distracting people's attention from the true goal, however briefly, so that it can be achieved openly but with impunity.

The principles involved in concealing one's actions are similar in many ways to those used to conceal oneself. The difference is merely one of scale. Such familiar factors as distance, lighting, and other ambient conditions can therefore be helpful in masking actions under the right conditions, but since this specific field of engagement tends to be much more limited in size, such factors may be somewhat less helpful. For instance, while low lighting may help mask a covert action, it is seldom sufficient to shield the truth from prying eyes altogether.

Let us take as an example the planting of a listening device, a common enough objective in investigations of all sorts. The critical issue here is, of course, that the operative must be able to place the device at the chosen location without being detected. When the tactic to be employed is concealment, the palm is one of the most effective tools. And while modern electronic eavesdropping devices, even those with video capability, can be miniaturized to an extraordinary degree, the techniques described herein can be applied to items as large as a golf ball.

The process of palming an item, as the name suggests, begins with hiding it in the palm of the hand. This much is fairly straight-forward. As long as there is flesh between the item and the observer, the line of sight is obstructed. The artistry lies not so much in concealing the object itself, but in concealing the fact that something is in the palm, for the hand that is holding something looks different from the empty hand. For most of the operation, simply concealing the hand itself in a pocket or behind the back can achieve this result. The critical moment occurs when the object has to be deployed in some fashion.

During the brief period of time the hand is exposed, the operative's hand must appear to be empty. This effect depends in large part on ensuring that it has a natural appearance. Clasping something in a tight fist tells everyone what is going on. Cupping it in the

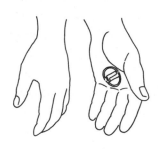

palm, or trapping it between the fingers, allows the hand to hang open, revealing nothing. With a little practice, a variety of objects can be held this way: coins, pens, folded pieces of paper, or anything of similar size. For larger items, keep the back of the hand facing any observers, lest they catch a glimpse of whatever is tucked inside.

As important as the way the hand appears is where it is held. It is quite natural to position a hand that is holding something a little differently than an empty one. Some people will keep a fistful of change out in front of them while walking to the vending machine. Others might rattle it at their sides. Whatever the impulse, the operative must recognize this tendency and eliminate it. The hand should hang at the side, moving in a carefree manner that will at first feel quite unnatural when it is gripping an item of some importance.

Another advantage of the palming method is that a release can be achieved unobtrusively. Whereas a closed fist must be opened to retrieve the object it contains, a relaxed hand can release a palmed object. It is a subtle distinction but an important one. Returning to our hypothetical mission, then, if the operative walks into the target's office, appearing not to be holding anything at all, leans up against a bookcase for a moment, pressing his palm against its side, and then excuses himself, the deed will be done with no one any the wiser. This is the art of concealment in action.

If concealment is the process of hiding what is, then illusion is the practice of showing what is not. It is the ability to create the impression that the feet sticking out of one end of the box the magician has just sawed in half belong to the head at the other end. It is the disembodied hand that the medium summons at a séance. It is the briefcase carried by the undercover narcotics agent filled with rectangular bundles of newspaper, each with a real hundred-dollar bill on top.

Unlike concealment, illusion often requires a certain amount of technological support. At one extreme of the spectrum is the next generation of military electronic countermeasures that use complex systems, including holographic projection, to create false images in the mind of the enemy. At the other is the low-tech but high-concept design from which these modern ideas sprang: the practice of dumping thousands of tiny strips of tinfoil known as "window" out of aircraft flying over hostile territory during World War II to create a massive, phantom radar contact.

Illusions, more or less by definition, tend not to be durable. The passage of time, a change in position, or the result of too close an examination will often reveal the truth. Thus, illusion is best employed in a limited capacity, to create a small window for the achievement of the next step in the operation. As applied to our hypothetical bugging mission, the illusion might be that the eavesdropping device is disguised as some other, innocuous item—a paperweight perhaps. Further scrutiny, either visual or electronic, may reveal its true nature, but over the short term it will serve its purpose.

Drawing another example from the historical record, during the

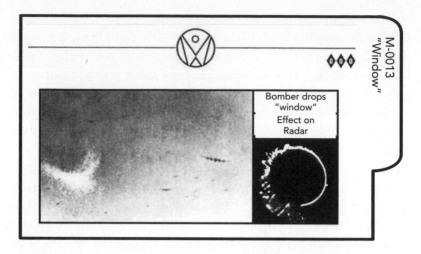

Bomber drops
"window"
Effect on
Radar

M-0013
"Window"

height of the Cold War, a certain Western intelligence agency wanted to eavesdrop on the office of a Soviet diplomat. Unfortunately, the cautious official had the interior of his office swept for electronic devices on a regular basis. After months of surveillance and many failed attempts, one of the agents on the case noticed that pigeons frequently perched on the ledge of the open window of the office in question. A bug was therefore installed on a stuffed bird, and the counterfeit was duly placed on the ledge. Any attention directed toward the window was thus caught up in the illusion, and the operation yielded a tremendous amount of valuable information while it lasted.

Illusion need not always be physical. Statements, confidences, loyalties, and promises can also be illusory. In this way, creating an illusion is not beyond the capabilities of the average person. When the mother of the six-year-old picks up the phone, dials the number for the recorded theater times, and proceeds to "talk" with Santa Claus or the homeroom teacher, this is illusion. When the used car salesman retreats into an empty office to "run the customer's final offer by his boss," this is illusion. When the police officer tells the codefendant that his partner in crime is singing like a bird in the next room, this is illusion.

Related to the practices of concealment and illusion is the art of misdirection, but there is an important conceptual distinction to be understood. When concealment or illusion deceives us, we may look, but we do not see the truth. When we are subject to skillful misdirection, we do not even get the chance to look, at least not in the right direction, at the right moment. Misdirection is perhaps the riskiest tactic in this category because the true goal is usually achieved without additional protection or camouflage of any kind, leaving nothing in the way of a fallback position should the ruse fail.

Broadly speaking, misdirection can be divided into two types or, more accurately, two time frames: momentary and lasting. Momentary misdirection usually relies on a startling event to distract the attention of observers. It is the flash of the magician's powder or the detonation of the special operations soldier's magnesium grenade. In our hypothetical eavesdropping mission, it might be as simple as a coin dropped to cover the sight or sound of placing the device. Even when the event is sufficiently startling to capture all the attention of all the observers, it is still, by its nature, fairly short-lived. This reality in turn gives rise to a very demanding set of imperatives with regard to the timing of the operative's objective. In order to be both successful and safe, it must be executed after the distraction has taken effect, but before it has worn off.

Further complicating this proposition is the fact that susceptibility to distraction varies by person and circumstances. The battle-hardened mercenary, for example, will likely anticipate the opposing force's attempt to soften the target with "thunder flashes" before entry, and he can prepare accordingly. He might entrench himself in a defensive position without windows, he may have ear and eye protection, and, above all, he will recognize the initial volley for what it is—an attempt to misdirect.

In its more lasting incarnation, misdirection overlaps significantly with the principles of illusion. But it is used not so much to deflect attention away from a subject as to focus it on a substitute target. It is a subtle distinction, but a valid one. This approach is exemplified by the resourceful art thieves who replace the objects they are stealing with replicas; the criminal defense attorney who points the finger at anyone other than his client; and the magician who substitutes a trick coin for the one provided by an audience member.

A peculiar kinship has evolved over time between the magician, the actor, and the spy. While their ultimate goals may differ, the tactics they employ to achieve them are often quite similar. During the Cold War between the Soviet Union and the United States, for example, American intelligence borrowed various techniques of disguise from Hollywood to assist in the dangerous process known as exfiltration. Elaborate pieces of theater and even prosthetic faces were devised to conceal subjects who had to be rescued from the clutches of the enemy. By changing hairlines and profiles and simulating wrinkles, facial hair, or girth, such assets could pass right under the watchful eye of the adversary undetected. And much of this was achieved using only transparent tape, spirit gum, and hair clipped from the subject's own head.

A critical aspect of implementing any of these techniques effectively is making sure that the target does not suspect even for a moment that he is being led astray or, to paraphrase Sun Tzu, is defeating the opponent before he realizes that the battle has been joined. In this regard, the operative may draw on another parallel to the world of the actor (as well as the magician, the salesman, and the trial lawyer): his performance must be believable. In addition to providing verbal "patter" to accompany the operation, the adoption of a normal, relaxed, and soothing rhythm will tend to lull the audience into accepting what is being presented. Keeping up a steady but by no means frantic pattern of speech and action will serve to distract observers from the techniques with which they are being misled.

For many, the task of acting naturally when they are in fact up to something untoward is a daunting one. It becomes difficult to imagine what would constitute normal behavior under the circumstances. In employing any of the techniques presented for installing a listening device, for example, it may be quite difficult to know how to manage the seemingly innocuous task of entering the target's office and conducting oneself once there. Even if the operative typically visits this office for legitimate reasons on a regular basis, his awareness of the additional, clandestine component of his mission may impede his ability to present a relaxed and natural demeanor.

Fortunately, he need look no further than the laboratory of the butterfly for his example. Anytime a covert action is to be concealed within an otherwise unremarkable course of conduct, it is helpful to practice the "cover" element by itself a few times. In the context of this controlled experiment, the operative can take note of natural tendencies and comfortable patterns of behavior. If it simply proves impossible to recapture the flavor of innocence, then he can always watch other people engaging in similar conduct. Threads of behavior can thus be gathered and woven into the cloak that conceals the intended action when the time arrives.

Gross motor movements and direct statements are two ways in which intentions can be conveyed or concealed. These are two factors that police officers rely on every day in developing and articulating levels of suspicion, but they are not the only ones. The scale of perception runs all the way from such obvious matters as these to the instinctive or intuitive reaction we have toward certain people and places. Along the way, it ascends into a more rarefied atmosphere, one in which the beat of a butterfly's wing can make all the difference in the world.

Could it have been the darting, but unmistakable, glance over the shoulders of the opponents directed toward the entranceway to the training hall—a look that suggested not only a presence behind them but an alarming one? Perhaps . . .

SPIRIT

In strategy your spiritual bearing must not be any different from normal. Both in fighting and in everyday life you should be determined though calm. Meet the situation without tenseness yet not recklessly, your spirit settled yet unbiased. Even when your spirit is calm do not let your body relax, and when your body is relaxed do not let your spirit slacken. Do not let your spirit be influenced by your body, or your body influenced by your spirit. Be neither insufficiently spirited nor over spirited. An elevated spirit is weak and a low spirit is weak. Do not let the enemy see your spirit. Small people must be completely familiar with the spirit of large people, and large people must be familiar with the spirit of small people. Whatever your size, do not be misled by the reactions of your own body. With your spirit open and unconstricted, look at things from a high point of view. You must cultivate your wisdom and spirit. Polish your wisdom: learn public justice, distinguish between good and evil, study the Ways of different arts one by one. When you cannot be deceived by men you will have realized the wisdom of strategy. The wisdom of strategy is different from other things. On the battlefield, even when you are hard-pressed, you should ceaselessly research the principles of strategy so that you can develop a steady spirit.

—Miyamoto Musashi, *The Book of Five Rings*

Thus far, the discussion has been limited to a set of relatively objective, empirically quantifiable phenomena. But a human being is more than a collection of shapes, colors, textures, and sounds. Ignition of the corporeal machine depends on the spark of life. The resulting fire—some may call it the spirit, others *chi*—can have at least as much effect on the perceptions of others as do the physical factors discussed in the preceding. This aspect of the human condition is difficult to measure or describe, but it is there nonetheless, noticeable perhaps only as a glint in the eye or a spring in the step at first glance. It is also a critical element in the process of managing perception.

In attempting to create a different persona, one intelligence officer's training manual advises operatives to observe how some people move with purpose while others waddle along seeming to have no goal in life and to take into consideration "upbringing . . . degree of ambition and outlook on life." Similarly, in our everyday lives, how often do we encounter someone whose arrival lights up the room, whose personality is larger than life, or who has a commanding presence? In such instances, it is not uncommon to find that the nature of such appeal cannot be accounted for merely by summing up the readily observable attributes. There is an altogether more subtle set of factors at play here, but their combined effect is both undeniable and profound. The gray man must understand this if he is to use it to his advantage.

Spirit is in many ways as immutable as it is indefinable. Under sustained scrutiny, its true nature will eventually come shining through. But by employing certain aspects of the butterfly art, it can at least be managed to a degree. For if the spirit is the fire that burns within the structure, then there are certain behavioral windows through which it can be most clearly seen. These include such detailed and related factors as posture, bearing, demeanor, eye contact, and even attitude. In the art of blending, the idea is, of course, to dim the fire or at least to obscure the view thereof to the extent that it is both necessary and possible to do so, or as the Japanese idiom renders it, "to make the spirit small."

Look around the classroom when the opportunity next presents itself, and try to determine which among the procession of humanity has military or police training; who is raring for a fight; how many are awake, alert, and observant; and how many are functionally asleep or impaired in some other way. How we carry ourselves speaks volumes about both our distant and our recent past. And as with virtually every other aspect of this particular art, context is critical. The ramrod bearing of the serviceman that will pass unnoticed on base is a virtual uniform in civilian quarters. The law enforcement officer's constant, sweeping gaze may be expected in a cop bar, but it will make patrons quite uncomfortable elsewhere.

In the realm of invisibility, special attention should be paid to the power of eye contact. As a rule, people tend to notice someone looking at them. To test this theory, try walking down the street behind an exceptionally beautiful woman, and notice the wake of activity that follows her path. Perhaps people are conditioned on some vestigial level to perceive a threat or an opportunity in such conduct, or maybe they are just socialized to acknowledge the apparent recognition. Strangely, however, this phenomenon often occurs even when the observer is located *outside* the subject's field of vision. Some characterize this as "a sixth sense." Others describe it as a "field of reflected awareness," theorizing that the subject is at some level conscious of *other* bystanders' awareness of the observer's attention to his target.

Whatever the explanation, this effect reproduces with surprising consistency under experimental conditions and holds tremendous value for those who appreciate its power. One skilled in the art of invisibility will avoid direct visual engagement with those around him. He will likewise avoid being conspicuously evasive in this regard. On occasion, he may encounter people for whom the opposite approach is appropriate: those whose nature or situation makes them shy away from direct engagement. In these cases, he may well lock his gaze on them. The art of the butterfly lies in knowing which course to take.

The manner in which a person breathes can say a lot about him. A hacking smoker's cough, a corpulent wheeze, and a drunken snore are significant attention getters. Gasping for breath is a sign of recent exertion, and mouth breathing may indicate congestion or other sinus problems. Forgetting to breathe is a sure sign of nervousness, and a sharp and inadvertent inhale may betoken surprise or shock. When the goal is to pass unseen, as opposed to merely unnoticed, even an audible nasal inhale can give away one's position. Silent breathing is not as easy as it sounds, particularly under pressure. Try it in a quiet place sometime. The first few breaths may be relatively silent, but maintaining the focus necessary to achieve this result consistently over time becomes quite difficult.

To avoid telegraphing information through one's manner of breathing, the process must be controlled. Those who practice the art of meditation have studied this subject over centuries, and the consensus appears to be that the respiratory cycle is at its most stable and controllable when the majority of the activity takes place low in the thoracic cavity. This so-called "belly breathing" requires the conscious suppression of the body's natural tendency to let the breath well up in the top of the lungs when under stress. One way to practice breathing from the abdomen is to cinch a belt around the chest so as to limit its ability to expand, forcing the locus of the respiratory process lower. In addition to its effectiveness in striving for invisibility, this practice is thought to be beneficial to one's health as well.

Related to the concept of controlled breathing, especially in the discipline of meditation, is the art of stillness. In the frenetic, workaday world, there is rarely time to get enough sleep, let alone to enjoy times of such profound tranquility. If you observe the immobility of the couch potato, the Internet surfer, and the person reading a book, they are not examples of true stillness. They are enabled by distractions and punctuated by occasional movements, however slight. True stillness, the stillness of the

butterfly, is a pure and total stillness, transmitting nothing and receiving nothing.

When someone achieves this state, it is as though he has stepped out of the present place and time. In the laboratory of everyday life, one's ability to identify a human shape is assisted by many other cues: motion, noise, eye contact, and the like. Collectively, these factors create what might be called a "human wake," much like that of a ship's hull cutting through the water. When these things are submerged in stillness, the wake disappears, and the ability of others to track the target is diminished proportionately.

This is a matter of significant complexity and requires years of practice to achieve. But the power of the principle at play can be much more easily observed under the exceptional circumstances that exist in the museum on Marylebone Road in North West London. Having fled from France in 1802, Madame Tussaud created a waxwork exhibition built on her collection of "death masks" of guillotined French aristocrats. Her museum is now filled with replicas of all manner of celebrities, living and dead. But observant visitors also come to realize that some of the "staff" and indeed a few of the other patrons are also mannequins.

It is not uncommon for those passing through the museum to stop for a period of time, either to examine an exhibit or to wait for a member of their group to catch up. Some will fidget or chatter or wheeze while they do this. Others will be still. And almost without fail, if a visitor remains motionless for too long, a group of tourists will approach, stare, take a photograph, and try, perhaps, to touch the person. The effect when the "exhibit" then moves or speaks is spectacular. For our purposes, it is also instructive.

In arriving at the next and final aspect of the art of blending, our analysis has progressed from the physical world to the wholly internal universe of attitude. Subjective, changeable, and completely unquantifiable, it is nevertheless an undeniable fact that peoples' attitudes affect the perceptions of others. We can all recognize the

angry young man who arrives at the bar intent on a fight without him having to say or do anything; likewise, we know the self-important "professional" who feels that he is too good to be associating with the other people at the party, and that the least they can do is acknowledge his inherent superiority.

Such people try to expand the dimensions of their personal space to make themselves feel more important, and in the process, they rub up against the territory of others. Whatever the reaction, they generally are noticed. Predictably, the gray man takes the opposite approach. He makes an effort to pull his personal space in on himself, to wrap it around him like a cloak. The material of his cloak depends on the impression he wishes to create—purpose, belonging, confidence, or boredom—but always the dimensions of the garment are kept to a minimum. He takes care to avoid having it even brush up against the person standing next to him, and thus, he simply fades from view. This is the art of the butterfly.

Or could it have been the way he seemed to grow in both presence and power while stepping onto the mat, but could fade away into the background and melt into the crowd as soon as the lesson was over? Perhaps. Perhaps it was a combination of all these skills. To the students, his technical abilities were magical. To him, they were simply examples of the principle underlying the practice. On this subject, he said:

Do not show your true face to the World. Your true face—your heart, your mind, your intention—is a private matter, not meant to satisfy the curiosity of any casual onlooker. You should no more bare your naked soul to all than you would your naked body. This is the first teaching in the art of the butterfly.

Mind Reading

In 1875 an English physiologist named Richard Caton discovered the existence of electrical fields in the brains of animals.[1] Half a century later, the German psychiatrist Hans Berger developed the first electroencephalogram. Since that time, this technology has become a mainstay of diagnosis and treatment in a number of medical fields. As the process of examining brainwaves has been refined, scientists have learned that certain stimuli will reliably produce the same observable and measurable patterns. The triggering conditions can be as specific as a clicking noise or a tap on the hand.

Over time, these characteristic waveforms, known in the scientific community as event-related potentials (ERPs) have been cataloged and coded with the letters N or P followed by a specific number.[2] For example, P300 is the surprise wave; N400 is known as the double-take wave; and N100 is the so-called "cocktail party" wave. While there are still many gaps in the alphabet—patterns corresponding to emotions, for example, have not yet been codified—a comprehensive language of brain waves is clearly emerging.

As the scientific community continues to classify and catalog these patterns, in much the same way that the human genome proj-

---

1. The historical and scientific data presented herein is documented in the article "Machines That Read Minds" by Gary Selden that appeared in the October 1981 issue of *Science Digest*.
2. The letters stand for negative or positive.

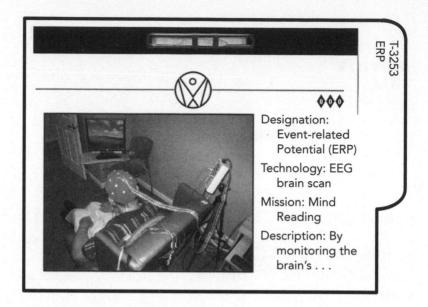

T-3253
ERP

Designation:
 · Event-related
   Potential (ERP)
Technology: EEG
   brain scan
Mission: Mind
   Reading
Description: By
   monitoring the
   brain's . . .

ect maps genetic material, the prospect of being able to develop a device that can literally read people's thoughts is becoming a reality. According to some commentators, the technology currently exists to develop a reliable lie detection machine: a possibility that is not lost on the scientific arm of the international intelligence community.

Like the optically transparent material and the stealth technology described in section 1, the wherewithal to look into people's thoughts in this fashion, if indeed it has already been developed, is likely to be well beyond the resources of most private parties and many government entities. But even without the aid of such sophisticated machinery, a similar result can be achieved with a sufficient amount of work by employing another aspect of the art of the butterfly: the skills of the detective. Careful research, observation, and deduction combined with a basic understanding of human psychology will allow the watchful observer to discover a significant amount of information about his target's thought processes. Proper analysis of this data can, in turn, provide a window into the subject's mind.

Following the Master's initial display of prowess in the engagement with multiple attackers, the nature of the combat training reverted to the more typical one-on-one scenario. His powers nevertheless, remained astonishing. On one occasion, he squared off against a lithe, fit young American. After throwing a few tentative feints, the student launched a beautiful snap kick aimed at his teacher's chin. The Master caught the foot in midair. It was an impossible move. He didn't just guard against the attack, allowing it to crash into his braced arms. He simply reached out one hand and cupped it under the opponent's heel in casual, almost lazy fashion. For a moment, their postures fused into a rigid statue. Then with a shrug, he pushed up, stretching the adversary's ligaments beyond their limit, causing him to pinwheel through the air and land in a pile on the mat, several yards away.

RESEARCH

Whether the object be to crush an army, to storm a city, or to assassinate an individual, it is always necessary to begin by finding out the names of the attendants, the aides-de-camp, and doorkeepers and sentries of the general in command. Our spies must be commissioned to ascertain these.

—Sun Tzu, *The Art of War*

Where the gray man strives to script the message conveyed by his appearance, his speech, his actions, and a variety of other tells, the detective or investigator aims to interpret these same signs in others. In performing this latter function, the practitioner of the butterfly art steps through the looking glass and, in so doing, must appreciate the operational distinctions between the two roles. For one thing, the detective has at his disposal certain tools that are generally inapplicable or irrelevant to the gray man's mission. Among these is the opportunity to gather information in advance of engaging with the target.

Information about the target, whether it be the enemy, the boss, or the competitor, is an invaluable resource. Each piece of data is a potential pane of the window into the subject's thought processes and therefore his likely actions and reactions under given circumstances. It is commonly thought that intelligence gathering is a uniquely governmental function, but this is merely a question of semantics. Asking the CEO's secretary what kind of mood he is in today is gathering intelligence. Checking out the venue for a future meeting or social function is gathering intelligence. Even switching on the weather channel to get the latest forecast can be considered intelligence gathering.

One of the most frequently overlooked resources available in this endeavor, even among professionals, is the wealth of valuable information that is readily available in the public domain. Some commentators claim, for example, that despite the failure of Western intelligence agencies to predict the fall of the Shah of Iran in 1979, the newspapers and even the word on the street at the time made it clear to anyone who chose to listen that this event was imminent. During the Gulf War in 1991, the point was more clearly illustrated by the way in which decision makers of all kinds remained glued to CNN to keep current on a variety of developments in the combat theater.

One final point must be made by way of introduction. It is almost impossible to tell what pieces of information may become important at some future point in the operation. While the target's politics, his temperament, and his general outlook on life will almost certainly bear on many or most aspects of his behavior, knowing his favorite color, his preferred drink, or the time he takes his afternoon nap may also prove valuable under certain circumstances. The cardinal rule of the detective, therefore, is that nothing should be deemed irrelevant.

When he is first assigned to a case, the wise investigator researches the subject as fully as possible. For example, with the dissolution of the Soviet Union during the 1990s, American law enforcement was confronted with the emergence of a new threat on the domestic front: the influx of Russian Mafia—the so-called "Redfellas." After decades of dealing with the Italian Mafia, Western police agencies had to learn about a distinctly different type of criminal enterprise. As one commentator put it, "Blending financial sophistication with bone-crunching violence, the Russian mob has become the FBI's most formidable criminal adversary, creating an international criminal colossus that has surpassed the Colombian cartels, the Japanese Yakuza, the Chinese Triads, and the Italian Mafia in wealth and weaponry."[3]

Born of an entirely closed and alien society, the so-called "Organyzatsia" presented Western authorities with a cultural phenomenon for which they had virtually no frame of reference. In 1993, therefore, American and Canadian law enforcement partnered with the Russian Ministry of the Interior (MVD) in undertaking the first significant investigation into activities of the Eurasian Organized Crime (EOC) syndicate in the United States. The primary target was Vyacheslav Kirillovich Ivankov, the senior coordinator for all EOC activity in the West, a boss who supervised operations in New York, Toronto, London, Vienna, Budapest, and several other cities in the United States, Canada, and Europe.

Traditionally, such investigations had begun with the compilation of a hierarchy, a cast of characters broken down along the lines of the chain of command. As federal authorities were about to learn, one of the chief obstacles to investigating and prosecuting the

3. Robert I. Friedman, *Red Mafiya* [sic]: How the Russian Mob Has Invaded America (Boston: Little, Brown, 2000).

Organyzatsia is the breadth and depth of its membership, a characteristic that renders such traditional flow charting methods obsolete. Unlike more familiar crime family models, almost anyone and everyone could be involved, at least to some extent, with the Russian Mafia. So pervasive was the corruption in Soviet society that criminal enterprises often involved representatives of the national government and leaders of private-sector industry as well as members of the mainstream criminal underworld. It is estimated, for example, that as many as 50,000 Russian companies accounting for 40 percent of the nation's GNP are still controlled directly or indirectly by the crime syndicates.

This unprecedented level of complicity is thought to be the result, at least in part, of the Russian Mafia having its roots in the Bolshevik Revolution. In the early 1900s, many professional criminals sided with the revolutionaries, giving rise to a strange affiliation between the government, the private sector, and the criminal underworld. This peculiar relationship, it seems, endured into and beyond the reign of Communism and became a common feature of both white-collar criminal enterprises as well as the more violent types of conduct typically associated with organizations of this kind.

Name: Vyacheslav Kirillovich Ivankov

AKA: "Japonchik" (Япончик)

Birth: 1940, Georgia

Affiliation: Eurasian Organized Crime (EOC) Syndicate

Operations: New York, Toronto, London, Vienna, Budapest

B-0219
Ivankov, Vyacheslav

Recognizing the importance of knowing their new enemy, Western law enforcement officers spent years learning as much as they could from their Russian counterparts about this emerging threat while at the same time monitoring ongoing Organyzatsia activity in the United States and elsewhere. Their newfound understanding, the fruit of patient research and cooperation involving many law enforcement organizations, coupled with the kind of surveillance techniques discussed in section 2, led to the arrest and conviction of Ivankov and five of his subordinates on extortion and conspiracy charges in July 1996.

As has been noted previously, the practitioner of the butterfly art neither has nor needs the kind of infrastructure necessary to execute operations of this magnitude. The lone detective must often rely on initiative, ingenuity, and hard work to achieve similar results. With respect to this research component of his mission, however, recent advances in the field of information technology have served to level the playing field considerably for such private investigators.

Every research assignment must begin with a subject. In the field of information gathering, this will commonly be a name. That name alone is often the key to identity. Unless confronted by a "Joe Smith," this single data point can be combined with other readily available facts to extrapolate a wealth of information about the target. For example, a mere name combined with an approximate location of residence allows the detective to search the phone book for an exact address and phone number. This finding, in turn, identifies the appropriate municipal subdivision in which to explore additional resources.

Once the approximate location of the target's residence has been identified, newspapers, especially those whose circulation is limited to the community at issue, may provide the detective with all sorts of additional information about his target, especially when that target has attained even a minimal level of stature or prominence in the community. Such publications will often feature stories about local businessmen and women as well as politicians, public servants, and other notable people. Whether this material is contained within the stories themselves, the op-ed pages, the public notices, or the advertisements, the local press can be a tremendous resource in the investigatory process.

Depending on the nature of the assignment, it may also be worth checking the alumni records of schools and colleges in the applicable area. If the target attended any of these, there is a good chance that a graduation photograph can be found and perhaps even more detailed information is in the institution's yearbooks, publications, or other records. It may also be helpful to see whether the alma mater in question can provide any writings either by or about the target. As is discussed in greater detail in the preceding, the way a person writes says a lot about the way he thinks.

Up to this point, the level of research described might be appropriate in preparing for an exceptionally important job interview. Investigations, both private and public, however, may sometimes require delving into a subject in far more detail. This process should not be undertaken without first appreciating the criminal and civil laws governing privacy and respecting their boundaries in a fashion consistent with the authority of the investigator in question.

Other ways of gathering detailed information about a target are available, either directly or indirectly, that are typically known only to those whose professions call for this kind of research. American Social Security numbers are coded to the state in which they were issued. A simple chart will reveal the place of issuance and may provide other valuable information about the subject as well.

Certain religious organizations, among them the Mormons, maintain vast databases of genealogical data about families and individuals residing in North America and elsewhere. And the number of state and federal agencies that can and will provide records about a given individual if approached in the right way could (and does) fill another volume altogether.

When the situation warrants it, public filings can provide the

Social Security Prefix Codes by State

001–003	New Hampshire	449–467	Texas
004–007	Maine	627–645	
008–009	Vermont	468–477	Minnesota
010–034	Massachusetts	478–485	Iowa
035–039	Rhode Island	486–500	Missouri
040–049	Connecticut	501–502	North Dakota
050–134	New York	503–504	South Dakota
135–158	New Jersey	505–508	Nebraska
159–211	Pennsylvania	509–515	Kansas
212–220	Maryland	516–517	Montana
221–222	Delaware	518–519	Idaho
223–231	Virginia	520	Wyoming
691–699		521–524	Colorado
232–236	West Virginia	650–653	
232	North Carolina	525, 585	New Mexico
237–246		648–649	
681–690		526–527	Arizona
247–251	South Carolina	600–601	
654–658		764–765	
252–260	Georgia	528–529	Utah
667–675		646–647	
261–267	Florida	530	Nevada
589–595		680	
766–772		531–539	Washington
268–302	Ohio	540–544	Oregon
303–317	Indiana	545–573	California
318–361	Illinois	602–626	
362–386	Michigan	574	Alaska
387–399	Wisconsin	575–576	Hawaii
400–407	Kentucky	750–751	
408–415	Tennessee	577–579	District of Columbia
756–763		580	Virgin Islands
416–424	Alabama	580–584	Puerto Rico
425–428	Mississippi	596–599	
587		586	Guam
588		586	American Samoa
752–755		586	Philippine Islands
429–432	Arkansas	700–728	Railroad Retirement Board
676–679			
433–439	Louisiana	729–733	Enumeration at Entry
659–665		000	Invalid
440–448	Oklahoma	4320–4329	Advertising

investigator with everything from deeds and corporate records to professional licenses and criminal histories. With the information age upon us, almost every aspect of our daily lives it seems is documented in some fashion and stored in a repository. At least until recently, conducting such intensive research would often require trips to offices like the recorder of deeds, the prothonotary, and the clerk of courts. With the advent of the Internet, all of this has changed.

Computer access to the World Wide Web has affected the availability of information of this kind on several fronts. The first of these simply relates to the ease with which the type of data previously available is now accessed. Conducting even a moderately thorough investigation used to require sending letters, making trips to many different locations, and sifting through massive quantities of data in search of the relevant material.

The same results can now be achieved in a fraction of the time and in the comfort of one's own home or office. In addition, most public and private entities are computerizing their records and providing online access to them when appropriate, and automated search features cut down tremendously on time spent locating the desired document. Most computerized record systems have search functions built into them, allowing users to scan records by name, date, or other pertinent characteristic. Moreover, specific words or phrases can be located in voluminous documents automatically by any home computer.

This increase in the rate of processing information is vital in the digital era since an explosion in the sheer quantity of data available accompanies it. Local, state, and national borders are becoming increasingly irrelevant; publicly and privately maintained databases coexist and overlap; and every person with access to the Internet is a potential provider. This last fact cuts both ways for the detective, in that the reliability of the information available must often be treated as suspect, but any reasonably intelligent user can learn to differentiate between reliable and potentially unreliable sources in time, and he can always cross-reference questionable material until a level of confidence is achieved.

Internet search engines can provide the detective with access to such useful services as global telephone and address information, reverse telephone number services, membership lists of all kinds, court records, and a host of other government and private sector databases. Specialized sites even provide profiles for members of particular professions. The website martindalehubbell.com, for instance, will give the user an overview of any attorney practicing in the United States, including such details as age, address, schooling, area of practice, and notable achievements.

Readily available investigative software packages claim to have access to an even broader range of information, including credit reports, unlisted telephone numbers, automobile ownership records, employment histories, driving records, and adoption papers. Likewise, legal software is used to locate hidden assets and missing witnesses every day. It must be kept in mind, however, that the legality of using such systems depends on both the nature of the inquiry and the identity of the user.

Increasingly, the process of researching an individual can be achieved simply by logging onto his personal web page or "MySpace" account. For vanity, publicity, or some other reason, more and more computer users are voluntarily placing personal information or original compositions in the public domain. For the detective, such sites are a veritable gold mine, not just for what they say, but also the way they say it.

The online computer age has not only increased both the amount and the availability of personal information dramatically but also created an entirely new source of information: user profiles. History logs, online activity reports, "cookies," and the like, can tell a great deal about the user. Likewise, codes embedded in electronic documents can be used to gather a surprising amount of information, including insertions, deletions, and prior drafts of the current composition. In certain instances, they can even provide the detective with the serial number of the device used to create them. Depending on the detective's level of sophistication and access to the target's Internet profiles, this emerging capability can provide a new and very important piece of the puzzle.

Notwithstanding tremendous advances in computer technology, it is generally agreed among law enforcement professionals that there is still no substitute for person-to-person contact. There are details and nuances to live communications that tend not to survive the translation into electronic format, as anyone who has ever had an e-mail message misinterpreted can attest. One of the most valuable resources for the detective is simply talking to people. Unless there is reason to believe that an inquiry is likely to frighten off the subject and thereby adversely affect the operation, just asking people to share their opinions can often yield much of the information sought.

In both the federal courts and those of many states, the rules of evidence prohibit the introduction of what is known as "character evidence." This term of art refers to information regarding a party's conduct on some occasion other than the one at issue in the suit. The potentially prejudicial effect of such evidence is thought to outweigh any probative value that it might have. Reputation for a specific character trait pertinent to the matter at hand is one of the few exceptions to this general prohibition. This is so, at least in part, because the law recognizes the value and reliability of reputation evidence. And if approached in the right way, people are often quite happy to share their opinions regarding the target's reputation with an interested third party.

In rare instances, the target's name may not be immediately available to the detective. Consider the example of the investigator whose primary target meets with an unknown, second party on a regular basis, perhaps at a restaurant or a hotel. This detective may not wish to risk exposing his mission by contacting the second person directly. He can try to investigate further by examining such resources as the restaurant's reservation list, the hotel's registry, or the target's monogrammed shirt or luggage in an effort to fill in this important blank. Should this approach fail, he must then avail himself of the skills detailed in the following section to put a name to the face of the secondary target.

At other times, the detective may encounter a name with no face, as in the case of coming into possession of a letter or other document. In such instances, he must begin with the known. What does the document say? In addition to the name of the sender and the date and location of the transmission, letterhead will often provide additional detail about the source. For example, many individuals include their professional accreditations on such documents, and firms often list the names of their partners in order of seniority. Some documents may even bear logos, coats of arms or mottos. There is even something to be learned from the type of paper on which the document is written.

Continuing with our dissection of documentary evidence, it is typical for correspondence from busy professionals of all kinds to end with the notation "XX:yy," indicating the initials of the person who dictated the letter and the person who typed it in that order. On occasion, this convention takes the form of "XX:yy:zz." In these cases, it is a fair assumption that the principal has both an assistant of some kind and a secretary. Similarly, the abbreviation "cc: _____ " lists every person to whom copies of the correspondence has been circulated. Collectively, these details ensure that the identities, or at least the initials of all parties to the writing are known. Thus, another tiny piece of the puzzle falls into place.

Among the specialties of the FBI and other law enforcement agencies are the twinned disciplines of content analysis and graphology. As their names suggest, the former deals with what can be learned from the way in which a document is written; the latter deals with the target's handwriting. Is the letter businesslike and to the point, or does it provide a wealth of background information in flowing prose? Does the writer use overly complicated constructions and unnecessarily long words, or does he speak plainly? Is it signed

```
                    LOGO
                     or
                    SEAL
                NAME OF OFFICE
                   ADDRESS
Name of Senior Person    TELEPHONE         Name of Senior Person
Title, Qualifications, Specialty  FACSIMILE   Title, Qualifications, Specialty
                 E-MAIL/WEBSITE
```

DATE

Manner of transmission (First Class Mail and Facsimile . . .)

Primary Recipient
Title
Address

Re: Subject Matter
Tone of salutation ("Dear"; "Name:";
"To Whom it May Concern" . . .)

Information contained in letter:
Tone of letter
Content analysis
Style of writing
Graphology if handwritten
        Tone of the closing

                        Choice of valediction
                        Signature (graphology)
                        Typed name and title
                        Contact Information

Cc: Other recipients, file (Copy to notation)
Enc.   Attachment A (Enclosure notation)
AB:cd (Reference initials)

with a flourish or a scrawl? Is it written or typed? Is it signed in ball-point or with a fountain pen? With sufficient study and practice, each of these factors can tell the detective many things about the writer.

Let us take as an example an actual callback letter for an interview with a law firm. From this document, we note that (1) the name indicates the interviewer is female; (2) the interviewer's name also appears on the firm's letterhead, toward the top of the list; (3) the correspondence went through two levels of assistants; (4) the directions therein are conveyed succinctly; and (5) the signature is tidy, but in ink and a little ostentatious. The Martindale-Hubbell profile indicates that the interviewer is (6) forty years of age; (7) a graduate of a state college and an Ivy League law school; and (8) specializes in personal injury suits.

It is a sad truth that even in the modern world, it can still be more difficult for a woman to make partner in an old-fashioned law firm. Here we have someone who is not only a partner but clearly a senior one, and at a surprisingly young age. Her educational history and preferred practice area indicate that she has worked hard to achieve this position. Her manner of communication suggests that she is all business. In the category of long shots, she probably drives an expensive car, dresses with a modicum of style, and might be a smoker.

Under these conditions, it would be best to expect some hardball questions, particularly in the field of tort law. Appearance should probably tend toward ultraconservative. Grades will likely be considered extremely important, and jokes are almost certainly a bad idea. As a matter of general practice, of course, all such suppositions could be wrong and should be verified in person before they are deemed reliable. As a matter of historical fact, every one of the assumptions reproduced in the preceding turned out to be correct.

In executing his breathtaking defense, the Master must have been expecting the kick. Was it simply that he had read the student's dossier and learned of his prior training in the Korean kicking arts? Perhaps . . .

OBSERVATION

Hence the saying: If you know the enemy and know
yourself, you need not fear the result of a hundred battles.
If you know yourself but not the enemy, for every victory
gained you will also suffer a defeat. If you know neither
the enemy nor yourself, you will succumb in every battle.

—Sun Tzu, *The Art of War*

Criminal prosecutions are commonly supported by direct evidence. For most crimes, a witness can identify the defendant, be it the victim, a bystander, an undercover police officer, or the defendant himself by way of a confession. Sometimes, however, no such witness is available to the investigator. In these cases, the services of a specialized kind of detective—the forensic analyst—may be required. The forensic specialist conducts an exhaustive examination of such trace evidence as hairs and fibers; entry and exit wounds; organic and chemical residues; latent prints and marks; and the content and pattern of stains from a variety of bodily fluids.

From these remnants, the examiner is able to piece together a picture of what happened, even though no living witness is available to him. Some of the most serious prosecutions can and do stand on such circumstantial evidence, meaning that society at large accepts the examiner's version as truth beyond a reasonable doubt. Thus, we learn that from detailed observation comes reliable understanding, and we recognize that such processes fall squarely within the province of the butterfly.

Before proceeding with this aspect of our studies, two issues of correctness must be addressed briefly: one statistical and the other political. First, for almost any of the observations discussed herein, there may be a variety of explanations. For example, a man may be overweight because of genetics or a medical condition or overeating or some combination perhaps of the three. It would therefore be both foolish and useless to base our conclusions on single interpretations of such individual characteristics. Rather, facts are to be cross-referenced and theories tested before they are accepted as reliable. Similarly, the tactics presented throughout this book may work on an individual basis to devastating effect on some occasions, but may yield unanticipated and entirely unavailing results on others. This is to be expected. This is why repetition and diversification are critical components of the process.

Second, it would be equally foolish as well as quite wrong to cling rigidly to national, ethnic, or socioeconomic stereotypes in the making of one's analysis. Common experience may yield useful rules of thumb, but it is the dogged unwillingness to allow preconceived notions to yield to empirical evidence to the contrary that breeds intolerance, racism, and ignorance. No ability is worth such a price. With these caveats in mind, we move on.

The ancient art of reading minds (or at least seeming to) has recently been resurrected on television by those "entertainers" who claim to be able to communicate with the dead. What these pretenders are really doing is expertly reading and manipulating their audiences so that they seem to know the unknowable. Many of the clues available to them are based on the way that the person with whom they are speaking looks and what they can deduce from this information. As a result, we return to the familiar ground of appearance, but this time as the observer, rather than the observed.

Dispensing with the obvious matters first, examine the subject as the medical examiner would a body, as yet undressed and unprepared. Open the file and note the vital statistics, as we did with our man on the side of the road at the outset: stature, frame, girth, coloring, and shading. What can be gleaned from these raw facts alone? A number of factors can provide clues as to the age of the subject, including hairline and color, skin condition, appearance of the teeth and eyes, and body alignment. Approximate weight and height as well as apparent physical condition can also be added to the list at this point for future reference.

Bone structure may appear aristocratic or common, and while

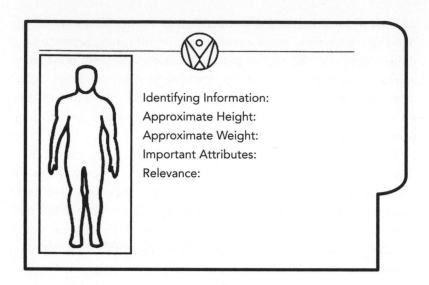

Identifying Information:
Approximate Height:
Approximate Weight:
Important Attributes:
Relevance:

this is by no means an accurate indicator of social standing, particularly in a meritocracy, it may be of some value in combination with other features. At least in some cases it may also be possible to hazard a guess at place of origin based on facial appearance. While it is a good bet that the gentleman of Hispanic appearance is likelier to speak Spanish than the young lady with Japanese features, do not count on it. In our highly mobile society, the birthplace of one's ancestors is often quite beside the point, and can on occasion be very deceiving.

It can also be difficult for the novice to recognize distinctions among the physical features common to certain geographically proximate nations, for example, China, Japan, and Korea. There are few sights more vicariously embarrassing than the overeager polyglot addressing others in what he supposes to be their native language, only to find that he is mistaken. Significant study must be devoted to these characteristics before they will be of any value at all, and, in any event, such superficial observations will yield at best a guess to be penciled on the margin of the file.

With regard to size, is it true that a tall person will exhibit confidence and authority and is likelier to hold a more successful position than his diminutive counterpart? Is it wise to assume that a tiny individual will try to overcompensate for his stature with an aggressive demeanor? Can it be said that the corpulent specimen will be ponderous and languid, preferring intellectual to physical activity? That the wiry subject will be quick and energetic? That a balding and bespectacled fellow will be more bookish than a bronzed specimen with flowing hair?

Perhaps and perhaps not. As just discussed, the complexities of the human condition cannot be defined by a single physical attribute or even a cluster of them. These characteristics may be the product of a number of factors, but further evidence is required in order to narrow down the available options. This does not mean such observations are useless; it is simply too soon to draw any reliable conclusions. File them for now.

What about the interplay of the subject's physical features? It is said that being beautiful is a matter of symmetry, but being striking is a matter of idiosyncrasy. Most people will agree that symmetrical features are generally pleasing, but what exactly constitutes bewitching looks will vary among beholders. Suffice it to say for present purposes that, extreme examples notwithstanding, subjects may be categorized as being of average looks, above or below.

Study after study seems to validate the proposition that others treat attractive people, especially attractive women, differently than their less fortunate counterparts in the genetic lottery. No matter how pure of heart they may be, the "beautiful people" will likely have become accustomed to enjoying a significant level of attention and appreciation over time. Sadly, the reverse is also true.

Of far greater weight and worth than peoples' genetic attributes, however, are the ways in which they choose to develop them. Natural physical characteristics may suggest certain attitudes and behaviors but controllable features define them. The individual with highly developed musculature has probably spent many hours in the gym to obtain this result. If this mass is further overlaid on a slight frame, the costs of achieving this effect are likely to have been even greater. The voluptuous lady with the narrow waist is likely engaged in a constant struggle to maintain these antithetical assets. And one can reach a level of thinness that is simply unnatural, metabolic variations notwithstanding.

There is always the possibility, of course, that the target's physical metamorphosis owes more to chemistry and surgery than it does to exercise and diet. While the artificial result may sometimes pass for its natural counterpart at first glance, the excessive symmetry of the surgeon's scalpel and the slight grotesqueness of steroid-assisted muscle are telltale signs for the observant onlooker. When confronted with such specimens, the detective is able to read both their underlying desires as well as their chosen approach to achieving these goals with ease.

As to facial appearance, all the cosmetics in the world cannot compare with the effortless appeal of a truly beautiful person. Nevertheless, the general preoccupation with improving appearance is evidenced by ever more elaborate hairstyles, outrageous makeup, and distracting accessories. The priorities of those for whom these adornments are prerequisites to going out of doors are plain for all to see. At the other extreme are efforts to downplay attractive characteristics, a practice that provides the detective with an equal measure of insight into his subject's motivations and state of mind.

Some people use lifts in their shoes to augment height; they employ comb-overs in a vain attempt to conceal receding hairlines; and they procure costly tans in an effort to offset natural paleness. While such efforts may add to the detective's understanding of the psychological attributes of the subject, they are, by their very nature, intended to mask genuine physical traits. From this fact, additional insight may be achieved.

Recalling the way in which the gray man is trained to control his appearance for a given purpose, the detective must ensure that his observations do not fall victim to the same techniques and tactics. He must maintain awareness at all times and look beyond the superficial. If he is successful in this regard, he can effectively double the amount of information at his disposal. By seeing past the façade, he will recognize the true nature of the subject, but he will also know what it is that the subject is attempting to conceal or become.

Take as an example the young man with the slicked back hair and the double-breasted suit, sitting at the bar in a Wall Street café, a stainless steel briefcase at his feet, a paper in his hand, and a cell phone at his ear. A successful securities trader? So it would seem at first glance, but take a closer look. The suit is off the rack and does not fit him well. The brief-case and hairstyle are yesterday's vogue. The cell phone is clunky, a far cry from the earpieces with which the real players hardwire themselves into their networks. And the market is just about to open; a real trader should be at his computer, poised to wheel and deal.

Moving in a little closer, we can see that this is his third cup of coffee, that he is smoking his fourth cigarette, and that he has ordered no food. He has clearly been here for some time. The paper is open to the employment pages, and his tone on the telephone is one of supplication, not command. His suit is too old for him to be a recent graduate looking for a position, and he is far too young to be a semiretired senior partner. The logical conclusion, therefore, is that he is one of the legions of financial consultants laid off during the recession, desperately trying to keep up appearances and regain a toehold in the cutthroat world of the market. The picture is now complete and, after brief interaction with the subject, confirmed as accurate.

So to avoid wasting time and space revisiting issues already addressed in the context of the gray man's appearance, it is sufficient for the moment to note that each of the myriad choices made by every person, every day, including such issues as grooming, clothing, and accessories, carry with them information for the trained observer of the human condition. Each such decision made by the target provides additional information for the detective's rapidly expanding file.

In striving to ensure that he is not misled, the detective should pay special attention to the inadvertent aspects of the subject's appearance: the things that are not susceptible to immediate conscious control. Among these is the character of the face. The story is told of Abraham Lincoln's rejection of a particular aspirant to a cabinet position simply on the grounds of facial appearance. When an advisor pointed out that this could not reasonably be held against the man, Lincoln is reputed to have replied, "On the contrary, every man over forty is responsible for his face." There is truth in this. Genetics may provide the canvas of physical form, but experience paints it.

Laugh and frown lines speak to the subject's internal condition in equal measure. Those who view the world with hostility tend to have a pinched and closed-in appearance, as though their faces, the

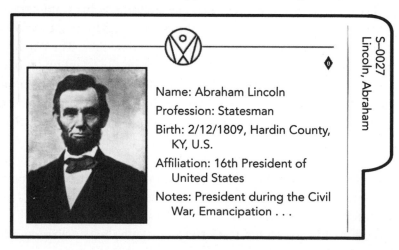

Name: Abraham Lincoln
Profession: Statesman
Birth: 2/12/1809, Hardin County, KY, U.S.
Affiliation: 16th President of United States
Notes: President during the Civil War, Emancipation . . .

S-0027
Lincoln, Abraham

organ through which they interact with the world at large, have become a battleground to be configured in a defensive fashion. The broad and open countenance of lovers of life, by contrast, exude warmth and welcome to all who see them. The tight and blotchy skin characteristic of a high-stress lifestyle is as telling as is the healthy glow of contentment.

After the face, the hands are perhaps the next most instructive feature. Are they strong and mobile or pale and limp? Do they bear the signs of an active lifestyle or the delicate manicure and expensive trophies of a life of luxury? Are they the clean and clipped instrument of the professional person or the scarred and sturdy tools of the laborer? Do they have the skeletal and vein-ridden appearance of the drug addict, the seriously unwell, or the extremely old? Finally, to differentiate the detective from the operative in this regard, do they show any indication of having been disguised to convey a particular impression?

In this particular endeavor, the investigator's sense of smell is another useful tool. Whether someone is a smoker, a drinker, or a user of certain drugs can be revealed by a good sniff. Information about the subject's type of work may also be discovered in this fashion. Can the smell of diesel, antiseptic, or the farm be detected? There are also certain activities that carry with them characteristic odors. The unmistakable scent of gunpowder, sweat, or sex can provide the detective with further insight. And even certain types of illnesses are capable of olfactory detection.

All of this can of course be masked by cologne or perfume, but even the subject's choice of type and quantity in this regard can be instructive. Is it expensive or cheap? Is it dabbed on or splashed? Is it used to augment or conceal? And in the latter case, even that which the subject is trying to conceal can often be detected in marked counterpoint to its chemical camouflage.

Finally, certain helpful physical characteristics change over time, but are not necessarily within the subject's conscious control, at least in an immediate sense. Dental work can provide clues about the nature and quality of one's upbringing. Tiny occlusions in the fingernails reveal dietary and health anomalies in the recent past, and even the subject's breath and waste can carry with it evidence of recent activity, especially regarding the consumption of certain foods and liquids. All these considerations, however distasteful they may be, are matters that the detective must keep in mind.

Up to this point, the detective is in no better position than a coroner examining a lifeless body. He may suppose, for example, that the little round fellow with the bushy mustache would present no real threat in a physical confrontation, but would be very much surprised to find that this subject moves with the stealth of a jungle cat and punches with the force of an irate mule. For this reason, prior to any direct engagement, the investigator should avail himself of the opportunity to examine the target's actions for at least a moment, if at all possible. In so doing, he will be able to factor observations regarding behavior into his assessment.

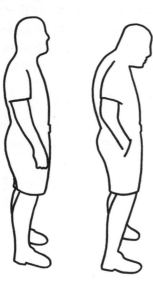

How does the subject carry himself? Does he walk tall or hunched over? Does he favor one leg? Does he wince when a particular body part is touched? Does he make eye contact with those around him, or does he cast his gaze downwards? Does he smile or frown at the world? When standing, does he shift from side to side out of fatigue or boredom? When seated, does he cross his legs or keep his heels firmly on the floor? All of these observations should be added to the file and cross-referenced against other considerations over time.

Had the Master observed the way that the American was able to drop effortlessly into a Chinese split when warming up before class? Perhaps . . .

DEDUCTION

The wish to acquire is in truth very natural and common, and men always do so when they can, and for this they will be praised not blamed; but when they cannot do so, yet wish to do so by any means, then there is folly and blame.

—Niccolò Machiavelli, *The Prince*

If research and observation provide the pieces of the puzzle, it is the process of deductive reasoning through which the detective determines how best to fit them together. In this regard, one historical example stands above all others: Sherlock Holmes. The fact that Holmes was the fictional creation of Sir Arthur Conan Doyle in no

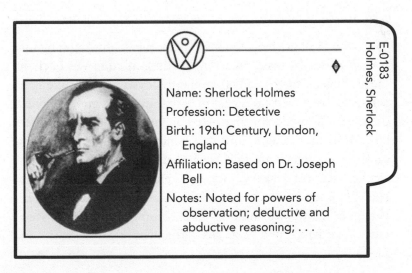

Name: Sherlock Holmes
Profession: Detective
Birth: 19th Century, London, England
Affiliation: Based on Dr. Joseph Bell
Notes: Noted for powers of observation; deductive and abductive reasoning; . . .

E-0183
Holmes, Sherlock

way diminishes the value of the lessons imparted through his approach to crime solving. This is especially true since the character, or more importantly his analytical approach, is based on the real-life teachings of Dr. Joseph Bell, a professor of clinical surgery at Edinburgh University, with whom Conan Doyle studied extensively.

According to several historical sources, including the seminal biography of Conan Doyle by Martin Booth, Bell was a tall, slender man with angular features. In addition to his medical expertise, he was also a keen sportsman and an amateur poet. As a diagnostician, Bell was a pioneer and some would say a genius. He believed that a doctor should avail himself of every sense in order to root out the cause of an illness. "Do not just look at a patient," he advised, "but feel him, probe him, listen to him, smell him." Using this approach, Bell was renowned for amazing his students during rounds with his ability to deduce facts, both medical and personal, from seemingly unremarkable details.

In the course of making a diagnosis, Bell would take into account every aspect of his patients' presentation, from the condition of their hands to the type of mud or dust on their shoes. In Conan Doyle's *A Study in Scarlet*, Holmes eloquently expands on this method, saying:

[B]y a man's finger-nails, by his coat sleeve, by his boot, by his trouser-knees, by his expression, by his shirt-cuffs—by each of these things a man's calling is plainly revealed. . . . Here is a gentleman of a medical type, but with the air of a military man. Clearly an army doctor then. He has just come from the tropics, for his face is dark, and that is not the natural tint of his skin, for his wrists are fair. He has undergone hardship and sickness, as his haggard face says clearly. His left arm has been injured. He holds it in a stiff and unnatural manner. Where in the tropics could an English army doctor have seen much hardship and got his arm wounded? Clearly in Afghanistan.

In following the Holmes-Bell approach, the detective moves beyond reliance on mere factual observations, and begins to extrapolate, to surmise, and to develop and verify theories regarding the target. From specific features and instances of conduct, he is able to derive a general understanding. There is substantial disagreement among students of logic as to whether this process should be defined as "deduction" or "induction." As a general proposition, deduction is argument leading from principles, and induction is argument leading toward principles. For our purposes, we will simply accept the colloquial use of the term "deduction" and focus instead on the fact that this aspect of the detective's art is intended to allow the drawing of general conclusions from specific observations.

It must be acknowledged again that this process is more art than science, for very few certainties exist in the realm of the butterfly. As the assessment begins to take shape, the detective's mission begins to shift from simply observing *what* the target is doing to asking *why* he is doing it. In this regard, he must avail himself of a second set of skills, borrowed this time from the psychiatrist and the psychologist. To further this analysis, we must have at least a passing familiarity with certain generally accepted motives and coping strategies that drive human behavior.

When we talk of psychiatry and psychology, we should be clear from the outset that these are complex sciences and that it takes years of study under expert tutelage to achieve any level of competence in such disciplines. Nevertheless, even to the lay analyst, it is obvious that people are driven to fulfill certain wants and desires and that they employ readily observable and definable coping mechanisms to deal with stress in their daily lives. Defining and examining the nature of these motivations and behaviors can be of tremendous assistance in the ongoing effort to look into the mind of a given subject.

Addressing the issue at its most fundamental level, people have needs. The exact nature of those needs varies by individual and situation, but it is a near-universal characteristic of human beings that they are engaged in a constant struggle to satisfy them. In the 1950s, renowned psychologist Dr. Abraham Maslow organized human needs into a hierarchy that has become a widely accepted paradigm in the study of human behavior.

Name: Abraham Harold Maslow
Profession: Psychologist
Birth: 4/1/1908, Brooklyn, NY, U.S.
Affiliation: Brandeis University
Research: Human need hierarchy,

P-0077
Maslow, Abraham

Maslow's "need hierarchy" as it is called has been recast many times to suit particular purposes and classes of people, but its fundamental structure is as follows:

1. The need to survive is paramount. This category is composed of biological necessities such as nutrition, sleep, and the reproductive drive.

2. The satisfaction of these core needs is required. When accomplished, humans are motivated to seek safety and security. It should be noted that the way in which these goals are realized has changed significantly over time as civilization has evolved.

3. The desire for love, affection, and a sense of belonging is next: needs that are analytically distinct from the primal urges discussed in level one

4. The fulfillment of the requirements just mentioned is necessary. Once satisfied, people tend to seek the esteem and recognition of others.

Hierarchy of Needs

First Level	Biological	Respiration, nourishment, sleep, reproduction
Second Level	Defensive	Physical, economic, situational security
Third Level	Social	Friendship, family, sexuality
Fourth Level	Hierarchical	Respect, esteem, achievement
Fifth Level	Transcendent	Morality, creativity, spontaneity

According to Maslow, only when all these categories have been fulfilled can the subject begin the process of self-realization. Unencumbered by the demands these needs create, the "actualized" person can come to grips with the "meta values"—ideals like truth, honor, and justice—thereby establishing a strong sense of self and place in society. Such a person, he posits, is self-reliant and resistant to various forms of social repression and indoctrination. Subjects who have achieved this level of function, therefore, present a far harder target for both the investigator and the manipulator.[4]

Whether or not we agree with the precise contours of Maslow's categories is not important. What is critical for our present purposes is the recognition that we are all engaged in quests of this nature. For if the detective can identify which need or needs are currently influencing the target's behavior most powerfully, he will have gained an analytical (and persuasive) tool of tremendous value.

Obviously, the person who is hungry is motivated to seek food; the one who is cold will search for shelter. In such situations, it is

4. The art of manipulation is discussed in detail in section 4 of this text.

not difficult to deduce the subject's primary motivation. At least in the mainstream society of Western democracies, it is rare that such basic necessities are wanting. Paradoxically, given the concentration of wealth and power in these same cultures, adequate sleep and nutrition are often lacking to a shocking degree among the same subjects. The target who is inactive but sleep deprived or overfed but undernourished is not hard to find.

There is another aspect to this most fundamental level of survival. It is the need, real or imagined, to reproduce. People in general and men in particular spend a remarkable amount of time in pursuit of attractive members of the opposite sex, often with a single purpose in mind. This is a normal aspect of the human condition, and a fundamental assumption in the practice of the detective. The difficulty arises when the seeker becomes unreasonably selective about the source or the nature of the companionship he desires. In certain situations, he may be striving for the unattainable in either an absolute or a relative sense. This way lies trouble for the subject and opportunity for the detective. The signs of unrequited love, for example, tend to be written large on the face of the unfortunate victim.

In ancient times, achieving a sense of safety might very well have involved equipping oneself with the skills and weapons of warfare. With limited exceptions, the battle for survival is merely figurative in modern society. For some, security is measured in material possessions; for others, by the size of their bank balances. Appearances to the contrary notwithstanding, the well-heeled, compulsive shopper and the single-minded corporate raider whose net worth is beyond the dreams of avarice are both mired at this secondary level, and the key to what drives them is obvious. They present targets that are far more accessible from the point of view of the detective and the manipulator alike than do those happy few whose means are sufficient to meet or exceed their desires.

The commodities of love and affection are not in such short supply, as many believe. They are attainable goals if one is willing to work at a relationship and to give as much or more than he receives. They can be found in a warm hug from a friend, a baby's smile, or the purr of a cat. Included in this category is the need to feel a sense of belonging and identification with others. Many people achieve and maintain this goal everyday, but many others do not. Whether they are socially inept or simply cast out by their peer group for some perceived defect, a so-called omega will do and say almost anything to ingratiate himself with the pack and is therefore an open book to the observant detective.

Esteem and recognition must be earned to be of any value. Even for those with no apparent natural gifts, there are many endeavors in which the sole ingredient of success is hard work. But problems arise when people crave a particular type of esteem and are unwilling or unable to bear the cost of achieving this goal in an honest fashion. Examples include the loudmouthed know-it-all, an expert on any subject that comes up in anyone else's conversation, and the intellectual thief, who is eager to take credit for the work and ideas of others. While such people may be nightmare colleagues, they are easy marks for the detective, for their needs are both clear and urgent.

Whereas the fulfillment of the four categories discussed in the preceding depends on interaction with outside influences, the process of self-realization is a largely self-contained matter. As a result, it is much more difficult for the detective to read or influence a target who has advanced to this level of functioning. The needs that would normally inform the analysis are of a much more elusive and ethereal variety. The subject is wrapped in a protective mantle, the material of which is introspection, growth, and self-discovery. When confronted with such a specimen, the detective must recognize that the needs in question are of an altogether different variety.

Interrogation specialists trained in the fundamentals of psychology also agree that the self-actualized individual presents a far greater challenge. Such a person has the ability and the wherewithal to assess and accept or alter his situation and the internal resources to withstand or deflect a tremendous amount of external pressure.

Fortunately, for those engaged in the process of reading or influencing others, such a person is the exception not the rule.

If life were as simple as identifying a need and then satisfying it, the hierarchy just presented, or some version thereof, would suffice to assist the detective in making any necessary deductions about a given target. Unfortunately, for both the detective and the subject, it's not that easy. There are many impediments to achieving what we desire and, as a result, most of us experience significant levels of stress, at least at certain points in our lives. While such situations may be painful for the target, they can be instructive for the detective, particularly if he has a fundamental understanding of the mechanisms that humans typically employ to cope with stress.

During the early twentieth century, Sigmund Freud, the father of modern psychoanalysis, articulated eight theories to explain the way in which people deal with anxiety. They are repression, rationalization, projection, displacement, reaction formation, compensation, sublimation, and identification. Given that a comprehensive treatment of these issues is well beyond the scope of this book, a brief overview of each may nevertheless prove useful, if for no other purpose than giving a name to the behavior in question.

Name: Sigismund Schlomo Freud
Profession: Psychiatrist
Birth: 5/6/1865, Freiberg, Moravia
Affiliation: University of Vienna
Research: Psychoanalysis . . .

P-0008
Freud, Sigmund

1. Repression involves the banishment of anxious thoughts from the consciousness. It is unlikely to be a successful strategy over the long term since it creates in the mind of the user a version of events that is at odds with reality to varying degrees (unless of course the source of the stress is itself imaginary). In so doing, it may create "blind spots." The blithely indifferent wife of the philandering businessman may be repressing the painful truth. Depending on the degree to which she relies on this mechanism, she may even cease to be aware of the lipstick marks on his collars or the smell of another woman's perfume. This evidence will have been rendered invisible to her for all practical purposes. In layman's terms such conduct is commonly referred to as "denial." Parenthetically, the investigator should also take note of the enabling effect this response will have on the husband's behavior.

2. Rationalization is the process of explaining away the problem to oneself, to others, or to oneself *through* others. In its simplest form, this can involve the offering of an excuse that may or may not be sincere: the man defrauding his insurance company but telling himself that "they can afford it." In more sophisticated incarnations, it may require the elaborate recasting of reality to justify one's actions, performance, or situation: the high school graduate who deals with his poor showing on the SAT by claiming that he was ill on the day of the test, or that such tests are inherently flawed, or that he would not want to attend any college that prioritizes such arbitrary evaluations. People are often familiar with this idea in the form of Aesop's "sour grapes" fable. Psychologists recognize a corollary to this concept, the so-called "sweet-lemons" approach in which the subject simply assumes that everything happens for the best.

3. Projection refers to the bizarre conduct of attributing unwelcome or unwanted feelings and behaviors to other people or

things. The misanthrope ascribes his outcast status to the ill motives and misconduct of the people with whom he comes into contact so that he does not have to face his own shortcomings in this regard. A more specific and common manifestation of this principle is the assumption that others are engaging in the same type of conduct that is the source of the anxiety: the cheating husband who comes to believe that his wife and perhaps even his mistress are also having extracurricular affairs, for instance. This process allows the subject to express concern and anger about the conduct at issue without having to direct these emotions inward. It is the embodiment of the theory that a good offense is the best defense. Obviously, this type of reaction to anxiety provides the interested observer with a direct line of sight into the innermost workings of the target himself.

4. Displacement is the rerouting of emotional impulses to a more acceptable destination. Rather than addressing frustration, anger, or dissatisfaction to the source of these feelings, the subject selects an alternate outlet. The classic example is the disgruntled worker who is too timid to confront his boss, so he kicks his dog or yells at his family when he returns home. In a perfect world, everyone would be free to deal with such stressors in a direct fashion. Unfortunately, many situations occur in which this is a genuinely impossible or at least unwise proposition. Thankfully, a variety of ways to release this pressure are available without taking it out on innocent third parties, including physical exertion and therapy sometimes. But in the analytical context, the inappropriate or disproportionate conduct of the displacer is a clue that the real problem lies elsewhere.

5. The term reaction formation refers to another peculiar tendency in humans: attempting to camouflage unacceptable behaviors by engaging in conduct of the opposite variety.

Examples of this reaction to internal stressors are ubiquitous: the wife beater who takes his duties as a church alderman very seriously; the greedy televangelist who rails against the evils of money; the homophobic bully who is struggling with his own sexual identity; and the mean-spirited do-gooder who is constantly bragging about charity work to anyone who will listen.

To produce an accurate analysis, it is important for the detective to distinguish between action by the subject who is motivated by a legitimate need and reaction formation in response to some other anxiety-producing behavior. Fortunately, there are often telltale signs that distinguish these two possibilities. Since reaction formation is artificial and intended to distract, it tends to be characterized by an excessive or exaggerated performance, almost as if the subject is secretly hoping to be discovered. As in that most infamous of Scottish tragedies, beware the lady who protests too much.

6. Compensation may be the most familiar of the coping strategies presented herein. It is a reaction to perceived weaknesses or failings that manifests as an effort to make up for the deficiency in some other way. The elaborately manicured beard may be a reaction to premature baldness. The muscle-bound torso may be a response to the teasing occasioned by the bodybuilder's diminutive stature. And the huge cigar and expensive sports car speak for themselves. In each of these examples, the subject may as well be holding a sign up that says, "I feel insecure about this aspect of my appearance."

Compensation is not, however, an inherently dysfunctional solution. According to Alfred Adler, a student of Freud's, feelings of powerlessness are common in the young, and efforts to remedy this state of affairs through a variety of endeavors is a necessary and appropriate part of growing up. The skinny street kid who goes on to become the heavyweight champion and the ugly duckling who strives to become a successful model are each engaged in a process of compensation. What impact this has on their respective mental states depends on how they have dealt with the process. Nonetheless, for the detective, the one who seems to be trying too hard is the easy mark.

7. The process of sublimation overlaps with both compensation and displacement to a degree—a sure sign that we are approaching the end of this particular analysis. Sublimation involves transforming unacceptable needs and impulses into more appropriate ones. Before proceeding, the distinctions between this mechanism and its close cousins should be explored. Unlike displacement, in sublimation it is the nature of the *conduct*, and not the *outlet*, that is undergoing change. Where displacement is kicking the dog, sublimation might be kicking the football. Unlike compensation, the subject is not so much trying to balance a deficit with a surplus as he is dealing with the effects of that deficit. Colloquially this might be called "blowing off steam." Sublimation tends to be one of the most healthy and straightforward ways of dealing with stress and, as such, provides very little purchase for the detective. Nevertheless, given a long enough lever . . .

8. The subject who engages in identification, on the other hand, is among the easiest of targets that the detective can hope to encounter. The identifier seeks to assuage his anxiety by sharing it with another or borrowing the characteristics of someone else. He is the embodiment of the maxim, "Misery loves company." For instance, most people can recall from their high school days the frenzied, pre-test comparison of notes with other students. The desire to affiliate one's own level of preparation or confidence with others is a common coping device.

Like compensation, identification is not necessarily a dysfunctional behavior. If the process of identification causes the subject to raise his standards, so much the better, but this is not always the way it works. From the detective's point of view, however, it does not really matter. He must simply remember that such a subject, more so than the average person, "gets like those he bides with." If the detective is himself a member of the identifier's peer group, his influence will be that much more pronounced, and his ability to read the subject that much improved. Finally, in the interests of completeness, note that those who willingly support the identifier's unhelpful behaviors, like those who tolerate repression, are enablers.

Ways to Deal with Anxiety

Repression	What is often colloquially called denial
Rationalization	Sour grapes and sweet lemons
Projection	The pot calling the kettle black
Displacement	Kick the dog
Reaction Formation	The lady doth protest too much
Compensation	Little man syndrome
Sublimation	Blowing off steam
Identification	Misery loves company

Helping the subject deal with his problems is decidedly not part of the detective's mandate. Without wishing to be unnecessarily callous, the target's difficulties and responses thereto are, in fact, the investigator's most valuable tools. By understanding people's needs, he can determine what general forces drive them. In the pursuit of their goals, any displacement or sublimation behaviors signal the existence of anxiety problems. Attempts to compensate or react in the opposite fashion help the detective to zero in on the source of the difficulty. Projection and rationalization can reveal the subject's innermost thoughts. Willingness to repress gives rise to blind spots. And the need to identify provides both insight into the target's current mental state and opportunity to exert influence over future behavior. Being able to read all these signs is an integral part of the butterfly art.

> *Had he noticed how the student enjoyed showing off his superb technique, and deduced that even in a match with a superior fighter, he would not be able to resist the temptation of attempting such a bold attack? Perhaps . . .*

SURVEILLANCE

To know the times means to know the enemy's disposition in battle. Is it flourishing or waning? By observing the spirit of the enemy's men and getting the best position, you can work out the enemy's disposition and move your men accordingly. You can win through this principle of strategy, fighting from a position of advantage. When in a duel, you must forestall the enemy and attack when you have first recognized his school of strategy, perceived his quality and his strong and weak points. Attack in an unsuspected manner, knowing his meter and modulation and the appropriate timing. Knowing the times means, if your ability is high, seeing right into things. If you are thoroughly conversant with strategy, you will recognize the enemy's intentions and thus have many opportunities to win. You must sufficiently study this.

—Miyamoto Musashi, *The Book of Five Rings*

The realm of the butterfly is a nexus of sorts, a place where students and teachers of various disciplines may meet from time to time to exchange notes. Its lessons are of value to the psychologist, the police officer, the attorney, and the agent alike. But this is not to suggest that every aspect of the art is equally applicable to all professions. The previous section, for example, will not tell the second-year student of psychiatry anything he does not already know. The overview presented therein is intended only to bring such matters to the attention of those whose professions would otherwise not touch on them.

Likewise, there are techniques and tactics that both reason and legality suggest are best left to law enforcement professionals. These people have the need, the expertise, and the authority to engage in such practices, and if the private citizen should try to follow in their footsteps in this regard, he may invite criminal and civil liability, not to mention any number of interpersonal difficulties. Among these potential danger zones is the point where observation becomes surveillance.

At the same time, it must be considered that there are occasions when surveillance is the only way to advance an inquiry. In the realm of law enforcement, there are many situations in which some evidence of wrongdoing must be obtained before more invasive investigative methods may be employed. Common examples include the development of reasonable suspicion before detaining an individual and probable cause before searching a location or arresting a suspect. Making such showings often depends on evidence gathered by means of surveillance.

In the late 1920s, celebrated federal agent Elliot Ness was at war with the notorious crime boss Al Capone. Among the many challenges the government faced was the highly secretive nature of Capone's bootlegging operation. Without concrete evidence of wrongdoing, Ness was limited in the actions he could take. At that time, Capone was using Chicago's Liberty Hotel as his base of operations. So secure was the location that federal agents realized there was no possibility of effectively monitoring the activities taking place there. By planting disinformation about an upcoming raid, the investigators manipulated Capone into switching to another site where it was possible to tap into the telephone line and overhear both critical investigative information and highly inculpatory statements as well.

More recently, during the mid-1980s, the FBI was again confronted with a similar wall of silence impeding their investigation of Mafia boss John Gotti. The so-called "Teflon Don" had come to command the Gambino crime family after publicly executing then boss Paul Castellano on the street outside New York's Sparks Steak House. As his moniker suggests, Gotti had proven an extremely elusive target for law enforcement. Like Capone, Gotti had followed the first rule of engagement in establishing a secure base at the Ravenite Social Club. Compounding the difficulty of monitoring Gotti's activities was that he usually met with his lieutenants either on the street or in the upstairs apartment of a Mafia widow who almost never left her home. Both of these situations made surveillance difficult—but not impossible. By employing a combination of advanced technology and old-fashioned police work, the government was able to gain access to the meeting place, install listening devices, and gather enough information about Gotti's operation to complete its investigation and secure a conviction.

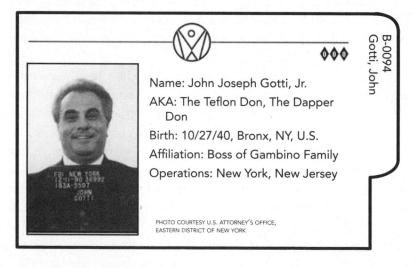

B-0094
Gotti, John

Name: John Joseph Gotti, Jr.
AKA: The Teflon Don, The Dapper Don
Birth: 10/27/40, Bronx, NY, U.S.
Affiliation: Boss of Gambino Family
Operations: New York, New Jersey

PHOTO COURTESY U.S. ATTORNEY'S OFFICE,
EASTERN DISTRICT OF NEW YORK

In its most benign form, surveillance is nothing more than taking note of what is going on around us. In the process of looking into a subject's mind, the way in which he organizes his life is a valuable gauge. If the opportunity presents itself to enter the target's home or office, either by invitation or by legal authority, clues will be everywhere. Beginning with the residence itself, is it a house, an apartment, or a condominium? Is it a typical three-bedroom, one-and-a-half bath on a half-acre lot in a neighborhood or a lavishly appointed, country manor in a rural area? How does this fit with the subject's probable income? Has he likely gone into debt to afford to keep up such appearances, or is he living well within his means? Is it too much or too little for his needs? Is it well maintained or run down? How far is it from the target's place of work?

Is the area intentionally secluded or densely populated? Is the lot wooded or clear-cut? How long is the driveway? Is there a No Trespassing sign or something even more menacing in the front yard, or is there a welcome mat at the door? Is the lawn manicured and painstakingly maintained or left to run wild? Is there a garden? A patio? A pool? A shed? A barn? A stable? Are there security lights? Are there signs of children? Pets? Wildlife? Are there any activity-specific items visible? A barbeque? An archery range? A horseshoe pit? A swing set? All these things may provide insight into the personality of the owners, without the detective ever having to set foot onto the property.

What kind of vehicles can be seen in the driveway? A sedan car? A pickup truck? A luxury vehicle? A Winnebago? A jeep? A sports car? Are there any boats or recreational vehicles? How many "work" cars are there? Do they appear to be well maintained? Are any up on blocks or in pieces? Is there evidence of a garage in which repairs are actually performed? Are the cars parked facing in or out? Are there bumper stickers, parking passes, or decals of any kind? Are they popular makes and recent models? Are all the license plates in the state and up to date? Choice and care of vehicles is another avenue of entry into the target's mind.

Does the house feel like a home or a residence? Does a family live there? Are there children, and if so, are their toys strewn around the house or kept in a tidy fashion? What ages might they be? Is the house neat and clean or would you think twice before sitting down. Or does it have the feel of a museum—sterile and barren? Is it well furnished? Spartan? Gaudy? Is the furniture sturdy and functional or ornamental and expensive? Can one detect the hand of a male, female, or professional decorator? Is there artwork? If so, is there a theme?

Of special importance are any photographs, certificates, or other displays. These are signs erected by the subject himself to tell you what he values. What or who is in each picture? Where are they placed? What do the certificates indicate? What dates do they bear? Has the homeowner chosen to hang a particular flag, or sporting pennant, or shelf filled with memorabilia in the recreation room? Is there a gun case? A safe? A bar? A computer? Plants? Animals?

Bookcases are another rich resource, as any "psychic" who makes house calls knows. How important are books to these people? What are the titles? What types of subject matter are covered? Law? Medicine? Accounting? Investing? Sports? Do the volumes look well worn or purchased by the yard, for effect? Are there college texts? Is there a dictionary? A set of encyclopedias? A Bible? A set of magazines or other periodicals? Similarly, what role does electronic entertainment play in this house? How many televisions are there? Is there a big-screen television? How many VCRs are there? DVD players? Video games? Is there a collection of films, and if so, what genre? How many telephones are in evidence, and whose number is on the speed dialer?

As the detective moves through the house, he will ask himself whether there is a sharp contrast between the appearance of rooms open to the public and the private areas. Are there any signs of home-improvement or do-it-yourself projects? Is there a workout room, study, darkroom, spa, sauna, or any other specialized area? What can be found in the kitchen? Health food? Junk food? Vitamins? Alcohol? Spices? Is there a wherewithal for cooking from scratch or TV dinners? What is in the fridge? What appliance looks as though it gets more use, the oven or the microwave? Are the dishes done or piled up in the sink?

If he should make it as far as the bedroom, does the couple appear to share the bed? Is there a lock on the bedroom door? Whose nightstand is on which side, and why? Is there a television in the bedroom? Is there a phone and on whose side of the bed is it? Is there a particular book on the bedside table? What types of medication can be found in the master bathroom cabinet? What can be found under the clothing in the top dresser drawer or taped to the underside of the desk—probably the two most commonly used hiding places.

If the residence in question is an apartment, is it so by choice or by design? Does it have the feel of a temporary accommodation or a stopgap while saving for a down payment, or does the resident seem comfortable in this kind of space? How long does the target appear to have been living there? Does it look as though it was rented already furnished? Is it a bachelor pad or a tight fit for a family of four? Are any of the bedrooms shared? Is there a spy hole in the door? Is there a buzzer to let people up? Is there a security system? Is there a mailbox or storage space key hanging on the wall?

While houses are often shared with other family members, and therefore tend to reflect a mixture of influences, offices are more individualized and typically far more accessible to the detective. Even a brief visit to such a location can provide a significant amount of information about the employee. Is the office private? Is it large and well appointed? Is the furniture expensive or cheap? Is it well equipped? Clean and well decorated? Is there a window? While many of these features depend on the type of work at issue, they may also speak to seniority. Furthermore, choice of profession is itself perhaps as useful a determinant of character as any other factor discussed thus far.

Based on the configuration of the office equipment, as well as signs of wear, how does the employee spend most of the workday? On the phone? Typing? Perusing paper files and books? Writing by hand? Is there an intercom? Is there a secretary's desk immediately outside the door? Is there a television set? A refrigerator? Are there certificates on the wall? Commendations? Blueprints? Schematics? Newspaper articles? Is there a bookcase? Is the office strictly a workspace, or are there signs of a blending of office and home? Are there personal items, like plants, posters, or pictures?

The office equivalent of the top dresser drawer for storing things the owner would rather not have everyone see is the back of the main or upper right-hand desk drawers, both of which can be easily locked. Another place that people put things they don't want others to find is in the garbage. Sifting through such material is known in the trade as "dumpster diving." While the discarding of an item means that the owner no longer has a valid expectation of privacy in the object, this degree of snooping certainly crosses the line between curiosity and invasion of privacy and is best left to law enforcement professionals.

As important to the detective as who the target is and how he lives is where he goes and what he does. This brings us to another activity appropriately left to the professionals—personal surveillance. While the principles at play here are similar in many ways to those discussed in the sections dealing with pursuit and evasion, the goal is different. Here, the detective is trying to learn about the target rather than merely keeping track of his movements; as a result, the calculus involved in determining when to abort the operation to avoid discovery changes significantly.[5]

Fixed personal surveillance is usually achieved by establishing an observation post with a direct line of sight to the subject's pri-

5. John Gotti was well aware of the presence of surveillance teams and even developed a somewhat friendly relationship with the supervising agent. Thus, when the time came for the eventual arrest and the agent in charge arrived at an establishment full of mobsters well in advance of his backup team, it was Gotti who ordered everyone to cooperate. Furthermore, the fact of a target's awareness of surveillance can even be used on occasion to force him to act or react in certain ways.

mary location: the home, the office, or both at times. As a result, the observer has the luxury of being able to choose a relatively comfortable and secure position. An apartment in an adjacent building or an empty house on the same block are ideal for fixed surveillance purposes, particularly if working in shifts with a team, but a sufficiently camouflaged position outdoors will also serve the purpose. A wooded lot or nearby public structure may work, as will the practice of innocently walking one's dog or jogging past the location on a semiregular basis.

From the fixed point of view, one can determine such fundamental things as what time the target rises, when he leaves for work, when he returns home, whether he goes out in the evening, what time he returns at night, and when he goes to sleep (or at least turns out the lights). Depending on whether windows are closed or curtains are drawn, much more may be observed as well. Even without resorting to high-tech imaging systems, the investigator can make a fair guess at what is going on behind closed doors or drawn curtains from a range of clues, such as the arrival of guests, the telltale glow of the television, the sound of music, and the movement of silhouettes behind the drapes. Also, the availability of affordable thermal and night vision systems has increased dramatically in recent years.

Roving surveillance, by contrast, can be much more demanding for the detective, but often carries with it a greater payoff in terms of information gathered. To keep the target in sight, the observation post employed in this capacity must, of course, be mobile. A motor vehicle of some sort is the most likely choice, but a bicycle or even an operative on foot may be appropriate under certain conditions. As previously discussed, it may not be possible or advisable to maintain constant contact with the target, but neither is it necessary. Humans are creatures of habit and routine, and they will typically fall into a regular pattern on a daily, weekly, or monthly basis at times. If the target makes an unexpected move and disappears on a particular Friday night, there is a fair chance that the trail can be picked up at the same time and place on the following week.

Exercise Seven:
Fixed-Point Surveillance (House, Car, Foot)

Notes: Fixed point surveillance can be most easily performed from an adjacent residence. A parked vehicle provides a less comfortable and secure option. Standing surveillance is the likeliest to attract unwanted attention . . .

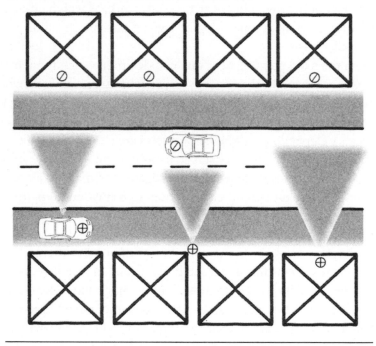

Among the questions that roving surveillance may be used to answer are, Does the target go to work every day? Does he leave early or late? Does he walk, drive, or take public transit? Where does he work? Does he go straight to the office? Does he put in a long or a short day? Does he take frequent coffee or cigarette breaks? Does he leave the building at lunch hour? Does he go to the gym or to the diner? Does he go there alone or with other people? Does he go straight home after work or stop at a bar? Or a shop? Or someone else's house?

Exercise Eight:
Roving Surveillance and Evasion

Notes: When pursuing (southbound lane) ensure at least one blind between the pursuit vehicle and the target; when being pursued, moving out of the lane and stopping briefly will force the pursuer to proceed past that position.

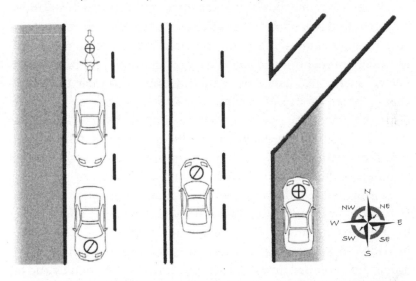

Where does he go in his free time, after work or on weekends? The movies? The game? A singles bar? The driving or the firing range? How does he travel for these purposes? Is he solitary or does he prefer company? Does he have a constant social group? Does he visit family? Does he receive visitors frequently? If so, of what kind? Couples? Same-sex friends? Dates? Does he ever stay out all night? Where? Does he travel far from home? Does he lock up every time he leaves? All these observations can help the detective in his ongoing effort to complete the human jigsaw puzzle.

Like many of the invasive measures discussed up to this point, the practice of eavesdropping clearly falls exclusively within the jurisdiction of law enforcement. The term hearkens back to the days in which a spy might conceal himself in the eaves of a house so as to overhear what is going on within. But whether the listening is achieved with or without the assistance of electronic devices, such conduct is unlawful under most circumstances unless specifically authorized by at least one (and sometimes both) of the parties to the conversation or by an appropriate government official.

Hidden camera exposés and consumer protection investigations have revealed that many of the so-called "psychics" who claim to be able to channel the spirits of the departed are able to come up with remarkably insightful comments as a result, in part, of having conducted such surveillance on certain members of their own audiences. Either by use of electronic listening devices or by agents dispersed among the crowd in advance of the show, they are able to overhear enough of people's comments and conversations to provide them with a significant amount of information about certain members of their audience. Their conduct in this regard, as well as the legality of the hidden camera shows that expose such practices, is a matter to be addressed by local law enforcement officials. The fact remains, however, that the technique works.

With the appropriate judicial authorizations, law enforcement agents are permitted to install listening devices in the homes and offices of suspects. These bugs come in a variety of shapes and sizes, and they can be concealed in almost any mundane item, including a human body. They can be spliced onto phone lines and draw power from the target's own electrical grid. They can transmit live feeds or record data for recovery later. More recently, the technology has existed to add a video component to these systems capable of taking a surprisingly clear picture through an aperture that is only as wide as a fiber-optic thread.

Technology specifically designed to intercept and record electronic transmissions is readily available in many catalogs and shops. It now includes products such as keystroke monitoring software that can track every press of a button on a computer and transmit the information to a remote location through the user's own e-mail server. While some argue that there is a legitimate purpose for such programs, in the form of parents monitoring computer activities of their children, the installation and use of such intercepts without authorization can and does result in criminal prosecution.

At the low-tech end of the spectrum, eavesdropping can also be achieved simply by keeping one's ears open, in the right place, at the right time. In addition to the noises that may be readily detectable from outside a room or structure—shouting, loud music, or words spoken at a sufficient volume—there are other ways for the detective to overhear useful pieces of information about his target. In this regard, two learned abilities are of particular importance:

The first, which is sometimes referred to as "filtering," is the ability to separate out a single conversation from a significant amount of ambient noise. When surrounded by other conversations, people will often discuss private matters secure in the belief that the background chatter will prevent anyone else from overhearing. And while it is true that a party atmosphere usually registers as an indistinct cacophony to the untrained ear, it is entirely possible to learn how to focus in on a single voice to the exclusion of all others. This ability takes time to develop of course and is much easier to learn as well as to employ if there is an unobstructed line of sight to the face of the speaker. Furthermore, even a relative beginner will find that there is a certain innate ability for divining meaning from some combination of lipreading and body-language reading.

The second and equally useful skill in this regard involves what we might call "auditory multitasking." Just as people suppose that the busy room will provide them with conversational cover, they also tend to assume that someone engaged in another conversation will be unable to hear what is being discussed in their own. While it is certainly more difficult to talk and listen at the same time, it is quite easy to appear to be listening to one conversation, nodding, and throwing in the occasional monosyllabic responsive platitude while at the same time focusing on what someone else is saying.

As spouses the world over can attest, the danger inherent in this technique is that if the partner in the cover conversation is an un-witting one, and further discovers what the detective is doing, the result may be less than satisfactory. But it is surprising how little attention many parties pay to what the other participant is actually saying. By way of illustration, a former U.S. president, evidently familiar with and perhaps amused by this phenomenon, is reputed to have greeted people at cocktail parties while shaking their hands, by smiling, nodding, and murmuring, "I killed my mother this morning." This technique worked well for a time, until one sharp visitor to the White House responded, "Well she certainly had it coming, Sir."

Under ordinary circumstances, most targets will tend to be more forthcoming with others than with the detective himself. This is so because it is unlikely (although not impossible) that the detective would also happen to be the target's closest confidante, at least with regard to the issue at hand. Were it otherwise, there would likely be no need for active investigative measures in the first place. Thus, the utility of eavesdropping measures under such circumstances is apparent.

But the person with whom the subject is likely to be most honest is himself. Accordingly, the target's internal dialogue, in whatever form the detective may have access to it, is perhaps the most reliable material of all to intercept. Such reflexive communication may take the form of journal or calendar entries, notes or reminders, or verbal statements made on rare occasions to oneself while either sleeping or waking.

Even when such obvious avenues into the subject's psyche do not present themselves, there is yet another way to divine the thoughts, feelings, and intentions of others: through carefully controlled interaction. This is the point in the analysis when the observer brings together all the data he has gathered thus far, forms his preliminary analysis and working conclusions, and prepares to engage the target directly.

> *Had he made it a point to watch some of the American's earlier bouts and seen him employ a similar gambit at a similar point in those matches? Perhaps . . .*

INTERACTION

In making tactical dispositions, the highest pitch you can attain is to conceal them; conceal your dispositions, and you will be safe from the prying of the subtlest spies, from the machinations of the wisest brains.

—Sun Tzu, *The Art of War*

The art of extracting information from a subject is as old as the profession of law enforcement itself. Statements, admissions, and confessions are among the most direct and persuasive types of evidence available to investigating authorities, if they bear the indicia of reliability. Thus, the process of obtaining information must be analyzed at two levels: sufficiency and accuracy. In other words, the subject must be persuaded to provide the information sought, but the interviewer must also be confident in the correctness of that which is provided.

With regard to sufficiency, one of the most obvious yet neglected avenues of interrogation involves exploitation of the willing subject or at least the potentially cooperative individual. Unless the target is already entrenched in an antithetical posture, a skillful interviewer should be able to gather a great deal of intelligence without causing alarm and defensive behavior. A degree of deception with respect to the reasons behind the questions may be required, but answers can often be procured by simply approaching the subject in a non-threatening fashion.

When the subject is hostile to the interviewer, the process becomes a little more complicated. Recently declassified government interrogation manuals provide guidance in such situations. The first step for the interviewer is to determine the source of the subject's resistance to be able to take steps to neutralize it. If the subject fears reprisal, protection can be offered. If the subject harbors ill will toward the interviewer or his organization, a rapport can be established and inducements offered. If, as is most often the case in the world of espionage, the subject feels a political obligation to remain silent, a convenient rationalization can be presented.[6]

If none of these inducements proves sufficient, the interviewer may have to resort to a degree of deception. For example, the law permits police officers to misrepresent facts under certain circumstances, in order to obtain information from suspects. Among the more commonly used tactics in this regard are the "prisoner's dilemma" and the "other side of the story" approach. The prisoner's dilemma occurs when two or more co-conspirators are placed in separate rooms and told that whichever of them offers to cooperate first will get the better deal. Unless each suspect is certain that none of his colleagues will "flip" on him, experience has shown that they are all likely to compete with each other to be the one to reap the benefit of cooperating.

The other-side-of-the-story approach involves telling the suspect that the police already know what happened and have sufficient evidence to secure a conviction, but that in the interests of fairness and completeness, the interviewer is prepared to hear this suspect's version of events. This technique has the dual advantages of reducing the perceived downside of coming clean while at the same time providing a significant inducement to do so.

---

6. Interrogators in the intelligence world have discovered that when significant pressure to talk is brought to bear on a politically motivated interviewee, his dilemma can be more easily resolved if the interviewer provides him with an intellectual rationalization that would justify his cooperation, such as claiming to have hypnotized the subject or administered a "truth serum" to him, even when this is not really the case.

One of the most labor-intensive possibilities available to the interrogator is the so-called "safe haven" deception. The idea here is to accept the fact that the target intends to be uncooperative with the interviewer, but to deceive him so that he believes that he is in a position to speak freely to someone else. Law enforcement officers often employ this tactic by introducing a "cell mate," who is actually cooperating with the authorities, into the suspect's holding area. In the intelligence world, such ruses can be more elaborate, involving staged "rescues," mock-ups of foreign hotels and other places, and, at least in one instance the use of a re-created Soviet "town" in the rural part of a particular New England state.

When the target still remains determined not to cooperate, more drastic measures may be required. Specialists in "hard target interrogation" generally agree that sufficient physical discomfort, whether applied externally or internally (as with the practice of "waterboarding") will usually cause a subject to break. This is especially true when combined with psychological or pharmacological disinhibitors. While the employment of such methods violates various legal and ethical rules, they have been used in the past and will continue to be used in the future, whether we approve of them or not.[7] But in addition to our general abhorrence of such practices on moral grounds, there are practical reasons that recommend against their employment as well.

The inherent weakness of these approaches is that any statements provided are given under duress and, as a direct result of the methods used to induce them, may be intentionally or unintentionally inaccurate. Experts agree that, especially when dealing with strategic intelligence, data obtained in this fashion should be viewed as highly suspect, even when the subject has been persuaded to try to cooperate as best he can.

More commonly, of course, the interviewee will actively resist the efforts of his captors, providing as little information as is necessary

7. It is fairly common practice for interrogators to employ such governmentally sanctioned practices as sleep and diet modification and the forced adoption of "stress positions" to assist in the extraction of information.

to keep them from hurting him. In one celebrated training example, an American POW threatened with such measures managed to devise and maintain fictional versions of his tactical and operational knowledge, successfully fooling his captors for years until his camp was finally liberated. Thus, the issues of sufficiency and accuracy begin to become inextricably entwined.

Of far greater reliability in seeking the truth, according to the experts, is the process of "regressing" a suspect to a point where he willingly submits to his captor's authority, in much the same way that a young child exhibits obedience to a parent. This effect takes time to achieve, but it can be accomplished through an assortment of disorientation techniques, including sleep or sensory deprivation, manipulation of lighting and other ambient conditions, confusion as to time and place, and noise bombardment occasionally. A few, well-documented but narrowly disseminated case studies ably demonstrate the frightening effectiveness of this technique.

While most people will never be required to engage in such involved and invasive methods of interrogation, many of the principles described in the preceding—adopting the right approach, neutralizing the target's resistance, playing subjects off against each other, encouraging dependency, and controlling perception—are currently employed by many people in the day-to-day business of gathering information.

Before commencing any operation of this nature, the practitioner of the butterfly art must appreciate the distinction between "reading" a subject's mind as a parlor trick and trying to look into his psyche for purposes that are more meaningful. To begin with, the former is a demonstration of the reader's powers of observation and deduction, and, as such, the ultimate objective is clear; the latter depends in large part on concealing the real purpose of the interaction from the subject. Furthermore, in the context of a demonstration, the subject is aware of the process, and he may therefore be guarded, resistant, and meticulous about accuracy to the point of contrariness. When the operation is covert and executed with a modicum of finesse, none of these obstacles is present.

As with so much of the other material presented herein, this rule is not absolute. Sometimes, even in the course of a surreptitious investigation, it may be helpful to reveal at least a portion of the intelligence that has been gathered thus far to the subject. Letting the figurative cat out of the bag may serve to create the impression that the interviewer possesses superior knowledge, thereby generating further interest on the part of the subject. Also, this tactic may be used to probe and test the accuracy of the conclusions that have already been drawn. Indeed, even when little is known about the subject at hand, an indication by the interrogator that he knows even one, albeit irrelevant, arcane fact about his target will suggest omniscience where in fact the reverse may be the truth.

"Reading" a person is similar in many ways to reading, or at least skimming, a book. While it is unwise to judge the contents wholly by the cover, the jacket and binding can provide some useful clues. Unfortunately, there is rarely time or opportunity for a complete and detailed study of the entire work. The reader may have to make do with a few glimpsed pages and some stolen glances at certain critical parts, such as the chapter headings and the summary on the back. Based on all these observations, he may nevertheless be able to fill in any blanks with a surprising degree of accuracy, as the interaction proceeds.

In engaging the target directly, experts agree that one of the most important considerations is the establishment of a comfortable rapport. Where the official interrogator's options in this regard will be quite limited, the undercover detective as an interviewer has the luxury of discovering or manufacturing any number of plausible points of contact so as not to arouse suspicion. While it is helpful to have a common acquaintance, experience, or objective in this regard, a shared seat on a train or adjacent tables in a café will often suffice.

Whatever the common ground may be, its effect should be maximized. Not only will this make the subject more relaxed and willing to talk, but it may also start the critical process of "identification," discussed at length previously. Should this happen, the target may actually begin trying to equate his beliefs, ideas, and theories with those of the detective, making the process of reading that much easier.

As the interaction develops, the detective must nurture the rapport, emphasizing shared views and experiences and minimizing points of opposition, all without seeming to be overreaching. If the interviewer's sincerely held beliefs are at odds with those of the target, a certain economy of truth is to be expected. The novice investigator should beware, however, for lying convincingly and maintaining the lie are specialized skills in their own right.

Once a good rapport has been established and maintained, the detective must next consider both the content and the form of his questions carefully. The idea here is to begin to gather information that can be cross-referenced with working conclusions and used to test assumptions. The question—"How are you today?"—is too common to be of any value; asking whether the subject is content or depressed with life is too obvious. Using a socially acceptable line of inquiry, perhaps regarding such matters as film or hobbies, is about right. What people enjoy watching or reading in their free time says a lot about who they are. The fellow who loves golf, screwball comedies, and the sports pages probably has a relatively happy if vacuous existence. The young man who is devoted to role-playing games, science-fiction film, and comics may be trying to escape from his real life.

Questions should be both oblique and nonthreatening if they are to yield the desired results. They must also be interspersed with answers by the detective so as not to appear to be part of an inquisition. There is a timing to good conversation, a give-and-take, a back-and-forth. Once this level of comfortable communication has been achieved, all manner of confidences may be shared, typically prefaced by the statement, "I can't believe I'm telling you this" or "I hardly know you, but you're a good listener." Under certain circumstances, achieving this effect will require the interviewer to "build a legend," to create a false persona so as not to reveal his true identity or intentions.

This process is greatly assisted by giving the appearance of insight as well as trustworthiness. The two must work in tandem. As previously discussed, insight can be demonstrated by selective disclosure of any of the intelligence that the detective has already gathered or suppositions that he has made. Trust is an even more delicate matter. While it is true that there is a certain comfort in revealing confidences to strangers, there is an equally powerful, countervailing defense mechanism to be overcome.

This is best achieved by adopting a nonthreatening demeanor. When speaking to the attractive, single person, this may take the form of a passing reference to one's happy marriage. When dealing with someone of a significantly different age group, the suggestion that he is reminiscent of a family member, a favorite uncle, or eldest child perhaps, may help in this regard. In virtually any situation, the offer of a confidence of one's own will assist in the forging of a degree of trust.

Sometimes the best question is silence. Interrogators the world over have learned that most humans experience an almost uncontrollable urge to fill the pregnant pause. It is so socially ingrained in them that silences, particularly uncomfortable ones in which someone is looking to them expectantly, must be filled. And even when silence is met with silence, this technique can sometimes be jump-started by beginning a sentence, but stopping at the midpoint to allow the target to fill in the blank. Next time you revisit the classroom café, see how long you can keep the other person talking, merely by saying nothing, perhaps nodding from time to time, or giving at most monosyllabic encouragement.

Before even considering the content of the subject's communications, the detective can gather a great deal of information simply by paying attention to his mode of speech. Is there a national or regional accent present? Does the word choice and diction suggest a good education? Are there terms of art or pieces of jargon sprinkled into the subject's everyday speech that provide clues to the nature of his employment? Are there recurring patterns of speech or expressions? Does the tone suggest confidence or timidity? Is the pitch too high or too low for the body type? And in rare instances, does the manner of talking suggest regression or a failure to progress beyond a certain developmental point in life?

With respect to the substance of a subject's responses, it is vital that the detective listens carefully to the answers given. It is surprising how many professional examiners fail to devote their entire attention to the subject's responses. Those interviewers who study the art of the butterfly must take care that they are hearing what the subject is saying and not simply what they themselves want to hear. This is not to imply that they must believe everything the target says, rather that they must keep their own beliefs separate in their minds from those of the subject. Police officers walk this delicate line on a daily basis. They usually have a good idea of how the crime occurred, but from their interview with the suspect, they are looking not just for confirmation but also for contradictions, levels of mental functioning, and clues to possible defenses.

As strange as it may sound, many people, including criminal suspects, demonstrate an irrepressible desire to reveal things that others might ordinarily expect them to want to keep secret. Whether this tendency is based on some deep-seated sense of right and wrong or on some efforts to skirt the periphery of the real issue in an attempt to ascertain what the interviewer already knows and to explore the pros and cons of coming clean or telling the other side of the story is not known. What has been shown repeatedly is that if the subject is allowed a little latitude, he will often steer the conversation, wittingly or otherwise, into the very area that the detective wishes to explore.

Even if the suspect cannot bring himself to address the issue head-on, clues can often be found in word choice, manner of speech, and linguistic constructions whether it is a murder suspect who keeps referring to his missing wife in the past tense; a malingerer who keeps referring to "my back pain" in the possessive; or a cheating spouse whose answers are vague and mumbled, these people are all hiding something, but at the same time, signposting its location. Likewise, an unnecessarily long pause between a question and answer suggests that the subject needs time to formulate his response and he is therefore unwilling or unable to proceed unscripted.

As important as what is said, is what is not. Where first offenders tend to want to come clean with police, career criminals often adopt the opposite approach. For the skilled interrogator, there is opportunity here also. While the invocation of the right to remain silent may be inadmissible in a court of law, it is controlling in the court of public opinion, and rightly so. When someone declines to comment about an important issue, there is usually a reason. Whether the subject expressly places the matter off-limits or simply redirects the conversation every time the issue is raised, it should be a signal to the detective that something important lies beneath.

There is wisdom in the expression "It's written all over his face." Emotions of all kinds show on the face. If the subject has a relaxed and faraway look with the trace of a smile, then the mental image is likely a fond memory. A wide grin and a sparkle in the eyes betoken joy, humor, and a little mischief occasionally. A furrowed brow, the pinched skin between the eyebrows, and a tightness to the face speak of stress, sorrow, or pain. And a genuine smile, one that demonstrates comfort, confidence, and forthrightness, is almost impossible to fake.

Therapists of all kinds report a vacant or listless appearance in the countenances of chronically depressed and even suicidal patients. It is difficult to describe the kind of emptiness of expression that this entails, but among its indicators is a certain slackness around the jaw and also in the cheeks. The faces of these unfortunates appear quite literally to have fallen. This type of despair also tends to manifest in the complexion. There is a paleness and a sallow quality that speaks of many short and angst-filled nights. In these cases, the gaze tends to be unfocused and glassy.

Furthermore, in addition merely to listening to the answers, the skillful interviewer will also watch the subject to determine whether there are nonverbal cues that may betray anxiety or duplicity or that even contradict the spoken response and point directly to the truth of the matter. Even experienced liars have trouble suppressing their physical reactions to questions that surprise or frighten them. However controlled they may be, a momentary physiological response to the stress of the lie is exhibited. This situation is in fact the principle on which polygraph technology is based. There are several places the detective can look to verify the truth of what he is hearing.

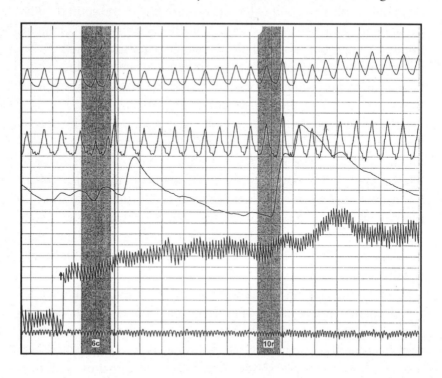

People use body language and physical gestures to amplify their words on a regular basis. With agreement comes nodding. With emphasis comes a decisive hand gesture. Leaning back and frowning indicates uncertainty. And shaking of the head means outright rejection. Under cross-examination, people tend to be even more emphatic and thus even more demonstrative in their statements, since there is usually something important at stake. Watching for agreement between the verbal statements and the associated physical punctuation, therefore, is one of the best determinants of accuracy.

Turning to individual physical signs, even those experienced dissemblers who are aware of and able to control the gross motor movements just described will have difficulty keeping more minor reactions in check under the stress of a lie. The so-called "shock reaction" may manifest only briefly, before it is suppressed and composure is regained, but it is long enough for the trained observer to take note. This is especially true when the detective has intentionally raised the issue for the very purpose of gauging the subject's instinctive and immediate reaction.[8]

Narrowing of the eyes can signify displeasure or distrust. Widening is more consistently observed when the subject is surprised. Failure to make and maintain eye contact suggests resistance or at least a lack of rapport. Many interrogators believe that rapid blinking is a sure sign that the subject is not being forthcoming. And looking up is thought to indicate a genuine attempt to remember something, whereas looking down is more consistent with fabrication.

If the eyes are the windows to the soul, then the mouth is oftentimes the door. Pursed lips suggest that the subject is determined to

---

8. One particular report advises the interrogator to watch for such signs as a flushed face, a "cold sweat," a pale face, a dry mouth, clenched hands, a visible pulse in the throat, a slight gasp, holding the breath, an unsteady voice, the fidgets, elbows drawn in to the sides, unnatural pauses as a result of self-monitoring, or a bobbing of the foot in time with an increased pulse rate when the subject has his legs crossed.

keep this potential point of entry sealed. General tightness of the mouth and jaw is indicative of stress or, at a minimum, concentration. The grotesque grimace that accompanies an involuntary wince is a sure giveaway that the issue raised is unpalatable in some way. Some interrogators claim that a wobbling of the Adam's apple is a reliable indicator that the subject is not being truthful. And licking the lips is an almost universal sign of desire in its many incarnations.

How the target holds his hands can often provide the investigator with additional insight. Squirming or wringing is associated with stress or discomfort. Covering the hands may signify a desire to conceal. Steepling the fingers is thought to carry with it a sense of superiority. Exposing the palms is more consistent with supplication. Tightly balled fists are often a precursor to conflict, either physical or verbal, and florid hand movements of all kinds are associated with lying.

As the analysis progresses from the common to the idiosyncratic, it should be remembered that people react to different stimuli in different ways. Physical responses, voluntary or otherwise, may vary by country, upbringing, and experience. These general guidelines collected from the experience of thousands of observers in a variety of fields simply provide a starting point. The mission of the detective, therefore, is to decode the verbal and nonverbal cues of the target in as short a time as possible so as to augment information derived from other sources.

While only a few people have actual ticks or nervous twitches that operate as reliable truth or stress detectors, almost everyone has tells of some kind. Whether the subject sniffs, sighs, touches his face, or engages in some more subtle or multifaceted behavior when he is lying, the clues will be there. And while cracking this code can be a tremendously valuable resource for the detective, discovering the reason behind the lie is perhaps the greatest analytical tool of all. If the detective can find the motive for the misrepresentation, he will be well on his way to mapping the mind of his target.

Or had the Master actually invited the kick by seeming oblivious to the opening feints and carrying his guard deliberately low? Perhaps. In all probability, many of these factors worked in concert to produce the spectacular result. Again, however, the demonstration served only as a technical analog of a deeper truth. What he said was this:

There are no coincidences. Each thing is a part of every other. When something happens, it happens for a reason. Just because you may not see the reason does not make it otherwise. Know this truth and you will see far. Know the reason and you will see all. This is the second teaching in the art of the butterfly.

SECTION THREE

Prognostication

During the 1970s, the American intelligence community learned that the Soviet military had been conducting experiments in the field of parapsychology for some time. In response to this perceived new threat, various programs were initiated to evaluate the effectiveness and potential tactical applications of such measures. Among these was a project known as "Star Gate." At Fort Meade, Maryland, and also at the Stanford Research Institute in Menlo Park, California, Star Gate researchers conducted experiments into the viability of such arcane intelligence-gathering techniques as remote viewing and precognition.[1]

After twenty years of experimentation under the direction of a number of different intelligence and defense agencies and of the expenditure of millions of dollars and thousands of man-hours, the results of the "psychic spying" initiative were deemed inconclusive. An independent review panel appointed in 1995 generated conflicting reports on this subject, and the decision was made to stop funding the program. Some evaluators felt that the project had been of

1. Remote viewing (RV) is a form of clairvoyance in which a subject is said to use his or her powers of extrasensory perception to perceive images of places or events that are hidden from the subject's direct view in space or even time. Precognition is a form of extrasensory perception that allows the subject to perceive information about future events before they happen (as opposed to merely predicting them based on past and present indicators and deductive reasoning). Presentiment refers to gathering information about future events in the form of emotions or feelings at the autonomic level.

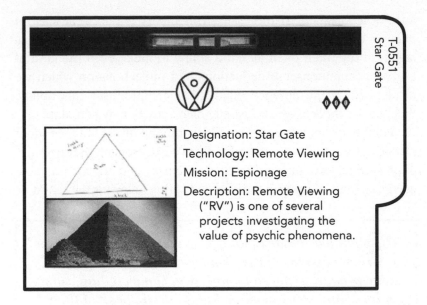

T-0551
Star Gate

Designation: Star Gate
Technology: Remote Viewing
Mission: Espionage
Description: Remote Viewing
("RV") is one of several
projects investigating the
value of psychic phenomena.

no assistance to the government. Others noted a statistically significant accuracy rate in the information provided by test subjects and advocated further research. One of the more conclusive findings of the review was as follows:

> Precognition, in which the answer is known to no one until a future time, appears to work quite well. Recent experiments suggest that if there is a psychic sense, then it works much like our other five senses, by detecting change. Given that physicists are currently grappling with an understanding of time, it may be that a psychic sense exists that scans the future for major change, much as our eyes scan the environment for visual change or our ears allow us to respond to sudden changes in sound.

More recently, some clinical researchers have begun to theorize that anomalies in the temporal-parietal area of the brain—the part that deals with such things as the comprehension of the denotative aspects of language and emotion—may contribute to the appearance of a so-called "sixth sense." This theory is based, at least in part, on evidence that patients who have sustained damage to this region of the brain often lack the ability to make even the kind of everyday, commonsense deductions and projections on which we all depend. If the absence of function compromises this ability, then, so the theory goes, unusually high activity may stimulate it.

Whether or not it is possible to look into the future in the manner just described, there are undoubtedly two extremes on the spectrum of predictability to be considered. At the near end are such reliable events as the sun rising in the east and spring following winter. At its

> *The class was made up of young men and women from a variety of walks of life. Some government employees, some private sector, some military, some civilian, some trained, and some novices, but all at the peak of their particular professions. There were two in the group of similar stature, skill, and demeanor—a Canadian and a Russian. To the casual observer, their relationship seemed no different than those of the rest of the group, but the Master saw more. On the fifth day, he ordered these two onto the mat. The match that ensued was bloody and protracted. The violence of their techniques betrayed a lurking animosity wholly out of proportion with the nature of the exercise. After many savage rounds, both combatants were exhausted but unrelenting. The look in their eyes suggested that this would be a fight to the finish. At that point, the Master intervened. Placing an arm on the shoulder of each and drawing them close, he whispered a few words. At that precise moment, their fury subsided like the passing of a sudden storm, and a bond of friendship was formed—one that endures to this day.*

farthest reaches, we are confronted with the fundamental truth of chaos theory: that especially in complex systems, nothing is certain. Somewhere in between may be found the kind of everyday predictions that can and must be made in a variety of contexts and therefore occupy the realm of the butterfly.

Professions of all kinds require looking into the future, near or far. Weathermen, stockbrokers, actuaries, insurance agents, doctors, lawyers, and many others must make predictions on a daily basis. But whereas the astrologer bases his prophecy on the position and alignment of the planets, the professionals just described employ empirical data to develop theories, which may then be tested and, if deemed sufficiently reliable, applied to the task at hand. And in some instances, the actions of the forecasters themselves may even affect the way in which the future unfolds.

INFORMATION

But to exercise the intellect the prince should read histories, and study there the actions of illustrious men, to see how they have borne themselves in war, to examine the causes of their victories and defeat, so as to avoid the latter and imitate the former; and above all do as an illustrious man did, who took as an exemplar one who had been praised and famous before him, and whose achievements and deeds he always kept in his mind, as it is said Alexander the Great imitated Achilles, Caesar Alexander, Scipio Cyrus. . . . A wise prince ought to observe some such rules, and never in peaceful times stand idle, but increase his resources with industry in such a way that they may be available to him in adversity, so that if fortune changes it may find him prepared to resist her blows.

—Niccolò Machiavelli, *The Prince*

Past Practices

At first, the task of looking into the future may seem a daunting one. But a moment's reflection will reveal that this undiscovered country is not as foreign as it might initially appear. Forecasting is a common, necessary, and often automatic part of most people's daily lives. By recognizing it as such, but taking a closer look at the mechanisms involved, the forecaster or analyst can learn to apply this ability to ever more complex and long-range issues.

By way of simple, everyday illustration, let us borrow again from the cinema. The film opens with a group of boisterous teenagers loading their car in preparation for a road trip. Even without knowing the title or genre of the movie, many audience members may begin to suspect that this excursion is unlikely to go well. They may associate the particulars of the cinematic episode with their own experience in similar situations and remember that problems of some kind arose along the way. Even if there is no direct match with their own histories, they may simply identify a few key factors—lack of adult supervision, group mentality, the combination of alcohol and vehicles—and recognize instinctively that this is a recipe for trouble.

As the plot advances, the group of travelers makes its way to a secluded cabin in the woods, perhaps the property of some distant relative or absentee parent. Now the viewers have a second resource at their disposal: historical and apocryphal material. From the fairy tales of *Hansel and Gretel* and *Little Red Riding Hood* to certain real-life crimes, both modern and ancient, the record is replete with examples of the bad things that happen to young people alone in the woods. At this point, most of the audience has a pretty good idea of what is coming next.

It has become apparent that some of the characters are thoroughly unlikable, thereby fitting precisely into the pattern that has emerged in such genres to explain or justify the evils that are about to befall them. As night draws in, the cycle completes itself when the party atmosphere is dampened by the discovery that the cell phones do not work, the car will not start, and strange noises are emanating from the tree line. Thus, the elements coalesce to make the future clear, and the audience is fairly shouting warnings at the screen at this point.

Real life is not a movie. The unscripted version tends to be far more complex and far less predictable. Yet the tools identified in this hypothetical example apply equally to the real world. Experience and instinct; historical data and examples; patterns and cycles; and present and future indicators are the suits in the deck of cards with which the forecaster makes his predictions.

While the experiences of others, whether conveyed directly or through a written record, can be a source of helpful information, the events of one's own history, in the form of direct experience, are perhaps the best teachers. This is so because even the most comprehensive documentation of an occurrence or situation cannot capture every nuance, flavor, and impression, and such details provide the shading and depth that distinguishes a living memory from a two-dimensional representation of someone else's experience. One's own memories are internalized to a degree that goes far beyond the conscious appreciation of statistical data. They are organic parts of someone's psychological outlook and are so familiar and comfortable that their lessons often manifest in the form of pure instinct. Response time is therefore that much quicker and that much more certain. In short, there is simply no substitute for being there.

While the depth of the senior analyst's experiential portfolio will be greater, by definition, than that of his junior counterpart, its breadth is a matter of individual discretion. This is to say, the more fields in which the forecaster has experience, the greater will be the resources at his disposal. Granted, there is a tradeoff to be considered: The study of several disciplines over a fixed period will, of necessity, be more abbreviated than concentration in a single area, but if he has learned his craft well, the student of the art of the butterfly can parley little into much. If he understands the rudiments of government, he will be better equipped to chart its future course. If he has a grasp of certain fundamentals of the market, his projections will be that much more reliable. And if he is a student of history generally, his overall ability to look into the future will be thereby significantly improved.

All that anyone can really know for certain is what has happened up until now. Fortunately, for the forecaster, life is cyclical. The sun rises in the east and sets in the west. The moon waxes and wanes in a reliable lunar cycle. The tides follow in kind. The axial tilt of the Earth tracks the same pattern every year. Weather conditions change accordingly. Certain comets and other heavenly bodies follow predictable patterns. And, at least according to some theorists, the universe itself is locked in a perpetual cycle of expansion and contraction, wherein the laws of physics are reversed at each inversion.[2]

While knowledge of these astronomical constants, at least in modern times, can hardly be described as privileged information, nevertheless, they remain important tactical variables. Timing one's approach from the east at dawn, as mentioned in a previous section, can ensure near invisibility. Covert nighttime maneuvers depend heavily on the phase of the moon, both in terms of seeing and being seen. Any kind of coastal, waterborne operation requires a working knowledge of tidal conditions. Had Napoleon or Hitler fully

---

2. This last theory has recently gained popularity as a result of the success of the Hubble telescope in determining the total number of galaxies and categorizing them based on their magnitudes so as to arrive at the so-called "density parameter." Using this value, according to astronomers, they are able to predict the future of our universe.

appreciated such natural imperatives when planning their invasions of Russia during the winter, we might inhabit a very different world today.

In the realm of human endeavor, there are various man-made cycles to be considered as well: the artificial construct of a week; the convention of using leap years and daylight savings time; annual holidays and festivals, both religious and secular; and periodic events like elections and Olympiads. Even the income tax filing deadline falls into this category. We are creatures of routine and we are most comfortable, as Maslow observes, when there is predictability to our existence.

In terms of tactical value, awareness of these synthetic cycles can serve to ensure that the escape route is not jammed by weekend getaway traffic or, reciprocally, that the operative can disappear into the mass exodus of holidaymakers heading to the shore. His awareness can also ensure that the queues at the post office do not prevent the timely filing of legal documents or, from the reverse perspective, that the opponent is forced to waste valuable time waiting in line; and that police presence in the area is significantly increased in anticipation of the Mardi Gras celebration or, in the alternative, that the attention of law enforcement is focused somewhere other than the site of the operative's objective.

Another type of cycle is governed by the complex interaction of multiple factors and is therefore somewhat less precisely predictable. It is the cycle of the ages. This cycle embraces such matters as the expansion and contraction of empires, the rise and fall of civilizations, and the evolution of the species as well as of the individual. These are gradual matters, of direct relevance only to those few generations or individuals who happen to find themselves living through a time of national or global crisis or a turning point in history.

Also, quotidian patterns are to be considered, such as rush hour traffic, the workday lunch rush, and the swelling of the television viewing audience at prime time. These are such common features of everyday life that they are well known to all and regularly relied on by many—commuters, restaurateurs, and television executives in the examples just provided—in making and executing their plans. As such, they are still useful, but provide little relative advantage to the forecaster in comparison with any given adversary.

Somewhere in between the daily and the annual lies the frequency that is of maximum value to the practitioner of the butterfly art, for it is in the periodicity of such intermediate matters, measured in months and years as opposed to days or decades, that maximum opportunity may be discovered. Markets improve and deteriorate, alliances form and dissolve, and political parties come and go. By studying such phenomena, the forecaster can predict, or at least make an educated guess, at what is about to come, and can use this knowledge to advantage.

For example, the financial analyst who always manages to stay one step ahead of the market will earn the respect of his employer, the admiration of his peers, and a comfortable living to boot. The political strategist who senses a change in the wind can switch sides if his ethics permit it or can at least advise his candidate appropriately. And the military commander or intelligence officer who foresees the collapse of a friendly regime in an otherwise hostile region can act quickly to save lives.

It is said that there is nothing new under the sun. Borders, cultures, languages, and technologies may change, but there are certain constants to the human condition: hunger for power, thirst for knowledge, the drive to procreate, and the desire to expand one's territory. These are enduring themes. With this in mind, chief among the tools available to the forecaster is the record of things past. While there is no guarantee that history will repeat itself, having a working knowledge of the applicable historical precedent will stand him in good stead.

In the realm of the market, for instance, there are innumerable sources of historical data and a variety of models of various cycles to boot. Undeniably, feast has typically followed famine, and bubbles eventually burst. Also, equally true is that since its inception the amplitude of the market wave has been growing at a tremendous rate. In pursuit of diversification, many analysts have observed that a decline in the domestic market, especially if that market is a global leader, often accompanies, and even occasions, a rise in the value of foreign issues, even if only in a relative sense.

History books scrutinize the evolution of various systems of government in infinite detail and examine the interplay among the political units of the day. The forecaster can find countless volumes dealing with subject matter as broad as the history of human conflict and as narrow as the span of a few days in the command center during a specific crisis. From these materials, he can develop a fair picture of how specific administrations and systems have dealt with almost any kind of challenge.

Of particular interest to students of history and politics alike is the subject of war. So much has been written about this endeavor that the analyst may find himself at a loss for a starting point. The idea, of course, is to look for principles of general applicability rather than becoming mired in the specific circumstances of a given conflict. The writings of Mao Zedong or Che Guevara, for example, will likely prove more useful to the analyst if read as manuals for guerilla warfare rather than historical records of particular revolutionary campaigns.

Library shelves are filled with volumes of material presenting various opinions, theories, and models regarding the way things have worked in the past, and such records can often yield useful present-day insight. What happened last time the Fed cut the interest rate? How long did the European Free Trade Association survive in competition with the European Economic Community? How many consecutive terms has one party ever served in a particular office? Remember that such raw data, as indigestible as it may seem at first, is among the forecaster's most valuable resources. In fact, intelligence agencies the world over employ a special kind of analyst known as a targeting officer, for the express purpose of wading through the oceans of available data so as to identify particular currents of interest.

On a more limited scale, what is the average high tide for a particular shoreline in the month of April? How many tons of wheat did the United States ship to third world countries in 1989? What was the coldest winter on record for a given New England state? Such seemingly mundane information may prove extremely valuable or even critical in forecasting the outcome of a particular operation. And if the library is unable to assist, then the Internet will surely provide. The analyst should employ all these resources to gather as much information as possible about past practices as they relate to his subject, before proceeding.

As noted in section 2, one of the most commonly overlooked sources of valuable intelligence, whether on the global or local level, is the public record. Of particular value to a practitioner of the butterfly art is that many of the media resources available to the international analyst also exist at the municipal or even departmental level, albeit in a somewhat abridged format. Local newspapers cover people and events of interest in the county. The organizational newsletter, while similarly limited in coverage, is likewise targeted in scope. Local television stations cover region-specific material, and national nightly newscasts will often feature segments of local interest. Geographical regions as small as a university campus will often have at least one amateur radio station. All of these are valuable sources of information for the analyst.

At an even higher level of analytical magnification, useful information can still be derived from the actual "post" from which many newspapers take their name. Like the Wanted posters common in frontier times, flyers and other documents and signs posted in public places constitute additional sources of potentially helpful information for the observant onlooker. A multitude of "For Sale" signs on homes and "Going Out of Business" banners on storefronts suggest bad economic times. "Help Wanted" can indicate either an increase in demand for labor or a dwindling supply. Numerous yard sales may mean that the neighborhood is well to do and that residents are able to replace their home furnishings routinely. And assuming that national franchises have not taken over altogether, family names on businesses of all kinds can be a clue to the identity of some of the major players in the community.

In organizations both large and small, one medium of communication eclipses all others: it is word of mouth. Discussion, complaining, gossip and information sharing, call it what you will, it is an undeniable fact of institutional life. Understanding how to exploit this resource is critical to navigating potentially dangerous political waters. And this is a skill that comes into play for a much larger percentage of the population than merely those who work in the specialized professions of "the faculty."

Anyone who believes that politics is purely a part of the electoral process or that espionage and intrigue are exclusively employed in the international arena has clearly never worked in an office setting or competed for a contract in the world of commerce. Paradoxically, the level of contention, competition, and concern is often far fiercer in the deceptively tranquil waters of these small ponds than in the ocean of global affairs.

There are two important and potentially competing channels through which the forecaster can keep abreast of what is being said in this realm: one is listening, but the other is encouraging people to talk. You walk a fine line between being viewed as a confidante and being dismissed as a gossip. Paramount among the characteristics of the former is the ability to keep a secret. It will not take long for others to identify the source of a leak, whether in the realm of personal confidences or national security. Information travels fast, but gossip travels faster, and if the source of the breach is not immediately apparent from the first disclosure, subsequent violations will quickly establish a pattern.

Yet as we have already discussed, the sharing of private information is one of the principle ways to engender trust and thereby reciprocity. How then is the forecaster to make use of this natural human tendency while retaining a reputation for trustworthiness? One way is to ensure that any disclosures offered deal only with one's own private affairs and not those of others. As the practitioner's skills grow, however, he may find that this violates one of the fundamental tenets of the gray man, in that it reveals too much about himself. As with all the points at which these discrete abilities and objectives converge, a certain amount of fancy footwork may be required to resolve this dilemma: fabricating a history, or "building a legend"—as the professionals term it—may be one solution.

Perhaps even more appealing to most people than the allure of the exchange is the security of the vault. People have a natural tendency, some might call it a need, to share information with others. This may be the result of a subconscious desire of people to unburden themselves, a need to appear knowledgeable, or a desire simply to interact. Whatever the motivation, they are far more likely to have such private conversations safe in the knowledge that what they reveal will go no further. It is for this reason that the attorney-client, doctor-patient, and priest-penitent privileges play such an important role in modern jurisprudence.

With this in mind, another way to maintain confidence while engaging in a bilateral exchange is to reveal facts and suppositions without attributing them to specific people. The disclaimer, "I can't tell you where I heard this; I'm sworn to secrecy," engenders both gratitude for the trust the speaker is placing in the listener and confidence that any subsequent disclosures will carry with them the same level of protection through anonymity. Moreover, it is easy to create the impression that a failure to disclose more specific information is based on prudence rather than ignorance, thereby adding to the mystique of the speaker.

In the intelligence world, agents are employed and assets recruited and paid specifically for providing information. In law enforcement, snitches and co-conspirators awaiting sentence serve the same function, hoping to secure a better deal for themselves when the day of reckoning finally comes. These are explicit examples of the information-gathering system at work, although such options are not customarily available to the private person.

But make no mistake, there is a gray area to be studied and exploited here too. News reporters are often tipped off about significant courtroom events by unscrupulous lawyers hoping to make a name for themselves. Lobbyists wine and dine captains of industry and leaders of government in an effort to get a look at the shape of things to come and to have a hand sometimes in the shaping. And the businessman who invites a colleague to join him for a round of golf at the club often has something more on his mind, and indeed his agenda, than the game.

If it would be unseemly or otherwise improper to recruit informants in this fashion, there is another more straightforward technique available to the forecaster. It is called "listening." Very few people will make themselves available at short notice, listen thoughtfully, avoid interrupting, think about the problem, and provide useful, helpful, and unbiased insight or commentary. Securing such a reputation is a tremendous asset in terms of gathering information. It is also an investment that yields rewards in an exponential fashion. For once the forecaster becomes known for this characteristic, his reputation will build itself. People will go to him because they have heard that their colleagues do, either to see if he can help or to tap into the wealth of information he has collected in the process of advising others. If the forecaster can become the informational nexus in his limited realm, he will have secured the best position possible.

Colleagues are not the only ones who may have useful information to provide. Relative strangers can be a tremendous source of insight as well. When arriving in a new town, almost every taxi driver is able and usually quite willing to provide his fare with the answers to a variety of questions at no additional charge. This is perhaps the appropriate juncture to note that information received must be filtered and assigned a level of confidence before being relied on, but at a minimum, the forecaster will have added one local asset's opinion to his understanding of the situation.

Police officers know that almost nothing happens on the street without someone seeing it. Among the most reliable sources of information in this regard, they say, are those for whom the street is either a home or a place of business. There is also the army of service workers, from bartenders to janitors, who are so often invisible to those preoccupied with their own concerns, but who nevertheless bear witness to everything that goes on around them. And it is the exceptional workplace in which the secretarial staff does not have the firmest grip on the pulse of the office. If approached the right way, such people are usually quite willing to share what they know.

One final source of potentially predictive information should be examined before progressing to the next stage in the art of prognostication. It is the readily available assortment of policies, procedures, protocols, and the like, which govern a wide variety of processes from the ordering of supplies by a small company to the declaration of war by the government. These provisions, at least when viewed in the most favorable light, are intended to make sure that a sensible course of action is pursued in matters of some importance. Assuming they are followed by the organization in question, they may be considered the institutional playbook.

This principle can be observed at play on a global scale in the explicit adoption of certain doctrines by the governments of nations. During the ascendancy of the doctrine of containment in Washington, DC, for example, the foreign policy of the United States was to react to any aggressive move by a foreign power in an equal and opposite fashion. The theory, at least for a time, was that even an indirect threat in a relatively inconsequential location could trigger a domino effect that would in turn jeopardize national security. Thus, American responsive measures under such circumstances could be predicted with some certainty.

Where many pilots may skimp on the preflight takeoff checks, the emergency landing procedures are usually followed to an exacting degree of precision. Homicide investigations are far more likely to be conducted by the book than are raids on underage drinking parties. Contracts memorializing major mergers will track the relevant law far more meticulously than will those dealing with lesser matters. Fortunately for the forecaster, all of this means that the more serious the subject at hand, the likelier it is that standard operating procedures will be followed scrupulously, and the easier it will be to foresee the next move.

Sometimes the playbook simply codifies common sense. On other occasions, it is expressly intended to prevent people from acting in the way their instincts suggest. For instance, a plummeting stock price often gives rise to mass selling, but internal or external regulatory policy may limit or foreclose this option for the express purpose of damage control. Similarly, in the shadow world of the intelligence operative, the natural reaction to a blown cover is to extricate oneself from hostile territory with all deliberate speed. Yet as the Gordievsky example demonstrates, the chances of escaping the surveillance team are sometimes increased by remaining in position for a period of time and by waiting for a moment of inattentiveness to facilitate getting "out of the loop." In such situations, knowing the book is not just helpful, but invaluable.

Even where the playbook does not provide the exact answer, the forecaster can benefit at least from knowing that his adversary has consulted it. By doing likewise, he can equip himself with the same information and guidance to which his opponent has access, thereby allowing him to assess more accurately the mindset and the general range of options with which the enemy is faced. This is a critical tool for knowing the enemy's mind, which, in turn, is a significant step toward forecasting what is to come.

Present Indicators

We now find ourselves at the point where the past and the future meet. Strictly speaking, this is a moment of infinite brevity, but for analytical purposes, we will relax this stranglehold and contemplate a slightly wider time frame. While the boundaries of this temporal position are somewhat flexible, it is perhaps best measured in hours and days as opposed to minutes or months. This time frame embraces what is current, what is present, and what is now. It is the point at which the pieces of the puzzle begin to fit together of their own accord.

Broadly speaking, the analyst should know what is going on in the world around us. In such fields as finance, politics, intelligence, and the military, we are increasingly becoming inhabitants of a global village. Depreciation in the value of a foreign currency may have a significant impact on the international component of the mutual fund on which many of the financier's clients depend. American casualties in a peacekeeping action on foreign soil may damage the approval rating of any politician who supported the initiative. And the unexpected death of an elderly despot may present the intelligence officer with opportunity or disaster, either of which will require the making of a quick decision.

Moreover, there is a significant and ever-increasing amount of overlap among the types of events just described. The deployment of troops can have a depressive effect on the economy over the short term because of such factors as decreased incomes for the families of reservists and increased uncertainty with respect to the stability of the markets. On the other hand, the so-called "postwar boom" tends to make up for such recessions with greater numbers of jobs and expenditures required to restock the nation's arsenal. And some commentators have even suggested that in times of domestic political crisis, a foreign campaign may serve to distract unwanted attention from matters at home.

Keeping one eye on the world stage is not enough, however, for domestic activity, especially in the country on which the forecaster's attention is presently focused, can be as important as international developments, and in many cases more so. While domestic affairs may have an attenuated effect on the global picture as a whole, their impact will likely be controlling at home. Such domestic matters can even expand beyond national borders on occasion. Major sporting

events, for example, and salacious scandals have the power to hyp-
notize the general public and all forms of media in equal measure.
Spillover must also be appreciated on the home front as well. It is well
known in financial circles, for instance, that an election year can have
a pronounced effect on the economy. Thus, each aspect of the analytical process depends on many others.

No one can hope to track every relevant condition, and even if
someone could, it would be impossible, as Lorenz discovered, to
predict with any degree of specificity the way in which the system as
a whole would evolve. But keeping track of the big picture assists
with identifying trends and potential turning points and will prove
useful in other ways as well. It is a matter of ensuring that both the
woods and the specific trees remain in sharp focus.

Fortunately for the forecaster, as the workings of politics and eco-
nomics on both foreign and domestic fronts become ever more complex, entire television networks have devoted themselves to
providing up-to-the-minute coverage of developing situations. Unlike regular news stations, these channels confine their coverage to
events of significance in financial and diplomatic arenas, dispensing
with the kind of shock-value pieces that are becoming the staple of
the so-called "infotainment" industry. Dry as it may be, such programming is an essential tool in the quest to stay current with evolving situations.

Networks of this type tend to offer their viewers explanations and
interpretations of the information they are reporting. Such opinions
can be very helpful, especially when time is short or experience is
lacking, but it must be kept in mind that these offerings are themselves just other people's best guesses. When the analyst has a
measure of expertise in the subject matter, the distinction between
fact and opinion is critical. Not only is the former a more reliable
commodity, but it is also the raw material from which original theories are constructed.

Opinions vary regarding what it is that drives developments on
the national and international level. Some commentators claim that

such matters depend wholly on the interplay of social, economic, political, and other such forces, and are so complex that they pass all understanding. Others espouse the "great man theory": the belief that certain powerful personalities determine, or at least direct, the course of history. Examining the historical record, particularly the conditions leading up to the two great wars of the twentieth century, it would seem that the truth lies somewhere in between.

In his role as detective, the forecaster has already developed some expertise in reading the thoughts and intentions of others. When seeking to forecast situations in which the will of the few is determinative, he may call on this ability again. But even if there are no clear, individual targets to be subjected to the analysis, the same techniques may nevertheless be applied to a political unit as a whole, for what is politics but psychology on the national level? Whether or not it is politically correct to say so, or accurate in every conceivable way, groups of people, be they an office or a country, tend to exhibit certain common characteristics: the conservative prosecutor's office; the liberal media; the high-pressure working environment on the East Coast of the United States; and the "no problem" attitude that dominates anywhere but the major cities of the island of Jamaica.[3]

By learning a little about the history, culture, and national character of certain major players on the international stage, the forecaster can begin to develop a sense of how they may react to certain events. Will they, for example, adopt the reserved and multilateral approach favored by many European countries or the aggressive and independent attitude of the former Soviet Union? Is their populace prosperous and peace loving or destitute and desperate? Is the government dependent on the military, or is it the other way around? Again, accuracy is not guaranteed, but in the intricate and ever-changing realm of international affairs, this method provides the forecaster with a useful analytical shortcut.

---

3. This idea that members of certain cultures may exhibit common characteristics is discussed, for example, in a 1963 CIA report dealing with methods of interrogation.

Glimpses of the Future

There is the present, there is the future, and then there is the twilight in between. Here lies opportunity, for the difference between victory and defeat is often a matter of inches and seconds, and the one who reacts both first and best is likelier to prevail. As situations emerge, the boundary between what is just about to happen and what has just happened begins to blur. In this special place, there are signs of what is to come for those who take the time to look, listen, smell, feel, and sense.

Superior pilots of all kinds of crafts develop the ability to keep one eye on what is immediately in front of them, and the other a fair bit farther downstream, taking in what awaits them in a moment's time. To achieve this advanced level of functioning, however, they must first master the present. It is useless to detect the wandering path of the big rig almost a mile down the road, only to collide with the minivan immediately in front. Nevertheless, if the figurative, or indeed literal, driver can safely maneuver his vehicle through traffic while at the same time gathering an impression of the conditions ahead, his chances of avoiding an oncoming difficulty will be greatly improved.

For the soldier leading his team on maneuvers, there may come a time when he finds himself on the verge of a clearing in the woods. The lay of the land suggests an obvious path, and conditions are clear and bright. But by sweeping the tree lines on either side before plowing blindly on, he may notice a slight irregularity in the color of the foliage, a curious absence of wildlife, or the glint of the sun off a piece of polished metal or glass. Any of these observations may save the life of every man in the squad.

The covert operative and the undercover law enforcement agent must both develop the ability to distinguish between the nervousness typically exhibited by criminals and confidential informants even under ordinary circumstances and the particular type of edginess that accompanies the double-cross. In this regard the smallest details, such as whether the subject's anxious gaze is directed at the people in front of him or toward some unknown presence concealed to one side, may be the only indicator of trouble. In these situations, the lives of the professionals involved may depend on their skill at detecting and interpreting such minutiae.

Visual cues come in many forms. On the road, brake lights in the distance mean that a decrease in speed ahead will likely be passed down the line. Dipping headlights coming in the opposite direction demonstrate that there may shortly be a reason to slow down. A slight swerve to one side may indicate an obstacle in the road or impairment on the part of the driver. And another driver's casual shoulder check is a sure sign that he is about to make a lane change, with or without the courtesy of signaling.

In the natural world, a sudden darkening of the sky can precede a torrential downpour. The flash of lightning will soon be followed by a rumble of thunder, during which other sounds will be temporarily obscured. Birds rising from the trees and animals pricking up their ears are reliable indicators that someone is approaching, and the rhythmic swaying of a single branch among several still ones is good evidence that something has just passed this way.

In the home or office, shadows passing across the window or silhouettes reflected on glass surfaces suggest that a knock on the door may be imminent. Flickering lights may indicate that the power is about to go out, and that it is a good time to save your work. A stirring of the curtains or other fine material reveals a disturbance in air currents, and the slightest spontaneous movement of an object or appliance can demonstrate that it is off balance in time to intercept it before it tumbles to the floor. And the car's engine rarely gives out completely without at least giving some form of auditory or tactile warning.

What we can hear is just as important in detecting things to come as what we see, and under some circumstances it may be more so. But acute hearing takes a readjustment of the level of sensitivity to which this sense is typically set to use it to maximum advantage.

Beset by the ever-growing volume of noise in modern society, people have a tendency to stop listening and to hear only those sounds specifically and repeatedly directed at them. While this may be a valuable defense against the excesses of the everyday world, the forecaster must remember to remove this filter when the need is no longer present if he is to take advantage of the additional information his ears can provide.

In ancient Japan, even the noble houses were not safe from attack by the most stealthy of assassins: the ninja. Often trained from birth in the arts of war and death, these ghosts, it was said, could walk through walls and disappear into thin air. By the time anyone knew that they had been there, it was too late. Among the security measures employed in response to this threat, at least by those who could afford it, was the "nightingale floor." This term referred to a construction method in which certain floorboards would be deliberately left a little loose so that when they were stepped on, they squeaked or chirped. Over time, the homeowner would come to know which boards made what noises so that he could both avoid them himself as well as pinpoint the location of any intruder.

In the homes of observant people, particularly if they inhabit older houses, this defensive measure is very much alive today. It is past midnight. There is a slight change in the pitch of the humming noise generated by cars passing on the main road. A moment passes. There is the soft crunch of tires on gravel. Another moment. Then a soft shudder is produced by the collective components of the building's structure—the walls, the windows, the roof tiles—as the seal to the outside world is broken. An intermittent creak filters up the stairs as someone pads across the living room's hardwood floor. This noise becomes more consistent as the stairs are mounted until the intruder hits the second to last step. It squeaks like a mouse in a trap. The homeowner has been meaning to take care of it for some time. And right at the moment, he does happen to have a hammer in his hand.

These general principles do not change much in an outdoor setting. Here it is the swishing of branches and the swaying of undergrowth ever so slightly out of synchronization with the rhythm of the wind that gives first warning. The reaction of the nocturnal hunters confirms these initial indications. The crunching of twigs and leaves underfoot means the intruder is drawing near to the practitioner's position. And the choice is perhaps a length of oak and not a hammer with which the defender plans to arm himself.

These types of naturally occurring security systems are of tremendous value, both as safety measures and as teaching tools. They warn of unexpected attacks, and, in the case of false alarms, at least provide an opportunity to hone one's powers of observation. But the forecaster is also at liberty to take more active measures as well. The chair back propped against the doorknob of the hotel room in which security detail is protecting an asset is a simple way to guard against unannounced visitors. The wind chimes hung in front of the door in such a way that opening it will cause the striker to graze the tubular bells is a subtler means to the same end.

Not only can sound betoken approach, but it can also signal departure, as with the slamming of a door or the fading of voices. It can reveal and track some kind of parallel motion, in the case of synchronous footfalls. And for those blessed with a good ear, it can even provide the approximate position of a target. In Western films, the Indian guide puts his ear to the ground to determine the strength of the approaching force. Similar information can be gathered in the modern-day road pursuit by gauging the tone, pitch, variety, and change in volume of the other party's engine(s).

Sound warns of imminent danger. The blast of a horn or, worse, the squealing of tires says, "Get out of the way." The piercing shriek of the smoke detector or the fire alarm means vacate the building. The shriek of a baby alerts the parents that something is seriously wrong. The insistent beep of the pager signifies that some emergent situation is developing. And while a ticking noise emanating from a package of unknown origin may indicate that it is a clock, the prudent person will probably exercise caution in dealing with the parcel.

Nature appreciates the value of sound as a warning as well. The sharp crack that typically precedes the opening of the ice or the falling of a tree can give the traveler enough time to remove himself from harm's way. The length of time between the flash and the crash of a thunderstorm gives some idea of how close the lightning strikes are to the listener's present position. And highly poisonous creatures like the rattlesnake may come equipped with their own sonic warning.

Sound is a useful medium for conveying alarm. It can reach people no matter what direction they happen to be facing and whether they are awake or asleep. Its differing tones can convey a variety of kinds of information. And if the sound is sufficiently shrill, it will draw someone's attention from almost any other distraction. All these qualities make it a useful tool for one who knows how to use it. For example, triggering a fire alarm will guarantee that even before evacuation is commenced, the concentration of anyone in earshot will be destroyed.

But sight and hearing are not the only senses that can assist in forecasting what is about to happen. What the analyst can feel, in both the literal and figurative senses of the word, can add to his quantum of knowledge significantly and thereby assist in his efforts to look into the immediate future. And while tactile sensations are often accompanied by visible or audible cues, the information that touch can convey should stand alone for analytical purposes.

Anyone who fails to understand the predictive value of feeling has never lived near railway tracks. The approach of a locomotive, perhaps best appreciated at nighttime, gives rise to several distinct stages of sensation: First, there is the tingling occasioned by far-off vibration that reaches down into the depths of slumber to let the sleeper know that activity is afoot. This is followed by the emergence of a rhythm as the moving mechanism resonates with the structure of the residence, causing a distinct vibration or even a disconcerting tremor in any freestanding furniture and, indeed, the building itself. Finally, if the home is located close enough to the tracks themselves, there comes the rattle of fixtures that means the juggernaut's arrival is imminent.

The same phenomenon manifests with the passage of vehicles over a bridge. When first encountered, the feeling is an unsettling experience indeed when one finds oneself fairly bouncing up and down on several tons of steel and concrete in the wake of a passing car. Likewise, the perceptible sway of tall buildings in winds of even moderate strength is a disturbing sight whether the observer finds himself in them or on the ground beneath. As the famous footage of the collapse of the Tacoma Narrows suspension bridge demonstrates, such structures can withstand a tremendous amount of stress before they collapse. But this same example also shows that when the point of perfect resonance is achieved, even the mighty will fall. As such, it is a prime example of the art of the butterfly in action.

Just as events that can be felt will often have sight and sound components as well, many of the visual or auditory examples already provided also carry with them tactile components. The sounds of the intruder entering the house, for example, will sometimes be accompanied by a noticeable change in air pressure. Progress up the stairs may produce minute but perceptible vibrations. Subsequent movements, at least at close proximity, will actually create and disturb patterns of airflow.

Likewise, the prediction that the scout makes after placing his ear to the ground is informed by both sound and feel in equal measure. The opening of treacherous leads in the ice, like earthquakes, is usually preceded by some shifting underfoot. The charging of the air in the path of an imminent lightning strike can actually be felt by any unfortunate person who happens to be at that location. The driver can often feel the presence or passage of other vehicles on the road before hearing or seeing them. And the businessman's pager will commonly have a vibration mode to be employed instead of, or in conjunction with, its audible signal.

Humans have a surprisingly well-developed ability to sense things through touch, overlooked in part because it is so rarely employed. They can feel changes in air pressure and water depth through the mechanism of rebalancing inner-ear pressure. By simply placing a hand on an appliance, they can tell if it is on, or by nudging a box, they can determine if there is anything inside. Healers of all kinds claim to be able to detect illness through the laying on of hands, from the concerned mother who feels her child's forehead to check his temperature to the therapist who treats chronic injury by touch.

As well as being able to detect the approach of people, vehicles, certain types of danger, and the symptoms of illness by touch, this sense can also warn that something is too hot or cold to grasp; that food is stale; that someone is shaking from cold or nerves; and even that a patient has expired. But the concept of feelings encompasses much more than these tactile stimuli. There is another type of feeling—some might call it gut sensation or intuition—that informs human decision making on a regular basis.

Whether this kind of feeling derives from some independent sensory capability or is simply the brain's response to combinations of stimuli from the five conventional sources is largely irrelevant to this analysis. What is important is that there exists, for example, an almost universally recognized sensation in the pit of the stomach that manifests when danger is imminent. It is a most useful evolutionary device and is of value in a variety of walks of life. Like any other ability, this faculty can be honed through experience and should be given due consideration when it manifests.

For the litigation attorney, it may be a look in the witness's eye or a moment of visual contact with opposing counsel. Whatever the clues are, he recognizes that the current line of inquiry may be fatal to his case. The psychologist may see listless, depressed, and suicidal patients on a regular basis, but something about the last client of the day informs him that this one must be committed or at least supervised if he is to make it through the night. And the seasoned bartender cannot define what it is about the fellows at table six that has caught his attention. The gentlemen seated there appear to be well behaved and of good humor, but he will bet the evening's tips that there will be a brawl before the night is out. And he will win that bet.

The final component of our examination of the power of physiological prediction is that most evocative of senses: smell. The olfactory faculty in humans cannot compete with those of the animals, but it can reveal a surprising amount about certain situations. Like touch, smell is often merely one of several stimuli that foreshadow the happening of a particular event, but it constitutes a good and reliable corroborative source nonetheless.

The intruder's odor, whether inside or out-of-doors, will certainly be detectable to a watchdog but may even be perceptible to the human residents as well, especially at close range. If the subject has been drinking or smoking recently, or has been sweating or is wearing a strong perfume or cologne, the effect is that much more pronounced. Likewise, the lingering of such smells can signify a recent presence and will, of course, provide a trail for any tracker with a sufficiently well developed sense of smell.

By no means is it certain that the acrid smell of smoke from a fire will set off an electronic "nose" before a human one, and detecting the smell of gasoline, propane, or other flammable material prior to striking a match has saved many lives. The smell of good food cooking can be one of the most powerful attractors to any who sense it. Conversely, the human body is conditioned to reject any food whose odor indicates that it is rotten or diseased. And once identified, the smell of death and decomposition is one of the most powerful deterrents in both human and animal behavior alike.

Comparison of Relative Strength of Senses Between Humans and Animals

SENSE	HUMAN	ANIMAL
Smell	10 cm² of olfactory epithelium	**Dog** ≈ 100,000 × human (olfactory epithelium up to 170 cm²)
Hearing	typical range ≈ 15 Hz and 20,000 Hz	**Cat** ≈ 10 × human (detects sounds between 100 and 60,000 Hz)
Sight	20/20 vision—200,000 photoreceptors/mm², 1 fovea per eye	**Hawk:** 20/5 vision—1,000,000 photoreceptors/mm², 2 fovea per eye
Touch	17,000 "large" nerve fibers (hand)	**Mole** ≈ 5 × human, 100,000 "large" nerve fibers (nose)
Taste	approximately 10,000 taste buds	**Butterfly** ≈ 12,000 × human (chemoreceptors on the tarsi)
Other	*(no human equivalent)*	**Scorpion:** Specialized hairs that can detect air moving at .04 mph
		Bee: Abdominal magnetite ring can detect magnetic fields
		Bat: Like dolphins can use sound for echolocation
		Viper: Organ for sensing temperature changes of 0.002° C
		Shark: Electrosensors can detect charges of 0.005 uV/cm

The degree to which this faculty can be effectively employed depends in large part on the sensitivity of the instrument. Most people can, for example, trust their noses to detect a degree of intoxication in others sufficient to suggest that they should not be entrusted with the keys to any vehicle or can tell that their baby needs to be changed despite being several feet away. But for a select few, this sense is far more acute. They can perceive such ethereal matters as increased ozone in the air following a heavy rain or during a lightning storm, or the faded scent of another person on a loved one. It is even said that some woodsmen can follow a scent trail like a bloodhound. Such people, of course, enjoy a natural advantage in the practice of the art of the butterfly.

In sensing that the clash of these two Titans was inevitable, had the Master known that each had lost a brother and that the pain of such a loss stoked the fire of a hot temper and fed the embers of a smoldering fury? Had he seen such a dynamic before? Had he even detected the first few sparks of the conflagration? Perhaps . . .

ANALYSIS

Which of the two sovereigns is imbued with the moral law? Which of the two generals has most ability? With whom lie the advantages derived from Heaven and Earth? On which side is discipline most rigorously enforced? Which army is stronger? On which side are officers and men more highly trained? In which army is there the greater constancy both in reward and punishment? By means of these seven considerations I can forecast victory or defeat.

—Sun Tzu, *The Art of War*

All the information gathered by the forecaster thus far is worth very little unless it is subjected to rigorous analysis. As analyst, the practitioner of the butterfly art must determine what each piece of data means standing alone, as well as how they fit together collectively, if he hopes to have them point the way to the future with any degree of accuracy. In so doing, techniques will range from the everyday process of ascribing obvious meaning to certain events, to the extrapolation of likely outcomes from existing data, to the complex social science of formulating and evaluating theories using statistical analysis.

By virtue of the skills developed in the process of looking into the minds of others, as well as those that can help to capture glimpses of the future, the analyst may have actual knowledge of events that have yet to take place. Such intelligence is not, strictly speaking, the product of prognostication, but rather of related but analytically distinct abilities. In its pure form, foreknowledge, as that term applies in the realm of the butterfly, requires the application of analysis to facts to improve the accuracy of conjecture or supposition. For instance, knowing that the boss will be on the warpath next week because he has told you so is the product of intelligence; deducing this from his demeanor, his tone, and the surrounding circumstances is prognostication.

Depending on the situation, the analytical process may be as simple as knowing from experience that a red sky to the west at dawn suggests rain, that a rise in inflation is usually accompanied by a corresponding rise in interest rates, or that a faltering economy is bad for the incumbent party. It may be as common as assuming that corporations act rationally to maximize their profits, that rivals will behave in a competitive fashion, and that consumers generally seek to buy at the lowest price. At the other end of the spectrum, it might be as nuanced and insubstantial as an instinctive reaction to a situation or person.

The twin processes of extrapolation and interpolation are the somewhat more scientific tools available to the analyst in his efforts to forecast future events. Extrapolation is defined as the process of estimating the value of a variable outside a range using known values within that range. Interpolation, by contrast, involves estimating unknown values that lie between two known points. Employing the analogy of a train in motion, its location partway through the trip could be *extrapolated* by looking at the stations at which it has already stopped or *interpolated* by knowing the departure and destination points.

As the practitioner's studies progress from the classroom to the real world, it will become increasingly apparent that the evolution of future events is far more complicated than mere straight-line extrapolation (or indeed interpolation). Most situations do not evolve in an easily predictable, linear fashion. Patterns, however, begin to emerge: One such is the "knock-on effect." Strictly speaking, this model can also trace a straight line, but the key here is that the analyst must consider that the impetus of the initial action—or indeed of the resulting effect—may continue past the intended destination, and cause downstream consequences of either a benign or a malevolent nature. For example, some critics argue that covert funding of the Mujahedeen by Western powers eventually contributed to the rise of the Taliban. In modern parlance, this is known as the law of unintended consequences. In the intelligence world, this is known as "blowback."

Another commonly accepted model is that of the pendulum effect: the tendency of many systems to wander toward one extreme and then correct to the other. This can be seen in economic, political, and social arenas of all kinds. Markets rise and fall. Leadership alternates among principle parties. People and ideas fall in and out of favor. Thus, the great wheel turns and turns again.

A third, helpful, if somewhat more complicated, analytical paradigm is known as the "billiard ball effect." Drawing on the image of the cue ball striking another at an oblique angle, with or without spin, and knocking it into one or several more balls to achieve the

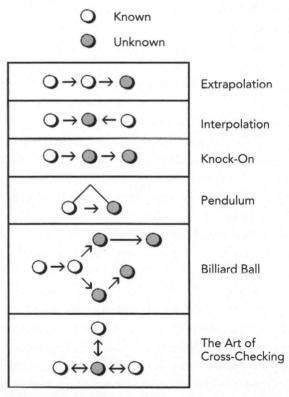

desired result, this model speaks to the kind of nonlinear, multifaceted analysis that is more commonly required to account for real-world events. And while such complex matters as the effect of a terrorist attack on the economy often elude exact calculations, simply having an awareness of the way in which the discrete components of these systems affect one another is a critical aspect of the forecaster's art.

Already discussed in the context of reading an individual's thoughts is the art of cross-referencing or cross-checking. This is a process whereby the analyst makes assumptions from a given piece of information, but requires corroboration from additional or independent sources before ascribing any significant weight to initial indications. In the world of the operative, this approach can be summed up by the expression "Once is happenstance; twice is coincidence; three times is enemy action."

Almost anyone with access to the relevant data can perform the types of simple analysis described thus far. This is not to suggest that such relatively straightforward processes are useless to the analyst, for the number of people who fail to avail themselves of these readily apparent clues is truly remarkable—it is not that they cannot figure out what is about to happen, it is just that they do not bother to try. But something more than this superficial level of analysis is required of the practitioner of the butterfly art, for the goal in this regard is not just to know what may be coming but also to know this better than the opponent.

In the context of this deeper type of analysis, the real payoff for the forecaster may be found. Financial experts, political consultants, and prognosticators of all kinds endeavor not only to peer into the future but also to see further or more clearly than their competitors. Or as the tourist said to the safari guide when told that he could never hope to outrun the attacking lions, "I don't have to outrun them; I just have to outrun you." But in seeking to outdistance the adversary in this way, the forecaster's level of uncertainty must increase. Because of the telescoping time horizon and the attendant increase in the number of factors to be considered, the process becomes far more complicated and the result less sure.

Fortunately, the statistician is a visiting member of the faculty in the study of the art of the butterfly. As an operative, the practitioner of the butterfly art has infiltrated the territory of the opposition; as a detective, he has gathered vast quantities of raw data; and as a statistician, he begins to make sense of all this, analyzing the data, formulating theories, and evaluating their validity later.

To isolate a particular current in the ocean of information with which he is presented, the analyst engages in a process that is sometimes known as data mining.[4] Either with the use of computers and sophisticated algorithms or with the use of more classical methods, the analyst sorts through the data to identify relevant trends. For the political agent, these may relate to voting patterns; for the financier, stock prices; for the soldier, victory or defeat in battle. But let us take as our working example in this case the law enforcement officer, who wishes to predict a change in the crime rate, to best deploy his assets over the months ahead.

Historical data shows that the crime rate changes appreciably over the course of a typical year. In the language of the statistician, the subject under examination—here, the crime rate—is known as the "dependent variable," because it *depends* on the interaction of some combination of "explanatory variables."

By virtue of having monitored the circumstances around him on several fronts, the practitioner has many choices when it comes to selecting one or more explanatory variables. Data mining helps him identify significant trends within the data pool, and common sense

---

4. This is to be distinguished from the way in which the term "data mining" is sometimes employed to describe the process of choosing the data that best supports the theory without considering or evaluating whether the resulting consistency is attributable to the validity of the theory or random chance. For example, it may turn out by pure chance that in one particular year, a surge in the crime rate happened to occur when the tide was at its highest. Such a finding would yield a 100% level of correlation, but would present a 0% level of reliability. Trusting these types of predictions is a recipe for inaccuracy and superstition.

helps him to eliminate those that seem unlikely to play a significant role in explaining the changing rate: in our example, things like the number of days in the particular month or the level of the high tide. Among the sensible options available for further examination is the temperature. From observation or anecdotal evidence, the analyst may theorize that an increase in the temperature brings with it an increase in the crime rate. Where personal experiences of this nature end the inquiry for many people, for the practitioner of the butterfly art, this is only the beginning.

To progress to the next level, the analyst then draws on the multitude of data obtained from sources described in the previous section to see whether it reveals any historical supports for his proposition. This process can be achieved simply by developing a sense of how often actual results have supported the underlying theory and to what degree. In our example, the analyst might look at the varying crime rate over the previous year and compare it to changing temperatures.

Statisticians, however, go so far as to plot points on a graph to produce a visual representation of the relationship between the dependent variable and the explanatory variables. For those with the ability to do so, the graphing approach yields a number of additional analytical tools.

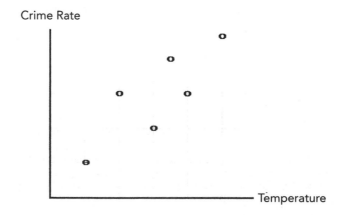

First, the resulting graph, produced with the help of a computer, or even a good eye and a steady hand, allows a line to be fitted to these data points, thereby approximating the average correlation of the variables at issue over time. This line will, in turn, reveal a slope, the steepness of which speaks to the strength of the relationship between the factors at issue. The steeper the slope, the more pronounced is the apparent effect of the explanatory variable (x-axis) on the dependent variable (y-axis).

Second, determining the slope allows for both the identification and the efficient expression of the trend in these many data points[5] and will have evaluative value downstream as well.

Third, by measuring the distance between each data point and the line itself, the statistician can determine the margin of error: that is, the average deviation from "normal" of each data point.[6] This "plus or minus" figure tells the analyst how precise the prediction is likely to be in practice. In some instances, a modest standard error

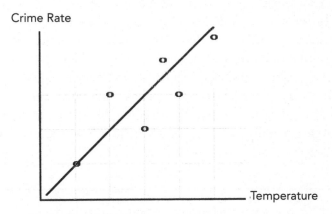

5. Sometimes known as "metadata."
6. By convention, and for mathematical reasons beyond the scope of this treatment, the standard error is actually produced by squaring the errors, summing the result, and dividing the total by the number that is two less than the total number of original data points (the two subtracted numbers representing each end of the line that was fitted to the data points in the first place). For a more detailed explanation, see Ray C. Fair, *Predicting Presidential Elections* (Palo Alto, CA: Stanford University Press, 2002).

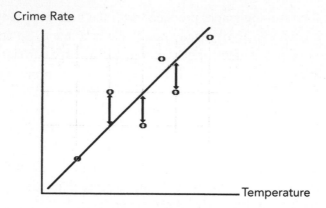

may be inconsequential. In others, like a close-run election campaign, this same variation may be decisive.

One limitation of this approach is that without the help of highly
sophisticated software or equations, only two variables can be compared in this fashion at any one time: A low-tech solution often employed by statisticians is the creation of a table in which the effect of
several explanatory variables on a single outcome, represented by
the slope of their respective lines, is displayed in numerical fashion
one atop the other. While this representation lacks the visual impact of its graphic counterpart, it does serve to get the point across.
And whether the analyst is more comfortable with charts, tables,
notes, or graphs, the process of subjecting his theory to some kind
of analytical scrutiny will serve to increase the reliability of his predictions significantly.

---

*Had his analysis indicated that the similarity of
appearance, attitude, demeanor, and training of the
two "alphas" made their eventual confrontation a
foregone conclusion? Perhaps . . .*

EVALUATION

The influence of theoretical principles upon real life
is produced more through criticism than through
doctrine, for criticism is an application of abstract truth
to real events, therefore it not only brings truth of
this description nearer to life, but also accustoms the
understanding more to such truths by the constant
repetition of their application. . . . In this critical, three
different operations of the mind may be observed. First,
the historical investigation and determining of doubtful
facts. This is properly historical research, and has
nothing in common with theory. Secondly, the tracing
of effects to causes. This is the real critical inquiry;
it is indispensable to theory, for everything which in
theory is to be established, supported, or even merely
explained by experience, can only be settled in this way.
Thirdly, the testing of the means employed. This is
criticism, properly speaking, in which praise and censure
is contained. This is where theory helps history, or rather,
the teaching to be derived from it.

—Carl von Clausewitz, *On War*

By beginning the analytical process with a thorough information-gathering initiative, formulating a sensible theory, and graphing the results, the forecaster reduces the possibility that his projections are based on mere coincidence without underlying meaning. Even after all of this, however, the cautious analyst may still question the accuracy of his initial findings, especially if, as the situation continues to evolve, things do not begin to turn out exactly as expected. This brings us then to the next step in the process: evaluation.

In its simplest form, this stage merely requires the keeping of an open mind with respect to the validity of the underlying theory. The forcaster is rash to abandon an otherwise sound hypothesis at the first sign of inconsistency, but there may come a point at which the contraindications are so numerous and compelling that there is no alternative but to go back to the drawing board. In the stock market, for example, the investor may believe that a "buy and hold" approach is the best way to guarantee consistent returns, and in adopting this strategy, he will have to be prepared to ride out the occasional downturn. But when recession begins to border on depression and the prospect of even moderate returns is evaporating rapidly, an entirely new approach may be required. The art lies in knowing when to blink.

At a more advanced level, as the statistician will explain, the forecaster may look to verify his theory using another pillar of the scientific method: experimental repeatability. A result that cannot be duplicated under similar conditions will be of little predictive value. In all kinds of statistical analysis, therefore, the reliability of an initial finding is calculated by determining its so-called "T-statistic." In fairness, it should be noted at this point that what follows is an exploration of a complicated aspect of statistical analysis that may be appreciated simply by understanding the importance of repeatability in making a determination of reliability.

For those with an eye for numbers and the stomach for a challenge, the question that T-statistic analysis answers is, "How likely is it that the true slope of the initial line (the correlation between the dependent and independent variable) is zero?" In other words, what are the chances that there is no real relationship between the variables at issue and that the analyst has been misled by a false positive? Without going into excruciating detail, this procedure involves dividing the intial slope of the line by the standard error of the estimated slope.

The numerator in this fraction is simply the "steepness" of the line that best fits the first set of data points showing the relationship between the dependent and the independent variables.[7] That is the easy

---

7. For example, if an increase in the temperature of 1% corresponds to a 2% rise in the crime rate, the slope of the line will be 2.

part. To derive the denominator, the analyst then takes multiple, additional samplings of the subject matter; in our working example, the crime and temperature rates are from many other years. From each of these, he is able to calculate additional alternative slopes. As an interim measure, as long as these slopes all seem to fall in the same general vicinity as the first, the chances are good that the analyst is on the right track. The statistician, however, then goes a step further. Each of the slopes derived by the statistician will have its own margin of error. By plotting all these different margins of error on a bell curve, the analyst can determine the maximum error of all the slopes falling within one standard deviation of zero. This number then becomes the denominator in the T-statistic fraction.

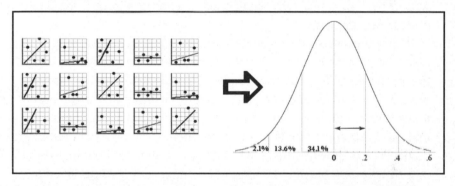

Since zero represents no correlation between the dependent and the explanatory variables, this explanation is a complicated way of saying that the denominator is simply a measure of how far from zero the majority of the errors of the slopes fall. By dividing the first slope by the majority of the average errors of all the other slopes, we are effectively dividing the apparent strength of the correlation in the initial example by the typical error rate.[8] We are, in effect, screening out the "noise" produced by random chance, in our example, perhaps the

8. As a technical matter, these additional slopes are then plotted on a bell curve. By measuring the value of the slopes falling within one standard deviation (defined as 34.1% plus or minus), the analyst arrives at the standard error of the estimated slope, which then becomes the denominator in the T-statistic ratio.

anomalous impact on the crime rate of the release of a large number of prisoners in one particular year.

Having calculated the T-statistic, the rest of the evaluation is relatively easy. When the denominator's value is small, it demonstrates that the majority of the additional slopes fall within narrow tolerances, meaning that there is consistency among the results. When it is large, by contrast, the values of the additional slopes vary significantly. The smaller the denominator, the higher the ultimate value of the fraction will be. By convention and sound logical reasoning, when the T-statistic thus derived is greater than two, we find that the original, theoretical relationship between the events at issue is deemed to be significant. If it is less than two, the result is said to be "not statistically significant" and should be discarded or at least reexamined.

If this process sounds confusing, it is only because it truly is. Also, the process is far more technically demanding than the practice of the art of the butterfly requires. Fortunately, the underlying principle can be reframed in a more digestible and practical fashion: imagine that the crime fighter has made the mistaken assumption that the rising crime rate is somehow related to the high tide. Parenthetically, it is precisely this type of illogical theory that the first step in the process—applying the filter of common sense—is designed to eliminate, but assuming that this does not happen for some reason, then subsequent T-statistic analysis should catch the error.

Compounding this error is the fact that the statistics for the single year he has chosen to examine corroborate that theory; by pure chance, every surge in the crime rate that year happened to occur when the tide was at a high point. Stepping outside the confines of this hypothetical for a moment, we know the assumption to be false, but the statistician needs a way to incorporate this "common sense effect" into his equations. It is here that repeatability will play a key role.

By examining the crime and tide statistics for several other years, the analyst will be able to graph additional data points, chart additional slopes, and calculate additional margins of error for each year. As a practical matter, the laws of probability are unlikely to continue to sustain the unusual result obtained in the first trial. Most of the time, the level of the tide will have nothing to do with the crime rate. Thus, the margins of error (and therefore the corresponding standard error of the slope) will be high. When the time comes to compare the initial slope with the standard error of the subsequent slopes, the result will be a high number divided by a high number, resulting, in all likelihood, in a value that is significantly less than two. All of this is a complicated way of saying that when the first result is not borne out by subsequent experimentation, the reliability of the initial finding is highly suspect.

Whether the forecaster is comfortable with the technical aspects of the statistical analysis outlined in the preceding or prefers merely to ask himself whether the results he anticipated are consistently reproduced, the key to this stage in the process is simply keeping an eye on the way that working conclusions and preliminary assumptions stack up against real-world events. In this regard, the analyst must be both vigilant and flexible, for even the most carefully constructed theory may be flawed in one critical respect or another. Rigidly clinging to an idea whose foundation is crumbling is anathema to the thinking person. One of the ways that the butterfly remains aloft is by respecting and responding to the way the wind is blowing.

> *Had he tested his initial theory by observing slight nuances and subtle signs in the interactions of these two competitors over the course of the previous days? Perhaps . . .*

PRESENTATION

I hold it to be true that Fortune is the arbiter of one-half
of our actions, but that she still leaves us to direct the
other half, or perhaps a little less. I compare her to one of
those raging rivers, which when in flood overflows the
plains, sweeping away trees and buildings, bearing away
the soil from place to place, everything flies before it, all
yield to its violence, without being able in any way to
withstand it; and yet, though its nature be such, it does
not follow therefore that men, when the weather becomes
fair, shall not make provision, both with defenses and
barriers, in such a manner that, rising again, the waters
may pass away by canal, and their force be neither so
unrestrained nor so dangerous.

—Niccolò Machiavelli, *The Prince*

Once the forecaster has gathered sufficient information and subjected it to rigorous analysis and evaluation, he is only partway
done. Even though he may now have a pretty shrewd idea of what is
about to happen next, he must still make the critical decision of
how best to use his newfound knowledge. As in the context of mind
reading, the initial question must be whether the insights developed
are for public consumption or are intended purely for private use.
Under the former condition, there is a degree of hedging, steering,
and showmanship required that is simply not necessary when keeping one's own counsel.

As with information deduced about an individual subject, this is
not to suggest that disclosing one's forecasts is a pointless act. For
certain practitioners of the butterfly art—the financial analyst, the
actuary, and consultants of all kinds—it is the very reason for their
elaborate prognostications. Furthermore, even when disclosure is
not the analyst's primary objective, modest revelations may serve
the collateral purpose of demonstrating a degree of analytical ability

or suggesting a level of inside knowledge that will intrigue, engage, or attract others.

When the forecaster does decide to share his insight, there are a few principles that should govern its presentation: First, he must choose wisely what he will reveal, when he will reveal it, and to whom. There should be some benefit to the revelation other than the pure fun of speculating. Showing one's cards when there is no money on the table is the hallmark of the amateur. Revealing them prematurely signifies lack of nerve or judgment. And sharing one's hand with the wrong person can have a devastating effect on one's reputation.

Having made the decision to speak on a given matter, you should follow the example of the carnival fortune-teller and avoid being too specific. Beginning with generalities allows for multiple interpretations, engaging the listeners in the process, and allowing them to supplement the prediction with their own knowledge and ideas. It also leaves open the opportunity for course corrections depending on the audience's reaction. If the analyst has made a critical error, there may still be an opportunity to recast a wide-ranging statement in a fashion consistent with the newfound discovery. Finally, such an approach betokens an altogether more dignified approach to the fairly common practice of exchanging gossip and may inspire confidence in the listener.

There are times when it will be in the forecaster's best interest to espouse predictions that are not necessarily consistent with his sincere beliefs. Sometimes this will merely serve the purpose of flattery: telling the subject what he wants to hear, in the pursuit of some other, more far-reaching goal. On other occasions, the specifics of the situation itself may favor leaning in a given direction. For example, a well-known professor of Russian history was asked during the Cuban missile crisis whether he believed the Soviets would actually fire on American ships or soil. His response was an unequivocal no. When asked about this prediction some years later, he admitted that he was not nearly as certain as he seemed, but he knew full well that if he turned out to be wrong, there would be no one left to say so.

While such apocalyptic scenarios are thankfully quite rare, the principle can apply to more common situations as well. The company commander who believes that an ambush is likely and the intelligence operative who suspects that his surveillance has been detected may both be mistaken. But their responsive reactions usually do no significant harm. The officer's men may benefit from a readiness drill, and the agent can usually hand off the operation to a colleague or reacquire the target at a later date. It should be considered, however, that in all things, the price of pursuing one path will include the opportunity cost of the road not taken.

Given the inherent uncertainty of the art of forecasting and the tremendous complexity of the underlying process, when the analyst can avoid being publicly pinned down to a specific prediction, he probably should. By playing his cards close to the vest, he may have to forgo the fun of impressing others with his powers of prognostication, but he will have the advantage of retaining total flexibility as events unfold, as well as the option of planning for multiple outcomes.

Contingency planning is commonly employed by such professional practitioners as the financier, the soldier, and the operative, to name just a few. In the wake of recent investment disasters, it has become common practice in the world of finance to favor balanced portfolios: ones in which the vagaries of the stock market are offset by a more stable bond component. Within the equity component, it is also fairly typical to prefer mutual funds to individual issues so that losses in one category are compensated for, or at least cushioned, by strong performances in others. Beyond this, conservative advisors often recommend further diversification among various stock and bond funds and even the inclusion of such purpose-built portfolio components as hedge funds, for similar reasons. The wider the net, the softer the fall.

In tactical operations of all kinds, a fallback position is a critical component of sound planning. Especially when there are lives at stake, the additional time spent preparing for several possible outcomes is well worth the effort. If enemy troops approach from an unexpected direction, the defensive line must be easily reversed. If they come from both sides, the troops must be capable of dealing with a two-front engagement. If they do not come at all, some other useful activity should be planned to avoid complacency.

In the world of the intelligence operative and the covert agent, contingency planning can make the difference between life and death. When infiltrating an organization in an undercover capacity, such people must be prepared to field a variety of questions and withstand a substantial amount of scrutiny, a skill referred to as maintaining "cover for status." If under observation, they must have plausible explanations for whatever operational tasks they have been or will be carrying out, or "cover for action." Both of these tasks require keeping as many options as possible available. Likewise, if discovered, they will need to have several different escape routes and plans at the ready.

Eventually, there will come a point of diminishing marginal returns. The energies expended in preparing to address every conceivable outcome could perhaps be better used by focusing on a few of the most promising possibilities and devoting any additional time to the pursuit of other mission-critical tasks. There is always a balance to be struck, for as we are coming to understand through our studies, no amount of analysis can replace good judgment; no level of research is a substitute for careful consideration.

Had the Master in some way encouraged, or at least permitted, the rivalry to grow by ensuring that the various challenges were always presented with the two combatants on opposite sides of the endeavor? Perhaps . . .

INTERVENTION

Thus, what enables the wise sovereign and the good general to strike and conquer, and achieve things beyond the reach of ordinary men, is foreknowledge. Now this foreknowledge cannot be elicited from spirits; it cannot be obtained inductively from experience, nor by any deductive calculation. Knowledge of the enemy's dispositions can only be obtained from other men. Hence the use of spies, of whom there are five classes. . . . When these five kinds of spys are all at work, none can discover the secret system. This is called "divine manipulation of the threads." It is the sovereign's most precious faculty.

—Sun Tzu, *The Art of War*

All of this brings us then to the final consideration in this process: the impact of the observer on the evolving situation. Strictly speaking, the theory of "observer-created reality" has only been tested at the quantum level, but its principles are equally applicable to the issues at hand. According to Niels Bohr's famous Copenhagen Interpretation, the very act of observing a system has an impact on that system. This theory is predicated on the notion that certain particles exist in a state of superposition in which they may occupy multiple locations at the same time.

In 1935, Viennese physicist Erwin Schrödinger wrote a letter to Albert Einstein in which he illustrated this concept in a fashion that made it more accessible to nonscientists. Imagine a box in which there is a cat and a mechanical device. The device is an execution mechanism that releases a poison into the box if triggered. The mechanism can be triggered by one of the aforementioned superpositioned particles. If the device is activated, the cat will, of course, die. If it is not, the cat will remain alive. The theory of observer-created reality dictates that until someone looks inside the box, the cat is both dead and alive at the same time, existing in some kind of limbo state between the two alternatives. Simply by opening the lid, the observer makes the particle fall into existence or nonexistence in the trigger mechanism, thereby forcing the feline's reality to fall into one category or the other, alive or dead.

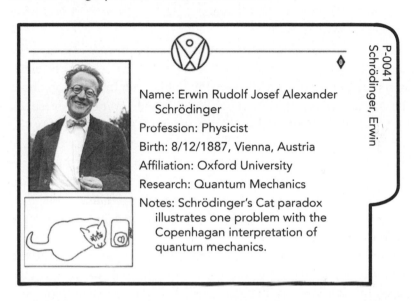

Name: Erwin Rudolf Josef Alexander Schrödinger
Profession: Physicist
Birth: 8/12/1887, Vienna, Austria
Affiliation: Oxford University
Research: Quantum Mechanics
Notes: Schrödinger's Cat paradox illustrates one problem with the Copenhagan interpretation of quantum mechanics.

P-0041
Schrödinger, Erwin

The lesson to be learned by the forecaster from this arcane scientific theory is that the one who is analyzing an evolving situation also has the potential to influence the outcome. For example, the surveillance team may be recognized by the target, causing him to change his route; the reconnaissance scout may be spotted by the enemy forces, thereby giving away the presence of his entire company; and the political commentator's words may reach enough ears and move enough hearts to change the outcome of the election.

Another way to gain appreciation of the power of this principle is through the story of the productivity consultant retained by a major firm to assess its employees' level of job satisfaction. For weeks the consultant watched the workers going about their daily tasks, and at the end of this process, he met with them individually. When it came time for his discussion with one particular vice president, he said, "I have been watching you over the past few weeks, and I noticed that every morning you drove to work you seemed unhappy, but when you walked to work, you seemed much more content; have you ever thought about why this might be the case?" To which the executive replied, "Yes, I have . . . since you arrived you have been parking in my spot."

One of the best illustrations of this principle at work occurs in the debt and equity markets. Financial experts often appear on television programs to provide the viewing public with information about the attractiveness of certain stocks or bonds. When they speak highly about the performance of a particular fund or commodity, the practical effect is that those who follow their advice may purchase shares in it. This in turn leads to an increase in demand, thereby increasing price and apparent performance, at least over the short term. The net result is often that the prophesy fulfills itself. Also true, of course, is that the opposite effect can be achieved when the cycle is vicious in nature.

Herein lies a tool of tremendous power for the prognosticator: the ability to manipulate the future to conform with his own predictions. Take for instance the goal of predicting who will be promoted within an organization of moderate size. It should be a relatively straightforward proposition to eliminate from consideration those candidates who are ineligible as a result of insufficient experience, lack of suitability for the position, general incompetence, or some other disqualification.

From the remaining field, the forecaster can identify certain front-runners: those whose credentials match his analysis of the requirements of the powers that be. At this point, there may be little left to distinguish those whose names appear on the short list, other than the forecaster's preference. Relying on the power of observer-created reality, the analyst may then make his prediction and set to work seeing that it does indeed come to pass.

His discussion and even argument regarding the relative merits of the candidates may have an effect on popular opinion at the grass-roots level. The achievement of even a substantial consensus in this regard may, in turn, have a knock-on effect at the management level, by virtue of direct interaction or general perception. Selective disclosures of information about the applicants may serve to strengthen the position of one or diminish the standing of another. The very act of endorsing a particular candidate may have a positive effect on his chances of success while at the same time causing that individual to increase his effort and improve his performance. Assuming that all other things remain equal, in this way, perception can become reality.

Of course, a dark side to this teaching, as well as to the art of the

---

Had the Master's command to fight been the catalyst for the ultimate engagement? Certainly. But the magic here was the ensuing peace, not the initial war. What had transpired in the Master's embrace? Had he told them that they shared a common grief? That they were equals, not rivals? That each should strive to make the other a better warrior? Perhaps . . .

The lesson he chose to share with the entire class at the conclusion of the hostilities, however, was this:

Everything is illusion. Nothing is what it appears to be. Just as you would hide your true face, so will others, and their designs may be of a darker kind. Therefore, do not simply trust what you are told. Do not merely accept what is presented to you. Listen critically. Watch carefully. Act wisely. Only then will you see the world as it truly exists. Only then will you be able to divine, and perhaps even change, what is to come. This is the third teaching in the art of the butterfly.

butterfly, exists. Where an atmosphere of support can build up a person, a campaign of negativity can tear him down. The fact that these abilities can be used for destructive as well as constructive purposes in no way endorses such practices. But as has been previously noted, the skills and techniques presented herein have been collected from a variety of walks of life. In the interest of completeness, they have been gathered from the attorney and the assassin; the detective and the thief; and the intelligence officer and the conman alike. How the student chooses to employ them depends on his own code of conduct. Fortunately, as we shall see in time, the probability of success is directly linked to the motives underlying the initiative.

SECTION
FOUR

Thought Control

Optically transparent metals and machines that can detect deceptiveness in human brainwaves can be found, if at all, at the outermost boundaries of human technology. Mechanisms for controlling behavior, however, have been under development and even in use for centuries. Power-hungry politicians, unscrupulous salespeople, and cult leaders, to name just a few, have spent vast quantities of resources and energy in trying to discover ways to control human behavior for their own benefit. Likewise, psychiatrists, psychologists, rehabilitative therapists, law enforcement professionals, and national security officials throughout the world have pursued similar means to ostensibly more altruistic ends.

In the world of espionage, possessing the ability to elicit guarded information, to increase suggestibility, to foster dependency, and to eliminate certain memories are incredibly powerful weapons. Research into such capabilities has involved the use of chemical agents, electronic devices, posthypnotic suggestion, subliminal communications, and psychological conditioning. In 1977, the 95th United States Congress conducted hearings into such initiatives by the American intelligence community. During the period at issue, these experimental projects fell under the umbrella of a program codenamed MK-ULTRA.

Today military research and development facilities in many nations have extensive extra low frequency (ELF) and other so-called "wide-

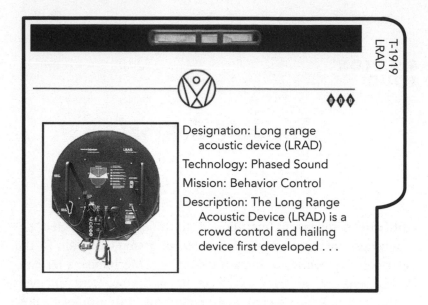

Designation: Long range
  acoustic device (LRAD)

Technology: Phased Sound

Mission: Behavior Control

Description: The Long Range
  Acoustic Device (LRAD) is a
  crowd control and hailing
  device first developed . . .

T-1919
LRAD

field weapons" programs. These systems are based on a range of observable behavioral reactions to the projection of certain energy waves at human subjects and are designed to allow for mass induction of specified mental states at will. In recognition of this emerging reality of modern warfare, bills dealing with the regulation of such systems have already been presented in the American legislature.

Such exotic technology is, of course, a relatively recent addition to the ancient practice of mind control. Long before the emergence of the hard science of thought direction and behavior control, the arts of persuasion, manipulation, and exploitation were evolving in the interrogation rooms of the intelligence community, the corridors of political power, the wards of mental health facilities, and the jury boxes of courthouses throughout the world. To call those who practice such arts "strategists" might be considered generous by some; to call them "manipulators" might perhaps be a little harsh. Appropriately, the truth can probably be found somewhere in the gray area in between.

Without the assistance of drugs and devices of various kinds, classical practitioners had to rely on certain fundamental truths of human behavior, among them are five of the following: First, even if they don't mean to, people often act without thinking. Second, even when there is thought behind an action, the catalyst for the idea may itself have been implanted by outside forces. Third, even internal motivations are predicated on what the actor perceives to be reality. Fourth, even under certain circumstances, a sufficiently persuasive argument can cause an actor to reassess his position and modify his actions. And fifth, even when this last approach fails, there are other, less subtle ways of inducing compliant behavior.

The legends of many nations tell of heroes defeating scores of enemy warriors single-handedly. The realities of combat, including fatigue and error, suggest that such accounts benefit, like any good story, from a degree of exaggeration. Yet employing the teachings of the butterfly art, one in the training hall was able to defeat thirty opponents, using only the power of the mind.

COERCION

The enemy's spies who have come to spy on us must be sought out, tempted with bribes, led away and comfortably housed. Thus they will become converted spies and available for our service.

—Sun Tzu, *The Art of War*

Progress in the art of the butterfly is a process of gradual refinement. In advancing, the student moves from the direct, the obvious, and the crude to the oblique, the subtle, and the delicate. But before the practitioner can hope to achieve the elegant simplicity of the art in its highest form, he must understand and appreciate some of the more rudimentary techniques from which these arts have evolved. Coercion is a necessary, if unfortunate, ancestor of the sophisticated art of persuasion and is to be examined, digested, and then filed away in some remote location with the hope that the need to use it rarely, if ever, arises.

At its most fundamental level, it is true that human behavior can be controlled, at least for a time, by the application of sufficient pressure to the subject. As discussed in the context of interrogation, when such pressure is applied in its most direct, physical form, for eliciting information, it is considered torture. When the means of compulsion is emotional, financial, or political and is intended to influence some future conduct, it is blackmail. When this technique is employed, the target is directed to perform or refrain from a specific act or course of conduct under the threat of retaliation. When the type of *retaliation* threatened is illegal, this is often referred to as extortion. When the nature of the *conduct* sought is against the law, it may be solicitation.

While any attempt to employ this approach may be morally repugnant to most people, there are versions of the technique that are neither illegal nor secret. Graymail, for example, generally refers to a type of threat, the performance of which is not technically illegal. Graymail is sometimes narrowly defined as a defensive tactic in an espionage trial wherein a witness threatens to disclose classified material in the public forum if called to testify. While such conduct may violate certain state secrets acts, it is sometimes argued that nondisclosure may be viewed as a breach of the public trust and contempt of court, thus placing this type of behavior in a gray area. Over time, this term has come to embrace many methods that skirt the boundaries of outright blackmail.[1]

---

1. It is common practice for spymasters, including, it is rumored, former FBI director J. Edgar Hoover, to collect files on a wide variety of targets for the express purpose of developing informational leverage that might prove useful someday.

In the world of finance, a corporate raider may agree to refrain from executing a legal hostile takeover in exchange for financial compensation in the form of overvalued stock repurchasing. This practice is known as "greenmail." In the context of criminal law, some defense attorneys refer to the position taken by police or prosecutors that they will seek the highest permissible punishment for a noncooperative codefendant as "bluemail." From the law enforcement standpoint, the rationale is, of course, that the target is not being punished for refusing to cooperate, rather clemency is being withheld. It may be a fine distinction, but courts have deemed it valid. And while there is, as yet, no catchy term for it, even a child who holds his breath until he gets what he wants is availing himself of this powerful technique.

Less direct pressure may also be brought to bear in such a way that it does not rise to the level of blackmail or even graymail. Behavioral psychologists discovered long ago that the actions of a variety of subjects could be controlled to a significant degree by either providing or withholding rewards. Where there is no duty to provide the inducement in question, there may be nothing inherently wrong with this approach. Annual bonuses, sliding compensation scales, and incentive programs of all kinds depend on this principle. Bribery and political patronage, of course, have no place in this category.

On the other side of the equation is the power of punishment as a motivator. The effectiveness of corporate compliance procedures, administrative sanctions, and criminal laws depends on the rational actor's aversion to unpleasant consequences. On the global stage, this strategy is evident in such national defense policies as massive retaliation or mutually assured destruction. In the classroom of everyday life, thankfully, the threatened punishment tends to be of a less terminal nature: people criticize, lecture, ignore, ostracize, and attack those whose conduct does not sit well with them, at least in part, in an effort to deter such behavior.

Centuries ago, Aristophanes told the tale of the soldiers' wives who ended a war by withholding their affections from their hus-

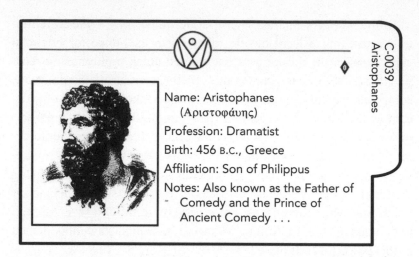

Name: Aristophanes
(Ἀριστοφάυης)
Profession: Dramatist
Birth: 456 B.C., Greece
Affiliation: Son of Philippus
Notes: Also known as the Father of
Comedy and the Prince of
Ancient Comedy . . .

C-0039
Aristophanes

bands until hostilities ceased. The effectiveness of this approach has not been lost on manipulators of all kinds through the centuries, as evidenced by the continued recruitment and employment of attractive female assets, among them one of Fidel Castro's former mistresses, for a variety of operational purposes. Whatever particular form it takes, when the adverse consequences of some future act are made known to the subject in an effort to control his present behavior, this principle of pressure is at play.

For the advanced practitioner, there are still subtler ways of inducing the desired behavior from a subject: "I don't think you want to do that; it might not be good for your career." "I'd think carefully before saying another word if I were you." "I'll pretend I didn't hear that." While none of these expressions makes an explicit threat, the speaker's meaning with respect to the probable consequences for the subject, at least in a general sense, is clear. Depending on the perceived power of the speaker, and the way in which such veiled threats are delivered, their effect can be equal to or, in some cases, far greater than that of direct and obvious pressure.

One of the few points of near uniform agreement among those who study methods of behavior control is that direct coercion has significant limitations, for which there are three reasons: First, since the target almost never truly submits to the will of the enforcer, his compliance will last only as long as the threat can be credibly maintained. Second, if the behavior sought can be performed at a variety of levels, coercion will elicit only the minimum required to avoid the unwanted consequence, and the target's performance of the required behavior may be lackluster, insincere, or sluggish. And third, under this approach, should the underlying threat ever be eliminated, the enforcer may himself become a target for retaliation.

All these problems can, of course, be eliminated if the practitioner is able to bend the target's true desires to his own will. Just as there are many ways to gain entry to a house, there are many approaches to eliciting the desired behavior from a subject. Coercive tactics may perhaps be best likened to knocking down the front door with a battering ram. There are better ways. The practitioner may simply knock and accept an invitation inside; he may create the illusion that his presence is required within; he may enter by stealth while the resident is home; or he may simply wait until the homeowner leaves.

Such restrained, graceful, and civilized approaches to the modification of human behavior are accurately classified as elements of the butterfly art. There is a specific term we shall use in referring to those who are capable of performing at such a sophisticated operational level—manipulating the behavior of others to their own advantage while remaining undiscovered themselves. This term hearkens back to seventeenth-century France, a place and time in which Cardinal Richelieu, known as the "Eminence Rouge" because of his red habit, was responsible for conducting important and delicate diplomatic negotiations, including those relating to the Thirty Years War.

The Cardinal was assisted in this capacity by his private secretary, François Leclerc du Tremblay. Customarily attired in a simple gray monk's cowl, Tremblay had no wish to share the limelight with his colorful superior, but rather preferred to blend against the stone walls of the castles in which such high-level discussions took place.

He nevertheless displayed an extraordinary facility for controlling the outcome of such negotiations, without drawing unnecessary and unwanted attention to himself. Among the cognoscenti, he therefore became known as the "Eminence Grise"—the gray eminence. In time, this moniker came to describe any who broker power from behind the scenes. Thus, we have returned to the gray man, this time in his capacity as "eminence grise."

Name: François Leclerc du Tremblay
  AKA: *L'Eminence Grise*
Profession: Politician
Birth: 11/4/1577, Paris, France
Affiliation: Capuchin Friar
Notes: As both advisor to and agent for Cardinal Richelieu, he maneuvered the Diet of Regensburg becoming Minister of War.

S-0004
Leclerc du Tremblay

Toward the end of their training, the Master informed the recruits that they would engage in a no-holds-barred exercise in which all would fight all. This was not a request. Given the combat proficiency and inherent toughness of those assembled, one-on-one bouts in the ring held little fear for them, but this was an entirely different proposition—a battle royal with no quarter asked or given. The corresponding surge of adrenaline caused their focus to narrow to a pinpoint, with one objective in mind: survival.

PERSUASION

A prince, therefore, ought always to take counsel, but only
when he wishes and not when others wish; he ought
rather to discourage every one from offering advice unless
he asks it; but, however, he ought to be a constant
inquirer, and afterwards a patient listener concerning the
things of which he inquired; also, on learning that any
one, on any consideration, has not told him the truth, he
should let his anger be felt.

—Niccolò Machiavelli, *The Prince*

Fortunately for the eminence grise, there are times when the subject
of his attention will be open to discussing future actions with others,
for the purpose of gauging their reactions or even seeking advice.
This useful situation is much more likely to develop if the strategist
has read his subject well and managed to foster a rapport or perhaps even a degree of identification with the target. Alternatively,
such opportunities can simply come down to being in the right place
at the right time. In either event, having a chance to engage the target's thought process directly is a tremendous opportunity, and one
to be managed with care.

As a threshold matter, distinctions must be drawn among the related issues of providing information, giving an opinion, and presenting argument intended to persuade. Furnishing raw data devoid
of commentary is typically expected in the report of the subordinate: the soldier scouting a forward position, the surveillance team
leader, the junior analyst or associate, and the field investigator.
While these situations afford an opportunity for the injection of disinformation or subtle spin, such measures may be detected if they
are not undertaken with extreme care and executed delicately.

Seeking counsel, by contrast, explicitly solicits an opinion, at
least in so far as it will assist the decision maker in achieving his
goals. This type of interaction is commonly sought from colleagues

of similar experience, senior advisors, and experts in a particular field. While the recipient of such advice remains the ultimate arbiter, he clearly believes that he may be able to benefit from the insight of another. Critically important to the eminence grise in exploiting such an opportunity to the fullest extent possible is maintaining an appearance of neutrality or disinterest. This is not to say that the counselor must seem unconcerned about the subject matter, but rather that he must not demonstrate any self-interest or partiality. If it becomes clear that the advisor has a stake in the outcome, his counsel becomes argument and the apparent objectivity of his opinion is diminished significantly.

Perhaps the most polished practitioners of this particular technique are the political advisors who pull the strings of some of the most powerful players in the realm of public policy. In democratic societies, leaders are elected for limited terms under the theory that such a system precludes the possibility of unacceptable concentrations of power amassing in any one person or office. But any rational student of government will realize that such complex systems simply cannot function efficiently if regulated solely by the disjointed and potentially contradictory policies of successive administrations.

As a result, at many levels of government there are certain key players: nonelected advisors whose tenure is measured in decades, not years. These so-called "mandarins" have tremendous influence over the direction of national policy in the intermediate and long runs. They have always been there, working patiently behind the scenes. Over the centuries, they have developed an entire art form devoted to the delicate manipulation of the masters whom they are supposed to serve.

Consistent with the gray man's practice, they have long ago identified the survival imperative of the elected representative: reelection. This is not to suggest that a desire to remain in office is the motivation of every public official, but it is a harsh reality that if the incumbent does not succeed in this primary endeavor, he will no longer be in a position to pursue any other goal. Both he and his advisors know that public opinion is the determinative factor in this regard and that the impact of any proposed initiative in the forum of public debate is therefore a matter of significant concern, hence their obsession with polling data. Here, then, is the strategist's weapon of choice.

An important skill in public life generally, and even more so when attempting to serve in an advisory capacity without revealing one's own agenda, is the ability to manipulate the language. A deployment of troops can be characterized as "an act of war" or a "peacekeeping initiative" depending on the intended effect on the listener. The leader of a faction within another government may likewise be called a "dangerous revolutionary" or a "courageous freedom fighter." Similarly, a cut in funding to a particular program may be described as "slimming down an unwieldy bureaucracy" or "turning one's back on a time-honored governmental responsibility."

So profound is the effect of such semantic distinctions that an entire language of politics and diplomacy has emerged over time, complete with certain heavily loaded expressions that make their meaning clear despite their relatively innocuous, objective definitions. News of "restructuring" in a governmental or departmental hierarchy can mean that mass firings are imminent. Such restructuring may follow hard on the revelation that "new information has come to light," or more plainly put, a substantial error was made. This may eventually lead to a press release to the effect that "present objectives are being reexamined and goals reprioritized"; in other words, a wholesale reversal of policy may be expected.

The political arena is not the only sphere in which such euphemism and circumlocution thrives. When someone is "assisting the police with their investigation," it typically means that he had better get himself a good lawyer. When medical records describe a patient as "complaining of generalized pain and exhibiting a hiatus between signs and symptoms," it usually means he is a malingerer. And if a matchmaker describes a blind date as "fun loving with a great personality," this speaks volumes by way of omission.

Common sense tells us that couching options in terms that enjoy certain positive connotations is an excellent way to put some spin on the matter. Advertisers have always known that people would rather purchase a handcrafted antique than a piece of old furniture; that they would prefer spending a fun-filled vacation in the cradle of civilization to taking a trip to Greece; and that they would be much happier to spend money to be a part of the longest-running live theater performance in London's history than simply to see an Agatha Christie play.

But positive reinforcement is not the only way to use this technique. In certain spheres, otherwise unobjectionable words and phrases carry with them thinly veiled warnings. Describing a politician's new policy as "bold" or "daring" may sound like a good thing, but implied in the comment is the idea that its implementation carries with it substantial risk. Hearing such an assessment from one who is in a position to know may be sufficient to force the abandonment of the initiative altogether and will certainly call for further consideration of the matter.

In the old boy network that still governs the membership and activity of certain institutions even to this day, describing an applicant as "able" is the equivalent of sounding his death knell. It may be that this is simply a manifestation of the principle of "damning by faint praise," or alternatively, this particular word may have developed a special meaning in such circles over time. Either way, its pronouncement is terminal. The term "interesting" as applied to observations, people, and ideas has roughly the same effect in common parlance. Despite its dictionary definition, time and use have imbued it with such additional meanings as boring, bizarre, or unrealistic.

Spin—the art of presenting facts in such a way that they favor a certain conclusion, interpretation, or position—is nothing new. It is a natural aspect of the human condition, at least when used in moderation. Everyone recognizes the impact of beginning a story with "There I was, minding my own business . . ." Those seven words cast the storyteller himself as the innocent victim while at the same time foreshadowing the affront that is to come. Even children quickly realize the value of such prefatory language as "all I said was" and "for no reason he . . ." And it is instructive to note that the word "attorney" is derived from the French verb *attourner*—to turn.

Spin is often used in subtle ways to alter perception by just a few degrees. For example, use of the passive voice, as in the expression "mistakes were made," admits error while failing to assign blame specifically. In the days when newspapers still accorded a measure of deference to the subjects of their stories, use of the term "tired and overwrought" was a far more palatable and professional way of describing a celebrity's episode of intoxication or a nervous break-down. But such semantic and euphemistic maneuvering usually constitutes only a minor course correction. The next logical question, then, is, How far can the situation be spun?

In the hands of a virtuoso, the answer is completely. At its highest level, this aspect of the art of the butterfly can be used to engineer a complete reversal of direction or to create a perception that is diametrically opposed to the current way of thinking. It can rescue a corporation from the precipice of insolvency and bring the ship of state about on the verge of international disaster. Nowhere is this artistry more readily apparent than in the related doctrines of "yes meaning no" and "no meaning yes."

While these twinned tactics have existed for centuries, they cannot be properly presented without at least a passing reference to the forum in which they were most recently, powerfully, and humorously presented: the BBC television programs *Yes, Minister* and *House of Cards.* The former tells the story of the trials and tribulations of an earnest if naïve member of Parliament whose attempts to implement policy are "assisted" at every turn by the archetypal mandarin: the minister's principle private secretary. So adept is this assistant at political maneuvering and psychological manipulation that the tagline, "Yes, Minister," almost invariably translates into a resounding no. In the end, the embattled MP succeeds only when

he too has learned the rules of the game and employs them to his own advantage.

In the latter series, the eminence grise is the chief whip, a tremendously powerful and trusted behind-the-scenes position in the parliamentary system of government. Exploiting his office, his acumen, and his relationship with the press, he, too, is able to control the behaviors and fortunes of those around him. Among his favored techniques is the anonymous leaking of certain inflammatory and potentially devastating pieces of information. Whenever he is subsequently asked to respond to such rumors on the record, he invariably replies, "You might think so. You might very well think so. I couldn't possibly comment." In the context of the piece, such a refusal in fact constitutes a ringing endorsement of the gossip at issue, thereby furthering his purpose while maintaining the appearance of meticulous and scrupulous propriety.

Lest any question the role of such fictional scenarios in the study of real-world abilities, it should be added that the inspiration for the *Yes, Minister* series arose from a lecture presented at the Civil Service College, and that *House of Cards* was written by a former aide to one of the most powerful and influential prime minister's of the twentieth century. Furthermore, as the latter series unfolded, it paralleled and often predicted real-life events in the British monarchy and politics to an extent that some commentators of the day described as "perilous."

Unlike a counselor, an advocate enjoys the distinct advantage of being able to champion a particular position without reservation. His partiality is a given, and thus, there is no need to maintain the pretense of neutrality. However, he must maintain credibility. By way of example, the attorney is expected, and in fact required, to represent his client with zeal. This duty requires him to explore every legal theory, pursue every piece of evidence, and make every argument that will, or even may, advance his client's position. But at least when the profession is practiced ethically, all these requirements are subject to higher duty: the mandate that they be within the bounds of the law.

To advance a frivolous legal theory, to present questionable or even fabricated evidence, and to make an argument without merit are all courses of action that can and should cost the lawyer his case, his reputation, and his license. They certainly have an impact on the way in which he, and his future clients, will be treated by members of the bench and bar alike. While the duty to see justice done above all else is only explicitly applied to government attorneys, the profession as a whole would benefit if all lawyers could be counted on to strive for this goal. And while it may serve the present client to cut corners and fudge facts, in the long run the damage done to individual and collective reputations serves no one well.

Just because the advocate is explicitly championing a given position does not mean that there is no place for subtlety in his practice. The young lawyer is taught that the path of persuasion is bifurcated. He must show the fact finders how to get to the destination, but he must also make them want to go there. In this way, it is important to

capture both their hearts and their minds. The first half of this for-
mula is largely dependent on fact and controlling law. It is in dealing
with the second part that the butterfly can show the way.

Mindful of the automatic suspicion with which the average person will typically view a clearly interested party, the advocate, whatever his profession, must strive to create and reinforce certain
perceptions in his audience. Chief among these is competence, for
after dishonesty, the most deadly sin in this milieu is ignorance. If
the listener detects even for a moment that the speaker does not
know his subject, confidence will be lost. It does not much matter
whether the misstatement is intentional or merely negligent, the result is the same: his argument is likely to be rejected.

There are two ways to ensure that this does not happen: The first
is to prepare sufficiently, a matter that I discuss at length in section
5. The second is to avoid overstating the case. No reasonable person expects another to have the answer to every question, all the
time. Such apparent ability is, in fact, by itself cause for concern.
The making of accurate statements is one way to foster credibility;
the avoidance of inaccuracies is another. Saying "I don't know the
answer to that specific question" lays the foundation for the follow-
up, "but I'll find out" or "but here's what I *can* tell you."

Making a connection with the listener is not exactly the same
thing as the rapport discussed in previous sections. While people
will only bare their souls to those with whom they feel a kinship,
they can and do take advice from a variety of other sources on a
daily basis without the benefit of any special feeling of affinity
toward the advisor. Thus, whether making a presentation to a judge,
an employer, a colleague, or a prospective client, it is *helpful* if the
presenter himself can capture their hearts, but it is *vital* that the issue does. In court, this may be achieved by demonstrating that the
result will be just; in the boardroom, that it will be profitable; and in
the consultation, that it will be safe or wise. In each case, it is a matter of showing the decision maker that the recommended course of
action will be good for him as well as for others.

> The Master explained that past classes had found it
> helpful to form alliances early on, faction fighting
> faction until only a few remained to battle among each
> other to the last, but the choice, of course, was entirely
> up to them. They were persuaded, and the hurried
> selection of teams and formation of coalitions absorbed
> what little concentration they had to spare.

PERCEPTION

Warfare is the Way of deception. Therefore, if able,
appear unable; if active, appear not active; if near, appear
far; if far, appear near; if they have advantage, entice
them; if they are confused, take them; if they are
substantial, prepare for them; if they are strong, avoid
them; if they are angry, disturb them; if they are humble,
make them haughty; if they are relaxed, toil them; if they
are united, separate them. Attack where they are not
prepared, go out to where they do not expect.

—Sun Tzu, *The Art of War*

In knowledge there is power, but in information there is motivation.
The various methods of obtaining information about a subject or an
emerging situation have already been discussed at length. It is to
the use of such insights, or indeed intentionally misleading versions
thereof, that our analysis now turns. Under the right circumstances,
disclosing or withholding data can be a powerful tool for controlling
behavior.

All decision making is limited by what is known at that particular
moment. The psychologist's prognosis is based on the specifics of
the patient's case history. The field officer's strategy is informed by
intelligence about the nature, position, and capability of the threat.

The prosecutor's plea offer is shaped by what he knows about the defendant and the surrounding circumstances of a case. And the financier's decision whether to buy depends on his understanding of a company's past performance and the general market conditions at that time.

The resulting judgment in any of these situations can be radically changed by providing additional detail. A review of the patient's previously sealed mental health commitment record may make a significant difference to the court-appointed psychiatrist. The detection of follow-on forces or hitherto undiscovered reserves turns the military tactician's lightning strike into a prudent and expeditious withdrawal from the field of engagement. Newly discovered evidence may implicate the criminal defendant in additional and more serious crimes or exculpate him altogether. Inside information about corporate earnings, even if obtained illegally, will not only prevent the purchase of additional equity but may also precipitate a frantic sell-off.

While withholding critical information may impede the decision-making process, providing disinformation misleads it altogether. One of the most stunning examples of the power of this technique occurred in 1943 toward the end of World War II. The Allies intended to recapture Europe, and it was agreed that Sicily presented one of the most strategically advantageous targets. Unfortunately, the attractiveness of this invasion point was readily apparent to the enemy as well, and the mountainous terrain presented an ideal medium for defensive entrenchment.

Operation *Mincemeat* was therefore devised with the goal of misleading the Axis powers into believing that a two-pronged attack was planned for Sardinia and Peloponnesia. In support of this elaborate ruse, a carefully prepared corpse was jettisoned from a British submarine just off the coast of Spain where the currents would wash it ashore and into the hands of the enemy. Handcuffed to the wrist was a briefcase containing military documents, which, after sufficient scrutiny, would reveal these false landing points to the enemy.

0-0115
Operation Mincemeat

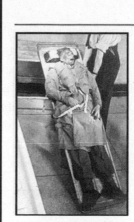

Code Name: *Mincemeat*
Target: German High Command
   (OKW)
Objective: Misdirection (Balkans)
Location: Huelva, Spain
Method: Disinformation
Sources: Major William Martin, . . .

Attention to detail in this operation was extraordinary, including the creation of an entire identity for the dead courier, complete with personal letters, overdue bills, keys, and theater ticket stubs. Records corresponding to his name and address were even planted into the files of various shops where the clothing he was wearing had been purchased. Meanwhile, on a grander scale, massive troop movements and the existence of large amounts of heavy equipment were simulated in places that corresponded to the disinformation contained in the briefcase. At the same time, great care was taken not to make the bait appear too attractive. Arriving at the desired conclusion would require a certain amount of analysis on the part of the adversary. In the end, the plan worked spectacularly, and the real invasion, codenamed Operation *Husky* was a success.

Any process that depends on receiving and assessing new information is vulnerable to disinformation. But implicit in the adoption of this technique are certain dangers, not least of which is the harm such practices work on one's own integrity and reputation. Chief among the tactical risks, however, is the possibility that the ruse will be discovered. This has the dual disadvantage of jeopardizing both the present operation as well as any plans that depend on deceptions of this nature.

In taking great care not to tip one's hand, compartmentalizing the mission to the greatest extent possible is an important aspect of tradecraft. Insurgent groups of many kinds use a three-man "cell" structure so that in the event that one or other operative is captured, the extent of the damage he can do to the entire network is minimized. In an analogous fashion, use of an often-unwitting third party—the "cutout"—to convey (dis)information and material alike, allows the strategist to ensure that his own credibility is not placed

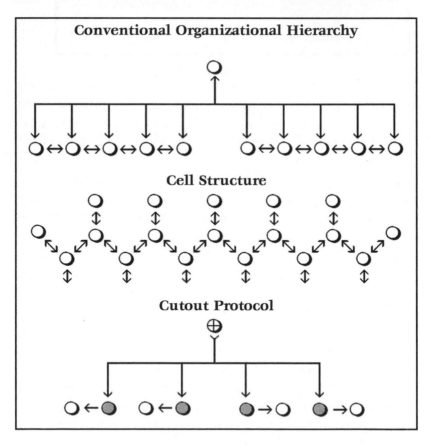

at risk. Furthermore, if several pieces of mutually reinforcing disinformation are conveyed through different channels, it reduces the chances that any single failing will be fatal to the overall objective.

Another significant concern when using disinformation is that the false impression may seem too obvious, too convenient, or too good to be true, and the target will therefore recognize it as part of a ploy. It was for this reason that the papers planted on the body floated from the British submarine in Operation *Mincemeat* did not purport to provide the Allied plan explicitly or even in its entirety. If the target must do some work himself to arrive at the conclusion, the disinformation will seem much more believable, and the analyst examining it may even take some ownership of the accuracy of the conclusion.

Many disinformation strategies are designed to distract the opponent's attention from some other subject. Care should be taken, therefore, that any discovery of the falsehood does not also serve to highlight the truth. In other words, the ruse should not be the polar opposite of reality. In fact, the best lie should incorporate many aspects of the truth and play on the target's existing beliefs and impressions. Thus, if the attack is to be from the west, the feint should not come from the east. Northwest or southwest, for example, may serve the purpose equally well without making it obvious that a complete reversal is imminent if the deception should be discovered.

Blood pounding in their ears at the prospect of what was to come, the students listened as the Master demonstrated. Each would wear a strip of red cloth tucked into his belt, like this. Once it was removed by anyone, in any way, the fighter would be deemed defeated. The prize would go to the last man standing.

MANIPULATION

> The important thing in strategy is to suppress the enemy's useful actions but allow his useless actions. However, doing this alone is defensive. First, you must act according to the Way, suppress the enemy's techniques, foiling his plans, and thence command him directly. When you can do this you will be a master of strategy.
>
> —Miyamoto Musashi, *The Book of Five Rings*

The power of suggestion has been recognized by advertisers for almost as long as there have been products to sell. Information conveyed about a product explicitly, whether or not it constitutes fact or mere puffery, is transmitted to the subject's conscious mind. At this destination, the product is examined and analyzed before being assigned a level of confidence. But there is a subtler path to be considered. That which is merely suggested or insinuated can often make its way past the intellectual gatekeeper and infiltrate the subject's heart or unconscious mind.[2]

Associating one's product with another desirable commodity—wealth, power, prestige, social standing, beauty, happiness, or sex—is the mainstay of the advertising business. Commercials are carefully crafted to convey such images and the promise of these results if the subject will only buy the product. But they do so with a whisper that fades into the background noise and rarely registers on the listener's analytical radar. Thus, while the subject is fully aware of what he is doing, he may not understand why he is doing it.

In the days before the advertising industry was subject to regulation, subliminal messages were sometimes flashed on the television or movie screen, too fast to be recognized by the human eye, but for

---

2. Avoiding such intellectual filters is among the principle goals identified by a number of treatises on the subject of behavior control.

just long enough to have an effect on the viewer.[3] And even without resorting to such visual trickery, the endorsement of the striking spokesmodels or the fresh scent of new leather beckon like sirens, enticing the subject without necessarily revealing their true natures.

A detailed examination of the power of subliminal perception was undertaken by the CIA under the umbrella of the MK-ULTRA project in the 1960s. Among the theories discussed in the ensuing report was the idea that much or most of the power of subliminal messaging derives from appealing to one of the strongest motivators of human behavior: the sex drive. Given that it would be inappropriate to satiate such urges in a public place, the theory goes, the target is forced to find a surrogate. Here, the manipulator has the opportunity to present his preferred substitute.

Noted was the possibility of "flashback"—the inadvertent triggering of precisely the opposite effect—was also raised in the agency study, as were concerns about the limited reliability of the method. Nevertheless, the report went on to provide a checklist of issues to be considered by any who would avail themselves of this technique, including selecting an appropriate cue or trigger, determining the appropriate strength of the stimulus, finding the best way to "tie" the trigger to the desired behavior, and tailoring the process to overcome the subject's natural resistance.

Notwithstanding the concerns just raised, the power of subliminal suggestion is a readily observable and verifiable phenomenon in

3. One such instance involved the sale of popcorn in a New Jersey movie theater, an event that later featured in a CIA report on the subject of subliminal perception.

the laboratory of life. When waiting for a friend or colleague to arrive at a given location, perhaps a restaurant or an office, take a moment to set the scene. On entering, determine which chair is the most inviting. If none suggests itself, choose one at random. Angle it out slightly, clear a space on the table in front of it, and adopt a position that most favors interaction with someone seated there. Next, place some object of interest in the open space on the table: perhaps a glass of water, a newspaper open to a specific story, or a pen and a blank sheet of paper. Finally, balance something in the immediate vicinity, like a pencil on the rim of a glass or an umbrella against the leg of the table.

Exercise Nine: Forcing the Draw ("Push")

Notes: By eliminating all other available options, the target can be pushed to select the desired seat. Below, the operative occupies one chair; a coat occupies the back of another; an obstacle blocks a third; the fourth and fifth are too hard (stool) and too soft (recliner) respectively, leaving only one choice . . .

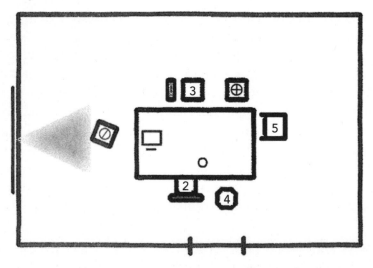

Almost without fail, when the subject arrives, he will take the intended seat, use or at least comment on the item before him, and knock over the precariously positioned object. On occasion, he may even make some apparently unrelated remark that corresponds to the paper's banner headline or the nature of one of the objects in view, without acknowledging its presence consciously.

Suggestion need not be achieved only by using physical props. Language can be an even more insidious medium. Using certain key words can place an idea in the mindscape of the listener without ever making any direct reference to the matter. According to a number of studies, peppering a business presentation with expressions such as "simmering on the backburner," "shopping for a fresh approach," "a menu of options," and "some key ingredients" may have a significant effect on the actual appetites of those in attendance. Will this work every time? Perhaps not. It is a delicate matter. Too little emphasis and the metaphoric theme will pass unnoticed. Too much, and it may be recognized and rejected. But at worst, it will make for a more interesting presentation. At best, the pieces will fall into place with an almost audible click.

Many other words and expressions are typically associated with particular endeavors and attributes. Nautical or military terminology implies order and precision and can be used to powerful effect on the right target. The retired army colonel sitting on the board of trustees may be far more inclined to favor the proposal that calls for "a rapid retrenchment of assets and the formation of contingency plans in the face of hostile market forces" than the one that merely seeks to "reorganize the corporate holdings and come up with alternatives in light of the anticipated recession."

The beauty of this technique is that even if the desired effect is not achieved straightaway, the experiment can be repeated as many times as it takes. There is strength in numbers, particularly in the realm of the butterfly. If confederates can be enlisted in the process of product or idea placement, the effect can be increased exponentially. But even when this option is not available, a series of subtle and well-executed suggestions in various forms will often do the trick. The presenter in the gastronomical example recently mentioned could, for example, bring a pot of fresh coffee to the meeting or open a window so that the smell of fresh-baked cookies from the factory next door washes over the proceeding. The possibilities are endless.

Placing ideas in the subconscious of others is one way. Cultivating their mindscapes is another. The philosopher tells us that there is altruism and selfishness; ambition and idleness; and good and evil in every person. The behaviorist maintains that the ascendancy of any one of these opposing forces is determined by experience. While the deep truth of these issues will continue to be the subject of much debate, the fact remains that it is possible to modify the behavior of others, however slightly, by the way in which we relate to them, to summon either the angel or the devil.

One of the primary techniques in this approach involves projecting the characteristic onto the target that will produce the desired response, before even asking the question. If the strategist wants to procure a yes, he may preface his question by saying, "I know you strive to keep an open mind, and I suspect that you are one of the few people in this organization who could really appreciate the complexity of this issue." In this single sentence, he has made it clear that (1) this is a matter of some importance to him; (2) the answer is not a simple one; (3) the obvious and instinctive reaction may be the wrong one; (4) the listener is valued and respected by the speaker; and (5) the listener can confirm all of the speaker's positive observations about him by simply agreeing with his position.

If he seeks the opposite result, he may say, "I hate to waste your time with this, but some of the others just don't seem to see the problem, and I think they'll respect your decision on the matter." This time, he has made it equally clear that (1) this is a matter of little consequence; (2) the solution is clear; (3) the immediate reaction is probably the correct one; (4) the speaker and others respect the listener's intelligence and authority; and (5) the listener can confirm all the speaker's positive observations about him by simply agreeing with his position.

The power of this technique can be augmented tremendously by the introduction of peer pressure into the equation. Not only do most people tend to go along with majority rule as a general matter, psychological studies suggest that they will often do so in the face of clear evidence that the majority is wrong. In the so-called "Line Length" study, the target is placed in a room with several other "subjects," who are in fact experimenters masquerading as participants. The entire group is then shown a series of pairs of lines of varying lengths and asked to indicate aloud which of the two is longer. The true subject of the test goes last.

As might be expected, when the lines in question are of similar length, the target is likelier to defer to the judgment of the collective. But even when the rest of the group is clearly and deliberately making the wrong selection, there is an alarming tendency for the target to go along with them anyway. Yet the injection of even one other legitimate subject has the effect of counteracting majority rule and empowering the target to voice the correct answer.

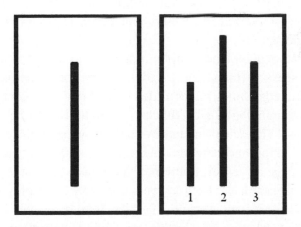

These techniques can work with very little advanced preparation or direct contact. Over a more prolonged period of engagement, it may even be possible for the process of identification—the mechanism for minimizing anxiety by finding points of commonality with others already touched on in an earlier section of this work—to take hold. Whether the subject's goal is to satisfy himself that he is in as good a position as those with whom he seeks to identify himself or that they are in as bad a situation as he is largely a matter of semantics. What is critically important to the exploitation of this phenomenon is appreciating how much easier it will be to achieve the desired behavior when the target himself can be engaged in the process of redefining his own position and outlook.

Like a truly excellent meal or a spectacular work of art, influencing the behavior of others has as much to do with presentation as with the substance of the matter. The way in which an agenda is constructed or an issue is framed can control the outcome in its entirety. In defining the field of engagement, one establishes acceptable boundaries. For example, one expert in the field of child social work suggests that parents might engineer much of their interaction with young children on the "Red Gloves, Blue Gloves" model. By asking the child to select which color he prefers, the caregiver affords an opportunity for individual expression within the safe confines of preestablished parameters, but either way, the child will be wearing gloves.

Negotiators of all kinds employ this tactic as well. The plaintiff's attorney seeks to frame the pretrial conference in terms of how many hundreds of thousands of dollars will make his client whole, and uses terminology like "publicity," "pain and suffering" and "future claims." The defense team, by contrast, wants to discuss theories of causation and potential cross-claims and prefers to employ such language as "expert opinion," "hard evidence," and "genuine issue of material fact." Both lawyers are likely to employ the term "attorney's fees" with alarming frequency, and all the while, the judge may be pushing for a settlement, while talking about "judicial economy" and "clogged dockets."

In the corporate world, the agenda strictly controls the permissible subject matter for shareholder meetings and voting. In numerous instances, it has been possible for a select group of directors, officers, or shareholders to pursue their preferred courses of action while effectively neutralizing any opposing opinions using this strategy, even when the dissenting voices are in the majority. This type of corporate filibuster works by making sure that the only issues tabled are those whose outcomes will further the purposes of the people in control of the agenda.

In the realm of buying and selling, being the first to name a price carries with it both advantages and disadvantages. On one hand, the initial pin in the map is what indicates where the starting point in the negotiation will be. To some degree, it will encourage the opposition, especially if they are lacking in experience, to respond with a number that is at least on a similar order of magnitude. On the other, it forces the disclosure of one's own position before the other side's figure is known. Either way, it serves to delineate at least one border of the ultimate field of engagement.

The techniques described thus far relate to the meaning of the words spoken by the manipulator. But as the old saying goes, what is actually said is often less important than how it is said. By paying close attention to such collateral matters as mode of expression, body language, comfort levels, and the type, tone, tenor, timbre, and timing of speech, the practitioner can increase the impact of his words significantly.

Neurolinguistics, as its name suggests, is the study of the way in which the brain receives and interprets verbal information. This discipline is becoming an increasingly popular part of psychology curricula at institutions of higher learning. It is also being exploited in the private sector by certain organizations offering courses in Neurolinguistic Programming (NLP). In both contexts, the focus is on paying attention to the way in which information is presented. In this regard, there are several principles that may be of assistance in the pursuits of the eminence grise.

The first step in the process involves categorizing subjects by the way in which they experience life. While most people are able to perceive events through all five senses, one sense tends to dominate. Which particular faculty enjoys preeminence varies by individual, but most people tend toward one of three principle modalities: visual, auditory, or kinesthetic. It is important to ascertain which of these applies best to the target. This determination can usually be made simply by paying close attention to the way in which the subject chooses to describe and interact with his environment. Does he tend to concentrate on what he has seen, what he has heard, or what he has felt. If the answer is not immediately apparent, the response to a seemingly innocuous question about a favorite place or time should clear up any doubt.

Having identified the subject's preferred modality, the practitioner must make every effort to communicate using this medium. This factor can be as important to achieving the desired outcome as is fluency in the target's native language. For the visual subject, appearance must assist in the process. The speaker must look credible, honest, interested, and engaged, and his body language and gestures will play an important part in the discussion. Such nonverbal cues as beckoning to induce an advance and holding up a palm to call for a halt will work well with such a person.

When dealing with a primarily auditory target, the speaker's voice must be powerful, the tone pleasing, and the pace sufficiently slow. He must choose his words with care and ensure that background noise is kept to a minimum. For the kinesthetic target, by contrast, the conversation must be augmented by physical stimuli. While direct physical contact with the subject during conversation is the most powerful option, such behavior may be inappropriate depending on the circumstances. If so, other, less aggressive options like frequent handshakes, pats on the back and shoulder, or the use of hands-on props can work wonders.

Whichever of these approaches the practitioner deems appropriate, the next step in the process is known as mirroring. It is a variation, or rather a manifestation, of a principle discussed in section 2:

establishing a rapport. Rather than verbally exploring the existence of past shared experiences, however, the goal here is to mirror the subject's actions in the present, but to do so subtly. Gradually, the practitioner begins to align his posture, his tone of voice, his facial expression, his manner of speech, his breathing pattern, and his mental outlook with those of the target. This goal must be achieved by degrees and with a certain amount of delicacy so as not to be obvious. But even if the technique is detected, it can usually be passed off as a kind of subconscious homage, thus potentially assisting in the process of identification.

In time, a symmetrical linkage should begin to govern the relationship between the parties thus paired. Not only are they now talking the same language, but they are discussing the same subject matter and doing so in the same dialect. If the link is strong, the eminence grise may even be able to begin controlling the subject's physical actions by leading the next movement in the pantomime. This effect can be more easily achieved by using actions previously exhibited by the subject, but over time, it may be possible to inject entirely new behaviors into the process. These physical techniques are, of course, ultimately intended to provide greater control over the target's mind.

Step One	Determine target's primary mode of perception (sound, sight, touch).
Step Two	Communicate to target emphasizing the preferred mode of perception.
Step Three	Mirror the target (words, actions) but not so much as to be detected.
Step Four	Once the link is established, practice leading the target's behavior.
Step Five	Identify positive emotional triggers and set anchors for those triggers.
Step Six	Link the desired behavior to the triggers using anchors and leading.

In the courtroom, trial lawyers sometimes use this approach to control testimony. When on the stand, the witness is more or less at the mercy of the examiner. If asked to stand up, to look at the jury, to draw on a piece of paper, or to hold an object, he must comply. A skilled attorney can exploit this opportunity for physical control to build a relationship with the witness that is based on compliance. He can also craft every question leading up to the vital one so as to reinforce the idea that the examiner is in charge and correct and that the only appropriate response is agreement. When the critical point is reached, the deck is thus stacked in the attorney's favor.

The penultimate phase in the process of neurolinguistic manipulation involves determining what ideas, memories, activities, phrases, and other stimuli are comfortable, reassuring, or pleasing to the target. This line of inquiry follows naturally from the threshold question often used to determine modality and can be pursued quite casually if the practitioner is patient and observant. The result is more sophisticated than merely buttering up the subject before asking for a favor. This situation involves the identification of certain triggers, which are words, concepts, or situations that are strongly associated with a positive emotional response, and the setting of anchors, which are key phrases or actions that become a shorthand for and shortcut to these trigger points.

Over time, the gray man will become adept at skillfully manipulating a conversation or, better yet, a series of interactions so as to be able to summon up the subject's state of maximum receptiveness at will. The final step in the process, then, involves simply tying the desired behavior, either temporally or conceptually, to this favorable, mental condition. Whether it be a promotion, a disclosure, or a sale he seeks, the practitioner knows that by inducing an affirmative and pleasant mental state, and associating the desired outcome with positive, past experiences, he can win the key to the door of the target's mind.

Where neurolinguistics depend on the power of positive association to engender receptiveness, hypnosis looks to relaxation. For centuries, mentalists of all kinds have claimed to be able to induce a trancelike state in their subjects using only a swinging object, a pulsing light, or the sound of their own voices. Once this condition has been achieved, the subjects are allegedly able to perform feats that they otherwise could not, and their behavior is subject to an amazing level of control from external influences. Not surprisingly, this phenomenon has been extensively studied by the intelligence community, the health care field, and the entertainment industry.

Studies conducted by various intelligence agencies generally agree on at least a few fundamental points. First, hypnosis is not sleep. Unlike a sleeping person, a hypnotized subject will, among other things, retain the patellar reflex and exhibit markedly different EEG readings. Second, hypnosis often works well to assist detailed recall and to work as a prophylaxis for pain, both of which are subjects of significant value to intelligence operatives. Third, hypnosis may be an effective tool for inducing selective amnesia or "wiping" certain recent memories.

Where opinions differ sharply is on the critical question for present purposes: can a subject's behavior be controlled using this method. At least one declassified report concludes that it can, citing J. Kroener's research in the mid-1950s, which detailed the case of a schoolteacher who fell under the hypnotic influence of his neighbor and was thereby induced to give him sums of money, to confess to certain crimes, and to shoot himself in the elbow.

The other, somewhat more commonly held view is that a subject cannot be forced to do anything in a hypnotic state that he would not do in reality. But even this school of thought makes allowance for the use of hypnosis in behavior modification under certain circumstances. If the subject is unaware of the hypnosis, for example, it may be likelier to have the desired effect. This might be accomplished by introducing the appropriate stimuli (detailed in the preceding) in a subtle fashion without revealing the true objective of the interaction. Furthermore, where hypnosis alone may be insufficient to achieve the desired result, it can be used as a stepping-stone to the final destination. As we have already seen, it can provide a rationalization for the captured enemy agent to succumb to the pressures of interrogation or it can even be a means to deceive him into thinking that he is in a safe environment so that he will disclose the information he has hitherto been guarding so fiercely.

Mental health professionals often use hypnosis to access memories that the conscious mind seems unable to retrieve. Whether they are blocked by mental or physical trauma or impeded simply by the passage of time, inducement of the hypnotic state can often serve to pave the way. Some studies suggest that this process can even access data that the patient would not have been able to perceive consciously at the time of the incident. While the precise physiological mechanisms at play are not yet fully understood, the consensus seems to be that relaxation is the key.

This phenomenon is readily observable in everyday life. Most people have experienced the kind of mental block or at least diminished capacity that often occurs in stressful situations. Pressures of many competing priorities and the constant bombardment of stimuli from a variety of sources greatly diminish our ability to focus. Familiar words elude us, objects seem to disappear, and recent memories evade recall. Often the remedy is to take a break from our regular activities, put aside other concerns, and relax into the response. For some people, it is simply a matter of pausing for breath; for others, it requires entering a meditative state.

Common to nearly every method of hypnosis are four main factors: general relaxation, a focal point of some kind, controlled breathing, and concentration without anxiety. Within these broad parameters, stylistic variations abound. Some people will kneel and chant. Others will sit and stare at an object. Still others require a voice to listen to. Whatever the preferred approach, almost anyone can achieve this state with sufficient practice. But while the ability to self-hypnotize is a useful skill, it is the other aspect of hypnosis—the ability to induce the condition known as hypersuggestibility in others—that is of critical importance in the realm of the butterfly.

Four Factors for Hypnosis

Relaxation	Find a sitting position that is comfortable without being soporific.
Focal Point	Choose any single object, sound, or image on which to focus.
Breathing	Ensure a relaxed, steady, and controlled rate of respiration.
Concentration	Do not become anxious if focus wanders; gently redirect to focal point.

In the health care field this phenomenon is used to help deter harmful behaviors like smoking or overeating, but in the entertainment industry and elsewhere, it is employed for more self-serving purposes. Those who hold that subjects will not perform any act under the influence of hypnosis that they would find repugnant in a conscious state explain the extreme behaviors witnessed in some public demonstrations as manifestations of the volunteer's natural exhibitionist tendencies or a desire simply to go along with the performance. But whatever the underlying motivation, its ultimate power to affect behavior is undeniable.

Furthermore, if the subject can choose within a range of possible behaviors that are acceptable, enhanced relaxation can be used to affect the selection. This can be observed on any given night at the local bar. At the point of significant intoxication, inhibitions are lowered, assertiveness is increased, and the truth is revealed. There is, in fact, a tradition among certain special operations teams that new recruits are never fully accepted into the group until their conduct has been observed in such an exposed state.

While it may facilitate the process, alcohol is not required to produce this condition. Careful planning, however, is. To open the door with this particular key, the practitioner must ensure that distractions are minimized, outside pressures are set aside, a relaxing atmosphere is created, and the focus on the subject at issue is maintained. If he is willing and able to take these steps, he too can benefit from the heightened state of suggestibility that this tends to produce in almost any subject.

Once the exercise had begun, the Master watched from a distance, seated at his writing table. At first, the competitors scattered, alone or in small teams, fearful of coming too close to any with whom a deal had not been struck. Skirmishes followed with many fighters observing conventional combat methods, but some making use of the environment and the objects it contained, as they had been taught to do.

After an hour or so, the factions had dissolved and the ranks had been thinned to three survivors. The eliminated competitors watched from the sidelines.

The Master scarcely looked up from his desk.

EXPLOITATION

Finally, combat begets the element of danger, in which all the activities of war must live and move, like the bird in the air, or the fish in the water. But the influences of danger all pass into the feelings, either directly—that is, instinctively—or through the medium of the understanding. . . . We should have to digress to show how often this instinct is prevented from going the direct road, how often it must yield in the difficulties arising from more important considerations: we shall, therefore, rest contented with affirming it to be a general natural law of the combat.

—Carl von Clausewitz, *On War*

The ultimate goal of the eminence grise is to bring about his preferred state of affairs while drawing as little attention to himself as possible. One important corollary to this principle is that the less he has to do, the better. Each overt action he takes represents an opportunity for him to be discovered and produces a possible clue to his agenda. The more he can exploit the natural tendencies and pre-existing motives of others, the safer his position will be.

Many times the practitioner may need to count on the fact that his subject will act or react in a certain way. If a distraction is needed, the target must be relied upon to make a scene. If the operation calls for luring someone to a certain location, that person will have to be curious enough to take the bait. When a compromise solution is required, the adversary will have to exhibit a willingness to concede, at least to some degree.

Without directly controlling the target's behavior, how is this goal to be achieved? The answer lies in choosing the right subject for the behavior desired or, indeed, the most appropriate behavior for the target at issue. For the skilled practitioner of the arts presented herein, any café, bar, street, city, country, or the world itself presents a veritable storehouse of potential assets, for an infinite number of situational variations. In filling the reactive requirements just discussed, the manipulator will need to look for one with a hot temper, a second with a powerful curiosity, and a third with a somewhat flexible approach to dispute resolution.

Such matchmaking can be expedited by categorizing and identifying the personality types available in any given situation. How these personalities are described and delineated is not terribly important, for we are all familiar with the critical characteristics at issue.[4]

---

4. One CIA manual, for example, uses the categories: orderly-obstinate, optimistic, greedy and demanding, anxious and self-centered, guilt-ridden, wrecked by success, schizoid or strange, exceptional, average, or normal. Given that these terms of art are somewhat less accessible than their psychological counterparts, the latter framework is employed for our purposes.

1. **The Performer:** This personality craves attention, whether good or bad, and thrives in the limelight. While the preferred mode of expression may vary by individual or situation, the driving force remains the same. Such people will pick a fight, sing a song, or take on a risky but high-profile assignment at the drop of a hat. They may be relied on to make a spectacle of themselves given the opportunity. They can usually be identified from the way in which their grooming, clothing, and behavior are intended to attract as much attention as possible. Showing an interest in them is the most powerful incentive the gray man has to offer, and disregard is the most stinging rebuke.

2. **The Follower:** Often seen in the company of the performer, these people yearn for acceptance and depend on the approval of the rest of the group. They will reliably go along with whatever everyone else is saying or doing and, as a result, can turn an individual initiative into a mass endeavor. Their appearance will often be modeled on some example drawn from their peer group or the fashions of the place and time, but they often fall short of the mark in this effort. Allowing them access to a select clique will satisfy their needs and secure their unquestioning loyalty.

3. **The Agitator:** This type enjoys nothing more than the spectacle of conflicts involving others. They are the world's gossips, stirrers, and complainers. They will breach confidences, spread rumors, and criticize anything going. They may be counted on to sow the seeds of discontent whenever possible. They are recognizable more by their conspiratorial and cynical demeanors than by any physical characteristic, but intellectual or physical limitations that might contribute to such behavior may be apparent. Providing them with a receptive ear and an equally poisonous tongue is the key to meeting their needs and gaining their favor.

4. **The Workhorse:** Whether by circumstance, natural limitation, or pure preference, this type is engaged in a constant struggle, actual or perceived, simply to satisfy the requirements of daily life. These people see themselves as the providers, the breadwinners, or the backbone of the office and will often manifest a martyr complex. Commonly overextended and exhausted, such people usually appear stressed and fatigued. The constant pressures they are experiencing will typically cause them to follow the path of least resistance, and herein lies the key to their behavior.

5. **The Iconoclast:** It is ironic that these people are so predictable in their efforts to rebel against conventionality and uniformity. They will automatically adopt the contrary position or approach just to be perceived as different or interesting. Unusual physical appearance is one of their preferred avenues of individual expression and may involve curious hairstyles and striking or unconventional attire. The key to controlling their behavior lies in encouraging them to reject the *opposite* course of action from the one desired, so that they believe that they are bucking the system, all the while falling neatly into place.

6. **The Crusader:** Often motivated by the best of intentions, the crusader has very little sense of moderation. He will tilt at windmills for days on end while neglecting other more pressing and realistic goals. Romantic, passionate, and enamored with the idea of the quest, he can be easily drawn into the most outlandish schemes and enterprises. He can be recognized by a stylish but somewhat unkempt appearance and a tendency to focus his gaze somewhere in the middle distance when reminiscing about past crusades or looking forward to future ones. Should a fair lady so much as drop her handkerchief, he will be there to retrieve it.

7. **The Mark:** There is really no polite way to say it: this category embraces the foolish, the ignorant, and the socially unsophisticated. These people are simply not equipped to deal with the complexities of the modern world and might not even have survived the evolutionary competitiveness of bygone times. Everything about them—their grooming, their clothing, their mannerisms, and their mode of speech—indicates that they are prey for interrogators, manipulators, and conmen of even moderate ability.

8. **The Observer:** Take care here, for you may find that while you are engaged in the process of watching others, you are also being watched. The one whose appearance gives away very little about his personality and whose position allows him to see everything around him without being easily seen is a potential threat. He may be engaged in an operation of his own, or he may simply be naturally aware of and attentive to life's subtleties. Either way, he will be of little use in the endeavor to control behavior.

Armed with this exemplary rather than exhaustive list and possessed of the ability to make additional, more detailed observations, the gray man, in his various incarnations is ready to proceed. On any given night, for example, in almost any public house on the planet, the well-trained intelligence officer can look around the place and identify several patrons who would happily volunteer to participate in a bar brawl of sufficient dimensions to occupy the attention of any onlookers for the requisite period of time.

All that he must do is select the right target(s) and manipulate the situation ever so slightly. With certain personalities, in certain establishments, all it would take to give rise to a confrontation is a period of prolonged eye contact. In a more reasonable setting, a little more rudeness—a deliberate collision or a spilled drink for instance—may be required. The more sophisticated approach, of course, is to create a disturbance between other people, thereby leaving oneself free to take advantage of the ensuing distraction. This goal can usually be achieved with a few choice comments or observations. Should the practitioner and the target be of opposite genders, some well-executed flirting can be a powerful tool in this regard.

In any military element, particularly one tasked and trained for special operations, there are likely to be soldiers whose self-images thrive on danger and daring. Such terms even appear in the mottoes of many of these units. Doubtless, commanding officers on either side of the battlefield can exploit this characteristic. When looking for volunteers in one's own ranks for a hazardous mission, these people can be relied on to lead the charge and inspire their comrades. When trying to draw the adversary into an ambush, these same personalities among the opposing forces will be the first to rush in.

For the detective investigating white-collar crime, determining which of any number of suspects to approach first is of the utmost importance. Once the fact of the investigation is revealed, documents may be shredded, physical evidence destroyed, and conversations carefully scripted. Wiretaps and search warrants will thus become useless. The suspect whom he attempts to "flip" must therefore be the one whose personality and circumstnaces make it likelier that he will cooperate than the one who will demand to speak to a lawyer and alert his confederates at the first opportunity.

When the case eventually goes to trial, the prosecutor must use similar judgment in determining whom to call. Several of the participants may know certain critical facts, but the probability that this evidence will be properly presented on the record depends in large part on which of several possible witnesses is actually called to the stand. The chairman of the board, for instance, may be far more concerned with preserving his reputation in the community than with protecting his subordinates from punishment for their misconduct. Conversely, upper management may be united in their denial of any wrongdoing, but the entry-level associate with no established ties to the organization may be quite willing to testify truthfully about what he has seen and heard.

The broker who sees the potential for incredible returns in an emerging but somewhat risky venture must select carefully the clients to whom he presents this opportunity. While almost anyone will express an interest in fast money, there are those whose temperament is simply too fragile for such endeavors. Despite their protestations to the contrary, the experienced financier will recognize that such people will recriminate bitterly if the most favorable result is not obtained and may react poorly to the fact that the prospect was even raised if they ultimately decide against getting on board. Those for whom speculation is a comfortable proposition, by contrast, will not only weather the eventual outcome but may even bring other, like-minded investors to the table.

Before leaving this subject, there is one further aspect of exploiting existing attitudes to be considered: execution. There is a critical difference between looking into a subject's thoughts and being able to rely on him to act on his desires and beliefs. In perhaps his most famous tragedy, Shakespeare explores this issue in extensive and delicate detail.

Hamlet's father, the king of Denmark, has been murdered by his own brother. The killer, Hamlet's uncle, has just married the recently widowed queen. The ghost of the murdered king appears to Hamlet on the battlements of Elsinore castle and commands the young prince to avenge this foul deed. Here then is motivation of a most compelling variety.

Hamlet's initial intent to seek revenge is clear. He swears an oath and speaks of his mission in several soliloquies; he confronts his mother on the issue; he leaves the country at one point; and he even feigns madness, all in support of carrying out this grave assignment. But when presented with the opportunity, he fails to act. Execution, in both senses of the word, is lacking. His hamartia, the flaw that puts him in the category of tragic hero, is that he allows thought to eclipse action. This is not an uncommon feature of the human condition.

The ability to recognize this tendency in others is a skill that the gray man, in his capacity as strategist, must be able to exercise reliably. He must learn to distinguish between the big talker and the serious contender. He must recognize the signs that indicate disagreement between what is said and what is truly meant. Likewise, when examining a given target for a particular purpose, he must be able to determine the difference between bluff and sincere intent. A failure in this regard can jeopardize the entire operation.

Past practice and present position are perhaps the best indicators of whether someone is likelier to talk about things or to get them done. A statement to the effect that the subject intends to give the present matter his full attention is somewhat suspect when coming from the junior executive whose desk is already buried beneath an avalanche of files. The believability of representations that immediate action will be forthcoming tends to be diminished when the speaker's appearance and presentation are clearly inconsistent with swiftness and efficiency. Threats of physical violence should be accorded a low level of reliability when they are issued by one whose physical condition suggests that he is wholly unsuited or unprepared to carry them out. These are subjects whose credibility is described in the vernacular of many different places using scatological imagery.

Yes, the average person exhibits a measure of bluster and bravado from time to time, but such episodes tend to be occasioned, or at least accompanied, by any of several factors that speak to diminished capacity. Statements made in the heat of passion—anger, frustration, jealousy, and the like—while they may provide insight into deeply seated feelings, tend not to be reliable predictors of future conduct. Once a cooling-off period has taken effect, prudence generally prevails. Similarly, intoxication in its many forms may give rise to an assortment of outlandish proclamations, but experience teaches that these too are to be taken with a rather large grain of salt.

At the other extreme is the phenomenon referred to by soldiers and police officers as "the thousand-mile stare." Peculiar to those who have fully committed to a course of action, often a dangerous or violent one, is a facial expression that evidences a mental disconnection from the current situation. There is an unfocussed quality to the eyes and an emptiness to the face that suggests that nothing in the present can prevent them from accomplishing their intended mission. Once seen, it can never be forgotten, and once recognized, it may be relied upon. This is one of the signs, in fact, that psychologists routinely rely on in determining whether a patient is sincere in his threats of homicidal or suicidal behavior.

When seeking to elicit specific behaviors, another, deeper level of functioning can be considered: it is the collection of instinctive, conditioned, or automatic responses that stem from the animal brain and are perhaps best introduced by the tale of the scorpion who wanted to cross a river. As the story goes, while the scorpion was pondering his predicament on the riverbank, a frog came swimming by. "Carry

me to the other side on your back," the scorpion said to the amphibian. "I cannot," the frog replied, "for you are a poisonous and aggressive creature, and you will sting me if I let you climb on my back." "If I did such a thing," the scorpion countered, "you would die almost instantly, and since Icannot swim, I would drown."

Having considered the logic of this statement, the frog agreed to do as he had been asked. At about the halfway point, the scorpion stung the frog. As they both began to sink below the waves, the frog asked, "Why did you do that, knowing that we both would die?" The scorpion replied, "Because it is my nature."

As much as we may like to think of ourselves as a highly evolved species, there are many situations in which we as human beings allow our actions to be governed by instinct. We flinch when we come into contact with something hot. We jump at a loud noise. We gasp when we enter cold water. These are helpful, physiological reactions, but they are also patterns that can be employed by those who wish to control the behavior of others. For example, many of the distraction techniques discussed in earlier sections of this text depend on predictable behavioral responses on the part of the subject. People's attention can reliably be captured, at least momentarily, by the flare of a match in a dark alley or the noise of a coin dropped on a hard surface in a quiet room.

Most people exhibit a natural tendency to wince at a painful prospect or memory and to smile at a pleasant or attractive sight. More minor physical reactions to such stimuli can also be measured with the aid of sensitive equipment. Based on this principle, psychologists will often show a series of images to a patient while monitoring his physiological responses to gauge his internal reaction to the subject matter presented. Even when the subject would prefer to conceal his true feelings on the issue, automatic responses of this nature are so ingrained that it is usually impossible to do so.[5]

In the realm of the emotional response, there are certain common reactions to given stimuli that can be anticipated and exploited by those who take the time to study such matters. One technique commonly employed by operatives of all kinds for creating an opening

5. While some such signs are detectable only by sophisticated machinery, others are plainly apparent to the human eye. In a recent side-by-side comparison of the performance of a polygraph machine and a live interviewer watching for such signs, the resulting measures of accuracy were surprisingly similar.

in an otherwise static situation is provoking the adversary. When confronted directly, people tend to adopt either a defensive or an aggressive posture. Either of these reactions can play into the hands of the tactician, the interrogator, or the captive.

Of necessity, the defensive response brings with it certain concessions. On the battlefield, for example, the enemy must give up his forward positions if he is to concentrate his assets in a rearguard action. In the courtroom, the witness may make admissions regarding peripheral matters so as to focus his concentration and credibility on what he sees as the critical aspects of the case. In captivity, it is unlikely that one's captors will simply back down if provoked, but it is not uncommon that limited concessions may be offered to prisoners for the purpose of keeping the peace.

If the adversary reacts with aggression, he will often expose his weaknesses in the process. In the theater of combat, an attack requires the commitment of assets in a particular location or direction, thereby reducing defensive capabilities elsewhere. Similarly, the witness who becomes angry will be far too preoccupied with responding to the immediate challenge to keep an eye out for more subtle threats emanating from different quarters. The prison guard who loses his composure in response to the actions of his prisoner also loses the appearance of professionalism and authority and may even lose control of the situation altogether; in so doing, he has allowed his behavior to be manipulated by someone in an objectively inferior position.

Having learned these lessons well, the practitioner of the butterfly art will favor a moderate or measured response in situations where he is himself the target of provocation. Such an approach, while contrary to human instinct in many cases, is far more effective in neutralizing attacks than is the natural tendency to meet force with equal force. It is also the best way to ensure that we do not fall victim to our own teachings.

Exploiting such tendencies in others seems to works better when the subject is in no position to evaluate or reassess and correct his initial, instinctive response. For some people, such a state of thoughtless behavior is the norm. For others it must be induced or the operation timed to coincide with its natural occurrence. Interrogators deprive their subjects of sleep in an effort to wear down their ability to deal intelligently with a verbal onslaught, and military tacticians time raids for the middle of the opponent's sleeping shift or at the end of an exhausting series of maneuvers to maximize this advantage.

Such timing is often employed in far less overtly adversarial situations as well. Children approach their parents in pursuit of some concession, and salesmen contact their prospective clients, first thing in the morning, before the target's critical faculties are fully engaged. Another favored time for initiating negotiations is toward the end of the day so as to benefit from the target's fatigue and corresponding desire to follow the path of least resistance to conclude the day's decision-making duties. At other times of day, it is merely the insistent interjection of the phone, the fax, the pager, or the crying infant that chips away at the subject's natural intellectual defenses.

Consistent with this principle of distraction, when laying a trap during cross-examination, the trial lawyer must strive to ensure that the tempo, timing, and content of his several lines of questioning are sufficient to consume all the witness's attention. If he asks questions too early, too slowly, or too simply, even a lying witness will be able to respond with caution and self-assurance. The target's ability in this regard, of course, depends greatly on his native intelligence, his familiarity with the system, and his awareness of the way in which the game is played. The superior attorney must therefore be able to increase the intensity of his attack to meet and defeat such defensive measures.

In some instances, the target's training or indoctrination can provide the most reliable indicators of what he will do under given circumstances. This is so, at least in part, because of the way in which training is often specifically designed to defeat independent thinking or the questioning of authority. In this regard, for example, those who specialize in the study of cults warn that people who adhere strictly to more orthodox faiths present far more attractive and accessible targets for cult recruiters. Perhaps nowhere, however, is this tendency more apparent than in the martial realm.

The soldier is trained to react according to standard operating procedures under almost any conditions. If the opponent is familiar with those procedures, he will have at his disposal a virtual mind-reading machine. Then, by simply performing a specific action, he will be able to induce the corresponding reaction with near certainty. If the commander of an extraction team needs to draw defensive elements away from his target, he can simply simulate a significant threat at a different location, knowing that his adversary must respond according to standing orders in this regard. With this very concern in mind, enlightened military commanders in many nations have taken care to avoid teaching this kind of rote reaction to given stimuli in the training of unconventional warfare units.

There is another type of conditioning to which people of all kinds, and not just those in certain specialized professions, are subjected. It is societal conditioning. Unless the target seems to exhibit deliberately antisocial behavior, it is a fair bet that he will react according to the conventions and protocols that apply in society at large. For instance, most people will instinctively respect the boundaries of personal space.

In a relatively empty movie theater, they will usually sit at least a few seats or rows away from the other audience members. Likewise, on a train or in a public bathroom, they will position themselves a respectable distance from other patrons, assuming that conditions permit it. By creatively deploying obstacles and selectively invading personal space, a target can be virtually led around by the nose. In so doing, it must be remembered that like many other such conventions, the precise dimensions of personal space may vary by culture.

Another powerful social convention is the exchange of pleasantries between those who come within a certain distance and angle of each other's positions. This automatic acknowledgment can be

Exercise Ten: Barstool Protocol

Notes: With practice, probable seating order can be predicted with remarkable accuracy. The first arrival generally picks neither extreme; the second leaves a respectable distance between himself and the first; the third must often choose which of the first two arrivals' space to approach, and can even precipitate a move by one of those present by sitting too close

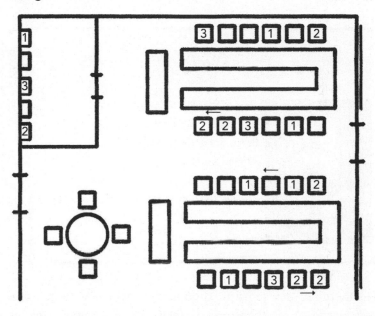

used for a variety of purposes, including close observation, distraction, or an initial contact. Likewise, the extension of the hand upon introduction is an automatic behavior in Western society, as is responding to a hand proffered in this way. The ensuing physical contact can then be used to control, delay, reorient, or mark the target.

Respect for authority is another typical and generally useful aspect of societal conditioning. People tend to respond obediently to directions that accompany flashing lights, warning signs, and badges and uniforms of all kinds, including the white lab coat and clipboard of the medical professional. The power of this principle was illustrated to a chilling degree in an experiment conducted during the early 1960s by a scientist named Stanley Milgram. Having grown up during World War II, Milgram was fascinated by the apparent willingness of the German people to acquiesce to, and in some cases actively participate in, the atrocities being perpetrated by the Nazis.

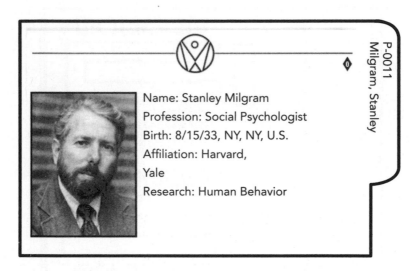

Name: Stanley Milgram
Profession: Social Psychologist
Birth: 8/15/33, NY, NY, U.S.
Affiliation: Harvard,
Yale
Research: Human Behavior

P-0011
Milgram, Stanley

He therefore devised an experiment in which volunteers were asked to report to a laboratory, ostensibly to assist with conducting clinical tests involving human memory. When the volunteers arrived, they were introduced to the professional-looking supervisors who were in charge of the study. The supervisors explained that their job was to administer progressively more powerful electrical shocks to the subjects of a memory test whenever any of these unfortunate souls gave an incorrect answer. In reality, the "subjects" of the trials and the "supervisors" were all actors playing their various parts for the sole purpose of observing the behavior of the assistants.

The machinery through which the punishments were to be administered was labeled to make it clear that there was significant danger to the subject after a certain level of intensity was reached. The highest setting was marked *XXX*. In case these written indicators were not sufficient to impress upon the assistants the power of the instrument at their disposal, as the experiment progressed, the subjects gave voice to the "pain" they were experiencing in ever more urgent ways, even though in reality no shocks of any kind were actually being administered.

To their credit, some of the assistants expressed reservations about continuing the experiment past the point where harm was clearly being done. But clothed in the appearance of authority, the supervisors simply reassured their helpers that everything was fine, that these measures were necessary, and that ultimate responsibility for any harmful results rested solely with the supervisors. Almost two thirds of those administering the shocks were appeased by the supervisor's responses, and they proceeded well into and beyond the danger point. Such is the power of societal conditioning.

In any of the endeavors described in the preceding, and a thousand more besides, taking advantage of the target's existing motivations may prove to be the better route to the intended destination. Letting people seek what they really want and be what they truly wish is the natural way. Things progress as they otherwise would, and if the eminence grise can benefit as a result, so much the better. But it should always be remembered that there may come times when the situation does not afford a sufficient range of options or the available assets are not well suited to the task, at least in their present form. At such times, a different approach must be considered.

*Two of the remaining students conspired to eliminate
the third. They fell on him like wolves and then turned
on each other, summoning every last ounce of strength
for the final battle. For several minutes they twisted
and turned, locked in each other limbs so as to
maintain their defenses while resting their exhausted
bodies to a degree. At last, the smaller of the two
managed to work a limb loose, and at the cost of one
hard blow to the body, snatched his opponent's tag
from his belt. To his credit, the victor managed to stay
standing as the Master approached, presumably to
award his prize. To his shock, the Master placed one
hand on his heaving shoulder and gently reached
down with the other, deftly extracting the strip of red
cloth from the remaining student's belt. It took a
moment for everyone to realize.*

This exercise was all in the training hall against all.

*The rules of engagement permitted the tag to be
removed by anyone in any way. Without throwing so
much as a single punch, the Master was the last man
standing.*

Predictably, the lesson followed:

The mind craves order. Man seeks direction. From
birth, we ask to know where we are to go and what we
are to do. Even those who reject order, do so in an
orderly and predictable fashion. Create the
appearance of order and the mind will follow. Show
the direction and others will choose to walk that path.
This is the fourth teaching in the art of the butterfly.

Invincibility

In ancient times, warriors wore suits of armor to protect them from bladed weapons of all kinds. Use of these steel skins was rendered obsolete by the advent of firearms, or so it was thought, but beginning in 1879, people began experimenting with the next generation of modern armor, intended to make the wearer impervious to bullets. Initial prototypes weighed almost one hundred pounds. More recently, a rating scale for body armor has been developed, using categories one through five. Level five armor, known as "dragon skin," is composed of a network of round, silver, overlapping discs of silicon carbide ceramic matrices and laminates that allow for flexibility while providing protection strong enough to withstand multiple rounds fired from assault rifles and a point-blank detonation of a hand grenade. Having said that, dragon skin is not available to anyone but certain select Special Forces units at the time of this writing.

During the late nineteenth century, in the gray area between the advent of modern armor and the obsolescence of its ancient forefather, foreign influences increasingly besieged China. The heavily armed military machines of European imperialism began to carve that nation into spheres of influence. Some Western powers went so far as to lay claim to territory within the country, while others simply declared an open-door policy on China's behalf with respect to foreign presence. In response, the Empress Dowager Tsu Hsi issued a royal edict to every province warning of this emerging threat.

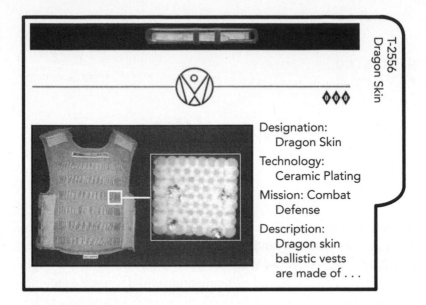

In Shandong province, a secret society known as "the Fists of Righteous Harmony" was formed to counter the invading menace. Many of its members were trained in ancient fighting arts, which, at their highest levels, involved arcane rituals and the use of secret spells and potions thought to make the practitioner invincible. These so-called "Boxers" were also taught to harden their bodies and control their energy fields so as to render themselves invulnerable to any attack.

In the early months of the year 1900, an army of Boxers numbering in the tens of thousands marched on the Forbidden City. At that time, the foreign diplomats of many European nations were present in the capital, under the protection of military garrisons equipped with modern weapons. As the Boxers approached the city walls, these Western soldiers banded together to form a defensive line. Armed with their swords, their fists, and their magical shields of invincibility, the Boxers' front line advanced to within twenty yards of the enemy riflemen. They were cut to shreds in a hail of gunfire.

No training, no practice, no spell can render someone impervious to attack. Unlike the specific arts and sciences discussed in earlier sections of this book, invincibility is an attribute, not a skill. But as with the other principles discussed herein, this term is capable of more than one semantic interpretation. It is a matter of degree. Many martial artists, for example, have succeeded in training their bodies to withstand blows that would cripple an ordinary person. They have conditioned their fists to break objects that would crush the knuckles of the uninitiated. And most significantly, they have learned to focus mind, body, and spirit unrelentingly on the task at hand.

It was perhaps because of these latter attributes, and not the illusion of invulnerability, that the Boxers returned after the initial massacre and managed to lay siege to the city for almost two months, launching assault after savage assault straight into the teeth of the well-entrenched, heavily armed opponent. Most historians agree that the capital would have fallen to them had it not been for the arrival of an international relief force of soldiers and sailors from eight different nations. At last, the Boxers were compelled to yield to superior firepower and vastly greater numbers.

In the history of physical competition, there have been only a very few competitors who have never been beaten. Rocky Marciano, the only heavyweight-boxing champion to retire undefeated is one. Johnny Weissmuller, the professional swimmer who went on to play Tarzan in the movies is another. Yukio Tani, ambassador for the sport of Judo in the early twentieth century is a third. These were men of iron. Men who were never bested. Not even on their worst day. In this sense, *they* were invincible.

But on occasion, circumstances can conspire to rob even the best and hardest working competitor of victory. With this in mind, there is another kind of invincibility to be considered. It is the absolute unwillingness of the spirit to yield in spite of the disasters that may befall the body. This spirit can be seen in the mettle of such fighters

> *At the conclusion of their studies, the Master selected one of the students for the honor of the final duel. He was not the strongest, the fastest, or the most skilled. Rather, he blended into the group, standing out as neither the best nor the worst. The Master's choice therefore came as something of a surprise. With a sense of reverence, the combatants stepped onto the mat. They gave a slight bow, neither taking his eyes off the adversary. Then the battle began. For several minutes they traded strikes, always delivered with control and intercepted with an appropriate defense. It was clear to all that the Master was allowing the contest to proceed across relatively even ground, but the student was at least holding his own. Then, the Master dropped his guard. Not by accident. He fixed his stance and lowered his arms. The student held off for a moment, anticipating a trap. The Master did not move. The student fired off a few feints. The Master did not flinch. It became clear that the ball was in the student's court. When he hesitated again, the Master even nodded his approval. The student summoned up all his strength to execute a strike worthy of this rarest of opportunities. And even as he began to coil his hip, he fully expected his punch to find its mark. It did not. There was no block. No deflection. No evasion. The strike simply withered in the air. The Master had not so much as blinked, but the disciple could not complete the attack.*

as George Chuvalo, a heavyweight champion who was *never* knocked down in almost a hundred professional fights, two of which were against Muhammad Ali. It is exemplified by the resolve of Britain's wartime leader, Sir Winston Churchill, who refused to concede when it seemed that almost the whole world was arrayed against his tiny island nation. And it is manifest in the steadfastness of Sir Thomas More, a loyal subject of the king who chose to die before he would abandon his conscience.

With a little luck, a significant amount of study, and a great deal of determination, it is possible to achieve this kind of invulnerability. It requires the warrior to secure his position carefully, to consider options thoughtfully, to research situations thoroughly, to wage his campaign wisely, and to do all these things with courage, integrity, and honor. The pursuit of these goals, particularly the latter few, is the embodiment of the noblest aspects of the art of the butterfly.

SECURE YOUR BASE

We have seen above how necessary it is for a prince to have his foundations well laid, otherwise it follows of necessity he will go to ruin. The chief foundations of all states, new as well as old or composite, are good laws and good arms; and as there cannot be good laws where the state is not well armed, it follows that where they are well armed they have good laws.

—Niccolò Machiavelli, *The Prince*

Sources as divergent as the gospel of the apostle Matthew and the treatises of the strategist Carl von Clausewitz agree that to secure one's base is of fundamental importance. As recently as February 2003, the Defense Advanced Research Project Agency generated a report for the U.S. military in which this was listed as the first objective of national security in the new millennium.

In its simplest form, this principle means that virtually any endeavor requires a safe center of operations. Unless there is a secure location for the project at issue, the practitioner will often fall victim to interruption, diversion, and the inconvenience of periodic relocation. Such intrusions will in turn compete for his attention, preventing him from focusing fully on the matter at hand, not to mention compromising the security of his workspace.

For the soldier his base is, of course, an armed fortification, a heavily defended perimeter inside which he can rearm, regenerate, and relax to a certain degree, protected from forces without that seek to do him harm. For the spy, it is the safe house, a refuge from prying eyes and potential threats. For most of the other members of the faculty, it is an office: either an entirely separate building or a room at least dedicated to the particular purposes of his profession.

The importance of having such a base is not just a matter of concentration, but it is also vital to the processes of decompressing and disentangling from the competing imperatives of the outside world and replenishing necessary commodities. As important to one's state of mind as sleep is the feeling of relaxation that accompanies closing the door upon returning to home base secure in the knowledge that the outside world can be held at bay for a period of time and that everything needed to face the next day is close at hand.

In addition to its importance from the point of view of psychic well-being, maintaining a base is also critical to the process of organization. The human mind can only juggle a limited number of facts or concepts at the same time. However brilliant the mind in question, the size of its random-access memory is finite. In the study of matters of significant complexity, therefore, people avail themselves of all manner of tools: lists, calendars, charts, files, notes, and computer programs. These things take up space, and the more cramped the quarters, the less readily accessible these resources will be.

At some time, everyone has experienced a move to a new home. For the first few weeks, every activity—switching on a light, going down the stairs, making dinner, doing the dishes, buying groceries—takes significantly longer than it did in more familiar surroundings. The resident must now adapt to the details of his new environment, such as switch placement, number of stairs, and position of the cutlery drawer. Internalizing these mundane matters to the point that they become second nature takes time.

Watching a professional deal with an emergent situation in familiar surroundings, by contrast, can be an almost artistic spectacle. The surgeon's hands retrieve, manipulate, and relinquish instruments without ever having to look at the tray. The pilot controls the aircraft by instinct, his hands flying over a dizzying array of switches and buttons with confidence and conviction. The soldier strips and reassembles his weapon blindfolded, under adverse conditions, with lighting speed and precision.

The principle of having a secure base is not simply a physical concept. In financial terms it may refer to ensuring that a company has enough working capital to accomplish its objectives. For the wise investor, it means placing sufficient funds in safe holdings so as to ensure that foreseeable future needs can be met, secure from swings in the market. For the family operating on a fixed income, it requires budgeting to cover essential costs. And even for the very wealthy, it involves protecting assets for future generations.

While the attorney's office is his physical base, the cases he takes and the arguments he makes must themselves be based on sound legal principle. He must have a good faith basis for making a claim or defense and should not even entertain arguments that are demonstrably lacking in merit. Not only is the presentation and litigation of a frivolous claim unethical, but it is also likely destined to fail. Even if it should survive initial consideration, the legal system is structured to provide levels of review and has at its disposal various sanctions expressly designed to safeguard against such practices.

The American constitution requires law enforcement officers to establish a reasonable suspicion based on objective and articulable facts before they may stop and question a suspect. That same document also requires a showing of probable cause before they may arrest a person, search a place, or seize an item. However heinous the crime at issue and however compelling the evidence discovered, prosecutions lacking this fundamental basis are likely to be dismissed by the courts.

The principle of securing a base resonates in the political arena as well. In this context, it speaks to garnering enough support for a particular contender before announcing his candidacy or generating sufficient backing for a proposition before it is presented for vote or ratification. Once the issue is in the public domain, the tide of popular opinion may toss it this way and that. By timing its launch to ride a supporting wave, success can be made that much more likely.

A strong base is also a critical component of clear analytical thinking. In crafting his philosophy, noted seventeenth-century mathematician, philosopher, and ex-soldier René Descartes abandoned the received wisdom of the day and started again with a blank slate, to ensure the solidity of the foundation of his theoretical construction of reality. Initially, all he could determine with certainty was, "I think, therefore I am."—a demonstrably sound base from which to proceed.

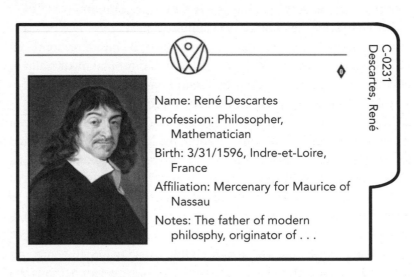

Name: René Descartes

Profession: Philosopher, Mathematician

Birth: 3/31/1596, Indre-et-Loire, France

Affiliation: Mercenary for Maurice of Nassau

Notes: The father of modern philosphy, originator of . . .

C-0231
Descartes, René

All people find themselves awash in a sea of uncertainty at some point in life. Whether trying to determine what move the opponent will make next, whether to commit assets in a particular endeavor, or how best to deal with a certain problem or person, it is always best to proceed from a firm foundation. Although the answer may be shrouded in a thick fog, there are always certain truths, analytical anchors to reality, that may be relied on in charting one's course through such perilous waters.

It is not enough that a base be secure merely for present purposes. Implicit in this principle is the idea of sustainability; otherwise defeat is simply a matter of time. The soldier must keep supply lines open, or he becomes vulnerable to siege. The spy must protect the secrecy of his hideaway. The offices of the several others must be staffed, stocked, and managed. Security cannot be viewed as a sometime thing.

Furthermore, merely relying on the appearance of security is not enough. Just because an attack is not presently underway, or none has succeeded in the past, does not mean that the base is adequately protected. Circumstances and methods change over time. Inspections of existing capabilities should be conducted and tools examined and cared for on a regular basis. For many this will simply require staying current with emerging technologies and developments in their particular fields. For others, a more literal application of this directive may be required.

Establishing an adequate defense depends in part on having a sound appreciation of the nature of the anticipated threat. In the military arena, entrenchment to meet a sustained ground campaign differs significantly from the emplacements best suited to ward off aerial attack. In the marketplace, a company may structure itself so as to address the threat of competitors while completely failing to safeguard against the danger of a takeover from within. And every parent knows that techniques that work with one child may prove useless when dealing with another.

In conducting this analysis, the defender must also look to his own flank for signs of weakness. The politician with the questionable past will want to focus on issues, not personalities, but he should nevertheless have a plan in place in the event that an uncomfortable question is raised at some point. In the legal world, the maxim is, "When the case is weak in law, argue fact; when it is weak in fact, argue law." And as the margin notes in the speech of one former U.S. president are said to have read, "Weak point so shout like hell!"

A truly rigorous inspection may, of course, reveal more than one potential point of entry. In *Sampson Agonistes*, John Milton wrote, "What boots it at one gate to make defence, and at the other to let in the foe." Part of the process of assessing defensive capabilities is being ruthlessly self-critical. It may be far more comfortable simply to continue following past practice and to concentrate on obvious and straightforward issues, but the true art lies in periodically reexamining the situation with a fresh and critical eye. Victory, fortune, and survival may hang in the balance.

During the height of the Cold War, the grand nuclear strategy of the superpowers alternated between variations on the principle of mutually assured destruction and ways of exploring the possibility of waging a survivable nuclear war. Part of the problem with the latter approach was the incredible devastation that a single warhead could cause if it were to reach its target unchecked. No single defensive system seemed capable of guaranteeing complete protection from this unthinkable consequence. Thus, the idea of layering existing strategic defense systems was devised.

In the process of having to bypass several waves of obstacles in order to reach its intended destination, the attacking force is whittled down, and at every stage, its overall chances of success are reduced significantly. The defender, by contrast, enjoys several different opportunities to destroy the incoming threat. Intelligence operatives employ this principle by ensuring that transactions go through several intermediaries, or cutouts, for making them untraceable. Financiers have funds available on short notice from a variety of sources so as to provide multiple liquidity buffers. Psychologists will often try several different therapies in concert with one another in an effort to address the same symptoms in a particular case.

There is no requirement that the layers of such a multitiered approach to defense be of the same kind. In fact, in this regard, variety is a valuable commodity. Just as warheads can be knocked off target by projectiles, electronic countermeasures, energy weapons, and command code overrides, offensive or unwanted behavior can be deterred by conveying the understanding that such conduct is unwanted, unwise, unhelpful, futile, or downright dangerous to the actor. Each of these approaches, in turn, involves a very different approach on the part of the defender.

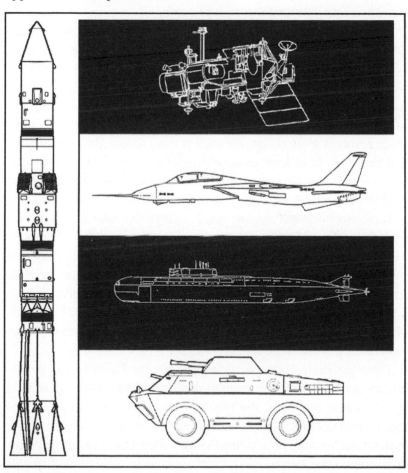

Securing a position in the safest way possible is often a matter of diversification. This concept is well known in the financial arena. The businessman with an iron in many fires can weather an adverse market reaction to any single enterprise. The attorney who is strong in reputation, knowledge, diligence, determination, and advocacy is much harder to defeat than one who possesses strength in only one such area. The soldier who is trained not only with his standard issue assault rifle but also in unarmed combat, edged weapons, small arms, and light artillery is the more formidable adversary. And while it is often said, "Beware the man of one book," for his knowledge in this specific arena is likely to be profound, in the long run, the man who is truly armed at all points presents the harder target.

Even when it comes to the art of living, people who enjoy a rewarding occupation, an active social calendar, a happy home life, a number of engaging hobbies, and an interest in new possibilities are much better equipped to face life's pitfalls than those whose existence revolves around just one such pursuit. Losses in one category will be offset, or at least assuaged to some degree, by gains in the others. They also have the distinct advantage of being able to bring their experiences in one sphere to bear on activities in another.

If the warrior waits to react until his base is under attack, it may already be too late to mount an effective defense. If the means employed by the adversary are unanticipated, the defender may find himself without any effective countermeasures. As a result, another important consideration in securing the base is the establishment of a perimeter. In an operational sense, this can be achieved using any of several early warning devices, such as tripwires, motion detectors, or thermal sensors.

From this literal example, analogies can be drawn to less deadly environments. Complex endeavors of all kinds, be it the management of investment portfolios, the administration of organizations, or the maintenance of machinery, benefit from the employment of feedback systems. Monitoring procedures that detect emerging problems before critical mass is achieved can prevent unexpected and unmanageable consequences. Periodic audits may reveal a financial sinkhole, a flawed policy, or an unbalanced mechanism not otherwise detectable to the human eye, long before any real harm has occurred.

More generally, by maintaining a state of constant awareness, the defender may be able to identify potential threats before they are upon him. The military uses scouts and sentries for this purpose. The market uses forecasters. With sufficient practice, there is no reason that the average person cannot perform the same function, albeit at a reduced level of specialization, in his daily life. Making such an effort can be the difference between success and failure in whatever the matter at hand may be and is imperative for any who wish to practice the way of the butterfly.

> *If the blow had landed, would it have injured the Master? Unlikely. He was a man of iron. But that was not the point. The Master was confident not only in his abilities but also in his judgment and in the student. His bases were secure.*

CHOOSE YOUR BATTLES

Now the general who wins a battle makes many calculations in his temple ere the battle is fought. The general who loses a battle makes but few calculations beforehand. Thus do many calculations lead to victory, and few calculations to defeat: how much more no calculation at all. It is by attention to this point that I can foresee who is likely to win or lose.

—Sun Tzu, *The Art of War*

In theory, if we could choose every battle, and do so wisely, we would probably never have to suffer defeat. The wise man would only enter into combat, as Sun Tzu counseled, when he knew that victory was a virtual inevitability. Sadly, this is not always possible. The fight is sometimes thrust on us, and even when it is not, our fallible judgment may inadvertently embroil us in conflicts under less than optimal conditions. Nevertheless, more than any other technique, the exercise of discrimination when deciding *whether* to enter into the fight is one of the best ways to secure victory.

In ancient times, physical battles for survival were more commonplace than they are today. Whether the threat emerged from the ranks of an invading force, the gangs of highwaymen, or the animal kingdom, our ancestors were often required to fight for their lives. Recent generations, by contrast, have only known this level of engagement in time of war or in those rare instances that they have hunted for or been hunted by dangerous criminals.

This does not mean that there are no more battlefields. In addition to the two exceptional circumstances just noted, people still engage in physical altercations with one another from time to time, typically at a somewhat reduced level of intensity. They also combat each other in a variety of nonphysical ways, including argument, debate, campaign, competition, and litigation. If the gridiron is today's battleground, then the boxing ring is the dueling field of honor and the courtroom is the gladiator's arena. Much of the strategy, philosophy, and terminology employed in waging a successful military campaign against an enemy army can in fact be applied to individual contests of this nature, either directly or by analogy.

Begin with the adversary himself. Using the skills discussed in previous sections of this book, what can be discovered just by observation? If he is an athlete or, more dangerous still, a trained fighter, a physical confrontation may not be advisable. If he speaks well, a verbal engagement may prove difficult to win. If he is a man of means, a bidding war is probably not the best course of action. If he is angry, bitter, or closed-minded, a negotiated solution is unlikely to be attainable.

In many cases, the opponent's identity may already be known. If he is a supervisor or superior, a confrontation may come down to the mere pulling of rank, and therefore, it is probably ill advised. If he is a subordinate, engaging in a mutual exchange of hostilities will lower the practitioner to the same level and may begin a quite inconvenient, long-term feud. If he is popular or influential in the community, then whether or not they are visible, his allies stand arrayed behind him for all practical purposes. And if he is a stranger or an unknown quantity, particular care should be taken.

What if anything is known of his reputation? Is he a hothead whose bark is known to be worse than his bite? Is he someone prone to violence, whose movements should be watched closely? Is he an egomaniac to whom every other point of view is the wrong one and with whom all rational debate is futile? Or is he known as a levelheaded and reasonable fellow who is generally well liked by all? In this last instance, the practitioner may sometimes discover that the true enemy lies within.

It is important from both an ethical and a practical standpoint for the warrior to consider the possibility that the fault may lie in himself, particularly if he seems to be beset by enemies on all sides. This is not to imply that the majority is invariably correct; rather that under such circumstances, the weight of the evidence does suggest that they may have a point, and that even if they are in error, the smarter and easier solution may be to consider modifying one's own behavior rather than seeking to change the rest of the world.

Of course, this should never be done at the cost of one's principles, but hearkening back to section 4, there are ways in which subtle modifications can yield a mutually agreeable result without transforming the underlying substance of the matter. For example, the hostile reaction that the statement, "You obviously don't understand," may well engender can be avoided altogether by changing the construction to "I must not be explaining clearly" without significantly altering the fundamental meaning.

As important as paying attention to who is on the other side, and in many ways more so, is giving sufficient consideration to the nature of the contest and the objective at issue, or more broadly, the question of "what." The threshold inquiry must be whether the engagement is defensive or offensive in nature. This is so because in the former case, options are often curtailed significantly. By making the first move, the opponent has already been able to determine such valuable, tactical matters as the type and timing of the attack as well as the territory at issue.

An unprovoked attack must be addressed in some fashion even if the ultimate decision is not to answer it in kind or at all for the time being. A total failure to respond permits the adversary to retain the initiative and may serve to spur him on to even more offensive conduct. A chilling historical example of this imperative is provided by Hitler's statement to the effect that if one French gendarme on a bicycle had challenged his aggressive move into the Rhineland, he would have withdrawn.

The nature of the attack, however, should in no way dictate the response. In fact, exercising some discretion in one's choice of retaliatory action can be a very powerful tactic indeed. It serves to retake the initiative as well as to seize control of the agenda. A prime example of this principle in operation occurred during the Cuban Missile Crisis of 1962 when Soviet leader Nikita Khrushchev ordered the deployment of nuclear ballistic missiles capable of striking American cities at bases in Cuba. Despite considerable urging to strike at these targets in force, American president John Kennedy instead ordered the implementation of a maritime blockade while holding measures that were more drastic in reserve, thereby responding to the threat without escalating it unnecessarily. While Khrushchev was the one who threw the gauntlet, Kennedy chose the dueling instruments.

While this technique of adopting the most measured and reasonable response possible *may* be appropriate under certain circumstances in the military theater, it *must* be the rule in the sphere of self-defense. The burgeoning canon of criminal and civil laws relat-

S-0115
Kennedy, John

Name: John Fitzgerald Kennedy
Profession: Statesman
Birth: 5/29/17 Brookline,
   Massachusetts, U.S.
Affiliation: 35th President of
   United States
Notes: President during the Cuban
   missile crisis . . .

ing to the use of force in self-defense consistently looks to the "reasonable man standard" in determining liability. Many jurisdictions limit the privilege to use lethal force to defend oneself to situations in which the defender is free from fault in provoking or continuing the difficulty and has tried to retreat from the confrontation if at all possible. And every court, whether criminal or civil, limits the use of force to that which appears reasonably necessary to counter the force of the attack.

Under other circumstances, the rule of reasonability may be inapplicable. The nation responding to a terrorist threat and the parent reacting to the dangerous conduct of a willful child may choose to do so with a massive show of force to deter any such actions in no uncertain terms. The corporate competitor may need to counter the unfair trading practices of the adversary by seeking immediate injunctive relief in a court of law if it is to weather the financial consequences. And the attorney or the espionage agent may have no choice but to respond to an aggressive move with an equal and opposite reaction so as to maintain the fragile balance of power. But common to all these scenarios is the tacit acknowledgment that the attack has found its mark.

At this point the concept of making a conscious decision to do nothing, at least for the time being, must be revisited. Under certain very special circumstances, the acknowledgment of an attack without any other overt response may prove to be the best course of all. This is so, for example, when the defender is secure in his position to such a degree that he can afford to be generous, at least once. The martial arts expert who turns the other cheek[1] or the police officer who overlooks a minor infraction both send a message to the actor that he is being given one more chance and would be well advised to take advantage of it. It should be kept in mind, however, that such restraint typically has the opposite effect when the failure to act results from fear or lack of ability.

When the warrior is contemplating *making* the attack rather than defending from it, he has at his disposal a wide-open field of possibilities. The nature, location, and timing of this first strike are entirely up to him. But before reaching this point, it is vital to take a moment to consider whether it makes sense from a tactical point of view to initiate hostilities in the first place.

With the notable exception of preemptive strikes, striking without provocation in any forum is rarely the smartest or the most ethical course of action. There might be scenarios in which such conduct is imperative to survival, but broadly speaking, if everyone

---

1. Or as one champion boxer remarked to the little fellow who kept bothering him at the bar, "If you hit me just once, and I find out about it . . ."

respected the guiding principle of nonaggression, there would be no conflict. Even so, there are times when the conduct of another is so deplorable that immediate, aggressive action is required. The short-sightedness of the citizens and governments of many nations that failed to respond to the Nazi menace during World War II simply because aggression had not yet targeted them directly is painfully apparent.

Likewise, the propriety and effectiveness of heading off an attack moments before it is launched must also be borne in mind. This principle is clearly illustrated by the swift victory of the Israeli air force during the Six-Day War in June 1967. In this particular engagement, acting on reliable intelligence that a massive attack was imminent, Israeli fighter pilots destroyed two thirds of the enemy's aircraft before they ever left the ground, thereby helping to conclude hostilities rapidly.

When is the right time to advance? At the time of *your* choosing, for the warrior who allows the enemy's provocation to determine his own timetable has already lost the initiative. An attack should ideally occur when one's own assets are in a state of maximum readiness while those of the enemy are most vulnerable. For this reason many raids are conducted at approximately four o'clock in the morning—the time when most people are fast asleep.

This tactic can be applied in virtually any context. Politicians are most vulnerable in the run-up to an election and most secure in a lame-duck term. Attorneys are at full stretch just prior to a trial but have the luxury of being able to bluff and bluster after the case has been continued. And in the corporate world, pressure mounts before the annual report date and during tax season.

Developing the ability to recognize and manipulate timing is perhaps more important when waging a defensive campaign. The natural inclination may be to respond immediately to an offensive measure, but biding one's time allows for the marshaling of resources and careful consideration of options. A simple example of this technique in the laboratory of everyday life may be found in telephone procedure. Those who answer calls immediately, especially without the ability to identify callers in advance, run this risk of being caught by surprise. They may not have the necessary tools and information at their disposal, or they might not have even considered the subject that the caller wants to discuss. This is especially true of those who are burdened with cellular telephones.

The person making or returning the call, on the other hand, has the luxury of doing so when conditions are at their most favorable. He can choose a quiet time, devoid of distractions. He can equip himself with the requisite information and materials. He can consider the issue in advance and prepare a list of questions or answers. And he can ensure that he is not out of breath, preoccupied, or in need of a bathroom.

Similarly, when circumstances afford a choice, deciding where an engagement should take place can be a critical factor in the eventual outcome. Everyone understands the concept of the home-field advantage; the familiarity and support implicit in such situations can often be decisive. The candidate for political office is likely to have significant connections and contacts in his hometown, district, or state. The resident lawyer is more likely to be familiar with the county judge's personality and the local rules of court. And the soldier knows the terrain of his home base in the same way that the street cop knows his beat.

In warfare, as illustrated by such historical examples as the twentieth-century conflicts in Vietnam, Korea, and Afghanistan, a small indigenous force can clearly exploit its knowledge of the terrain and location so as to confound a much larger and better-equipped adversary effectively. In much the same way, a skilled woodsman can virtually disappear into the bush and evade capture or detection by even the most sophisticated modern technologies. And even such geographic variables as temperature and altitude can have a significant impact on the performance of any operation.

Selecting the theater of engagement is not necessarily just a matter of geography. It also encompasses the decision to fight on metaphorically familiar ground. While the civil attorney may not be properly equipped to defend a client in a homicide prosecution, he may be the ideal representative in a wrongful death suit. Also, the tech stock guru may be useless when it comes to managing institutional fund portfolios; the police department's most favored forensic psychiatrist might not have the first idea of how to deal with a juvenile delinquent; and the rapid reaction element of a Special Forces command is not the right choice for waging a sustained ground war.

Even when the practitioner is capable of performing in several different areas, the best results are often achieved by focusing on areas of specialized expertise. If dissatisfied with a particular circumstance, the negotiator should debate the matter, the leader can mobilize a wave of opposition, the manipulator might try to effect change from within, and the fighter will perhaps be the only one to mount a full frontal assault. The lesson here is, play to your strengths.

Where strategy begins to border on philosophy is in the realm of "why." Before embarking on any campaign, the practitioner of the art of the butterfly will ask himself why he is doing so. This is a subtly different question from the one posed earlier in the context of whether it makes sense to launch an attack. The warrior will first identify the triggering event. Has there been a direct and obvious attack, or has there been a potentially threatening move? Is the threat a real and significant one, or might it be illusory or insubstantial? Does the matter even rise to the level that a response is warranted? If so, where does the real battleground lie?

Everyone recognizes that the bickering of couples is rarely about whether the top is left off the toothpaste. The substitution of less weighty issues in an argument can sometimes even be a helpful way of relieving stress. But in order to manage such situations effectively, it is important to recognize that the ostensible point of contention is merely a surrogate for a deeper issue or is, at a minimum, just the tip of the iceberg.

For the attorney, a client's desire to sue may simply be the manifestation of the pain of a loss he has experienced and one for which no amount of money can provide compensation. For the captain of industry, the drive to acquire ever more obscene amounts of capital is likely motivated by a deeper need that such pursuits will never satisfy. And in the cutthroat realm of office politics, competition for a corner office is rarely about the view. In the process of conducting such probing analyses, remember to focus the inquiry on one's own motivations from time to time.

In the scenarios just outlined, addressing the superficial concerns may bring a measure of temporary relief in the same way that medication can dull the symptoms of disease for a time, but no real satisfaction can be had until a more invasive or aggressive type of therapy is pursued. In the previous examples, the lawyer may want to suggest counseling to his insistent client or even a cooling-off period; the financial advisor might suggest that the corporate raider considers donating some of his time, energy, or resources to a charitable organization; and the employee who feels that worth is measured by such collateral matters as office placement might simply address the issue with his superiors directly.

Prior to becoming party to a conflict, it is also important to ask oneself if there is any real benefit to be had even if victory is achieved. In short, is it really worth it? The opponent, the disagreement, or the prize may be so petty that there is simply no percentage in compet-

> *Methinks I could not die any where so contented as in the king's company; his cause being just and his quarrel honourable . . .*
>
> *But if the cause be not good, the king himself hath a heavy reckoning to make, when all those legs and arms and heads, chopped off in battle, shall join together at the latter day and cry all "We died at such a place" . . .*
>
> —Henry V, act 4, scene 1

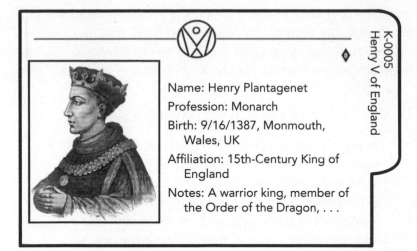

Name: Henry Plantagenet
Profession: Monarch
Birth: 9/16/1387, Monmouth,
    Wales, UK
Affiliation: 15th-Century King of
    England
Notes: A warrior king, member of
    the Order of the Dragon, . . .

K-0005
Henry V of England

ing for it, or as one clever commentator put it, "Even when you win the rat race, you're still a rat." There are certain arguments—squabbling over bequests, rehashing ancient grievances, or trying to assign blame for past misfortunes—the very pursuit of which debases the participants and lowers the tone of the company in which they take place as a whole.

Related to this is the calculus of right and wrong. There is rarely room for such absolute concepts in the realm of the butterfly, but this is one exception. Granted, opinions and interpretations vary as to where the line of demarcation lies, but what is critical is that the warrior strives to champion the side of right as he sees it. The man who

Why did the Master choose this student, this approach, this moment? It was the end of their time together, of course, and there was little left to teach or time to teach it. The students had absorbed as much of his art as they were able. And, perhaps, the final lesson—the most important for one for all of them—was that sometimes the right decision is not to strike.

truly believes that right is on his side will invariably fight more powerfully; his strength will be renewed by his faith, and his determination will be fueled by his spirit. And if he has truly followed his heart in battle, even in those rare instances where he may lose, he *still* wins.

DO YOUR HOMEWORK

As regards action, [the Prince] ought above all things to keep his men well organized and drilled, to follow incessantly the chase, by which he accustoms his body to hardships, and learns something of the nature of localities, and gets to find out how the mountains rise, how the valleys open out, how the plains lie, and to understand the nature of rivers and marshes, and in all this to take the greatest care. Which knowledge is useful in two ways. Firstly, he learns to know his country, and is better able to undertake its defense; afterwards, by means of the knowledge and observation of that locality, he understands with ease any other which it may be necessary for him to study hereafter; because the hills, valleys, and plains, and rivers and marshes that are, for instance, in Tuscany, have a certain resemblance to those of other countries, so that with a knowledge of the aspect of one country one can easily arrive at a knowledge of others. And the prince that lacks this skill lacks the essential which it is desirable that a captain should possess, for it teaches him to surprise his enemy, to select quarters, to lead armies, to array the battle, to besiege towns to advantage.

—Niccolò Machiavelli, *The Prince*

In examining the scene of a tragic firefight between armed felons and rookie officers, investigators were at first puzzled and then troubled by the discovery of brass casings in the pockets of their fallen comrades. Why in the heat of a gun battle had these officers taken the time to pocket the spent casings, an additional step in the process of reloading their revolvers that might very well have been responsible for their deaths? The answer was frighteningly simple: this is the way they had been trained at the academy.

The importance of proper preparation in the quest for a measure of invincibility cannot be overestimated, but as this tragic example illustrates, that training must be consistent with the actual challenges to be faced. It is not enough simply to develop a general understanding of the way in which a specific task should be performed, nor are occasional simulations under controlled circumstances sufficient. In the heat of the moment and subject to any number of unanticipated variables, the superficial layers of understanding are stripped away, forcing the warrior to rely on teachings that have been thoroughly absorbed, internalized, and imprinted on muscle memory.

When encountering gunfire or the detonation of explosives for the first time, many people close their eyes and shrink from the source. New students in the arena of unarmed combat tend to turn away from the attack. Turbulence can disorient a student pilot to the degree that he loses faith in his instruments. In such situations, the body's instinctive reaction is of no help, and for the police officer, the soldier, and the pilot, these natural tendencies can be fatal.

The warrior must therefore learn to override or, more accurately, train out such unhelpful behaviors without neglecting the value of the underlying motivation. The weapons expert can distinguish between the backfire of a car and small arms fire, fireworks and munitions, and artillery and construction blasting and can gauge his safety relative to their position in an instant. If he determines that his location is secure, he can gather further information about the source of the explosion, including direction, distance, and line of fire. Similarly, trained fighters quickly discover how to cover their vital areas while keeping the opponent in sight, and veteran pilots have learned by experience and anecdote to trust their instruments at all times.

The danger of training that fails to simulate real-world conditions adequately is apparent. Tactical teams that are not able to conduct live fire exercises because of budgetary constraints will find that the situation changes significantly when real bullets are flying. Fighters who spar for points have an alarming tendency to continue to pull their techniques out of habit when actual contact is required. And practicing the delivery of lectures and arguments to an empty room wholly fails to prepare the speaker for the challenge of presenting these same matters to an audience.

The art of preparedness requires constant attention. By the time the threat has actually appeared, it is often too late to draw on this account. The amount of repetition required to develop sufficient expertise takes time, and there are no shortcuts to the destination. This is not to suggest that the practitioner must devote himself singlemindedly to honing his skills; such a level of intensity can rarely be maintained over the long term, and even if it could, at what cost? Rather, a nexus must be developed between training and everyday activity. As the legendary master-swordsman Miyamoto Musashi ex-

Name: Miyamoto Musashi　宮本武蔵
Profession: Soldier, Strategist
Birth: 6/13/1584, Harima Province, Japan
Affiliation: Daimyo Hosokawa Tadatoshi
Notes: Master swordsman, fought in Battle of Sekigahara; Author of *Heiho Sanjugo* and *Go Rin No Sho*; fought over sixty duels, including duel with Sasaki Kojiro; had several disciples . . .

C-0093
Musashi, Miyamoto

plains in his *Book of Five Rings*, the combat walk must become the everyday walk, and vice versa.

Given the power of perception discussed in the preceding, there is an additional advantage to continuous preparation. Such measures rarely go unnoticed by others, and as a result, they contribute to the formation of one's reputation. An attacker is less likely to initiate a confrontation with one he knows to be a trained fighter. A company that is reputed to enjoy proactive and attentive management presents a far less attractive target to a corporate raider. And the mere fact that a tactical team's reputation is known to the enemy can have a powerful effect on the nature and outcome of the engagement.

But simply preparing oneself is not enough. While taking care to monitor his own progress, the enlightened warrior will keep his other eye on the horizon. As has already been discussed at length, there are many signs of an impending attack: changes in the natural rhythm or pattern, behavioral cues, and physical clues. While attention to these subtleties may not provide a complete picture of the emerging threat from the outset, they can assist in the process of pinning it down and making specific preparations in that regard.

For example, the scattering of woodland creatures indicates that something is coming, even though the precise nature of what is not yet known. If a swaying of the treetops follows this, it suggests the approach of something large on the ground. If on the other hand, it is accompanied by a whiff of smoke, the cause may more likely be a fast-moving fire. The rumble of a diesel engine next would serve to confirm the former supposition, whereas the crackle of burning wood and a glow on the horizon would be more consistent with the latter. At each step in this progression, the observant person has a better idea of how best to prepare to meet the imminent threat.

The signs are often not as obvious as these. Depending on the situation, a greater degree of observation and analysis may be required. In the realms of politics and finance, for example, the systems at issue are so complex that everything from weather patterns to emerging technologies can have a significant impact on their evolution. As a result, there may be many false positives—misinterpreted signals or signs of emerging trends that never in fact materialize. But the cost of taking the time to pay attention to such possibilities is inconsequential when compared to the benefit of having advanced warning when a true threat emerges.

Moving from the realms of the possible to the probable, many aspects of any given endeavor are ascertainable in advance. A chess match will require an open move, an endgame, and a number of gambits in between. A trial will involve presenting an opening, an examination and cross-examination of witnesses, and a summation and arguments over the admissibility of certain pieces of evidence. Managing a portfolio will require buying and selling assets, recognizing and compensating for trends in the market, and addressing the tax consequences of the particular investment strategy.

From such known quantities, the practitioner can then anticipate a limited number of possible scenarios, thereby allowing him to concentrate his attention and energies in these specific areas. It helps him narrow things down. He may, of course, find that he is mistaken and should not cling rigidly to the tactics he has planned to rely on in the face of overwhelming evidence that they are no longer viable, but anticipation is nevertheless a useful tool in the process of preparation.

Once the nature of the threat or challenge becomes apparent, the practitioner is no longer limited to speculation. He has a clear target at which to aim. It is now time to apply the skills discussed in previous sections to learn everything possible about the object of his attention. Intelligence gathering in its many forms can provide a tremendous amount of insight into one's target. Careful analysis may open a window into his mind. And attention to surrounding circumstances will provide some idea of how the environment will affect the eventual engagement.

The principle difference between the analytical and the operational aspects of the butterfly arts is that the former involve gathering information generally, to be filed away for future use, whereas the latter aim to identify specific weaknesses and possible points of entry that can be exploited in an imminent or current engagement. By keeping track of a company whose stock comprises a significant portion of his portfolio, the financier can remain abreast of issues relevant to the health of his overall portfolio. Should the situation change and should this same company become a target for a potential hostile takeover, his inquiry will shift to focusing on specific areas of potential vulnerability such as capitalization and voting bylaws.

As the situation unfolds, the greatest danger may not always be the opponent; it may be the environment in which the battle takes place. But fortunately, such an adversary can often be made into a powerful ally with sufficient preparation. The rules of legal procedure can be powerful weapons or significant liabilities to the trial lawyer, depending on his knowledge of them. Inclement weather and adverse conditions can help the soldier, at least in a relative sense, if he has anticipated and prepared for them and his opponent has not. And the covert operative's level of familiarity with the details of his cover can either conceal or betray his true identity.

Sun Tzu counsels that the wise strategist should know not only the enemy but also himself. This idea has already been touched on in the context of developing an appreciation of one's own abilities and weaknesses so as to be able to play to strength. But such introspection also provides the clearest guidance in determining where the need for additional preparation is most pronounced. The tremendous criminal investigator whose cases are routinely thrown out of court for failure to abide by rules of procedure should spend more time in the library than on the firing range. The brilliant legal orator whose exhibits are nevertheless often denied admission by the presiding judge should be studying the rules of evidence rather than the art of public speaking. And the scientist whose theories dominate the journals of the day but has trouble talking about his findings with others should perhaps spend more time on his feet than at his keyboard.

There is a difference between preparation, at least as the term is used in this context, and rehearsal. While preparation embraces such general activities as training and research, rehearsal speaks to the use of practice runs for specific operations. In some circles, such run-throughs may involve elaborate mock-ups of the target and even the use of "extras" to make the scenario more realistic. This is the case, for example, in counterterrorist training exercises and emergency services preparedness drills. These operations often involve the use of appropriate buildings and vehicles or may even call for the creation of purpose-built replicas. During the height of the Cold War, the superpowers even went so far as to create entire towns in isolated areas designed to simulate those of the adversary in excruciating detail, for just such training purposes.

Broadly speaking, hands-on training is better suited to physical objectives, whereas mental analysis is more appropriate for intellectual challenges, but this is not always the case. Lives may be saved or lost depending on the amount of thinking that has gone into crafting the operational plan. Conversely, clinical studies suggest that the process of repeatedly imagining the performance of a particular action can have an impact on the subject's real-world abilities in that regard. In one such study, for example, shooting accuracy on the basketball court was increased significantly merely by thinking about it. In addressing matters that are governed more by the cerebral than the physical, the process of turning the matter over and over again in one's head may also reveal potential alternatives and hitherto undiscovered problems.

METHOD OF PRACTICE	IMPROVEMENT
None for 30 days	0%
One actual hour per day for 30 days	24%
One hour of mental rehearsal per day for 30 days	23%

In many walks of life, there are virtuosos who are able to perform at the highest levels of their respective professions seemingly by instinct. But the naturally gifted musician who does not need sheet music, the child prodigy who can compute to several decimal places without the aid of a calculator, and the student with the photographic memory are all exceptions to the rule. The rest of humanity needs to prepare for such challenges, and among the more important aspects of the process is the development of a plan.

There is a certain appeal to the unscripted speech, the accidental discovery, and the off-the-cuff remark, but more often than not, such spontaneous events depend on, or at least proceed from, the general exercise of due diligence. The presenter with a genuine interest and a firm base of knowledge in his subject is far better equipped to speak on the matter impromptu. The thorough researcher will find that his careful labors place him in the right position for providence to lend a helping hand. It is said that Winston Churchill spent many hours in his bathtub crafting the "spontaneous" quips for which he was so well known.

Planning, even in broad strokes, serves to move much of the time-consuming business of analysis to an earlier and somewhat less pressurized position in the process. If it can shave even a few moments off the time it takes the warrior to act or react to emerging situations, it may make the difference between success and failure. And even when circumstances conspire to make the execution of a given plan unworkable, the fact of having given the matter prior consideration at least serves to establish the right state of mind and may also expedite matters by ruling out nonviable options.

There is such a thing as too much planning. No amount of preparation is sufficient to allow the actor to disengage his critical faculties and react by the book. Those who wed themselves to the plan or whose lack of confidence or creativity leads them to follow the written directive in an unquestioning fashion, even when its futility becomes apparent, are prime targets for the practitioner of the butterfly art.

The recipe for conducting a thorough examination of an adverse witness in a court of law, for example, requires the employment of both prepared questions and "opportunity cross." It is quite simply impossible to anticipate every twist and turn in the testimony and to script an appropriate reaction at each stage. Even if this were possible, the opportunity cost of doing so in terms of time and attention far outweighs the likely benefit. Similarly, no matter how many steps ahead of the current position the chess master is able to envisage, there will come a limit, a kind of intellectual terminal velocity, based in part on mental capacity and in part on the logic of diminishing marginal returns.

As in the game of chess, a single plan is rarely enough. Options evolve at an exponential rate, and the likelihood that surrounding circumstances will trace the contours of any one forecast accurately is minimal. Likewise, every plan, by its very nature, forecloses other options. Thus, having a backup or contingency plan is essential to success, and if this seems like a lot of work, it is. It can consume significant quantities of time and energy, but it is the cost of safeguarding victory.

> *How had he known that he could count on the student—this particular student—not to strike, because he knew the man's character? While he often affected a kind of aloofness, the Master never failed to call a student by his name and often gave individualized advice that drew on some aspect of the student's particular background. In short, he knew his stuff.*

FIGHT SMART

When you engage in actual fighting, if victory is long in coming, then men's weapons will grow dull and their ardor will be damped. If you lay siege to a town, you will exhaust your strength. Again, if the campaign is protracted, the resources of the State will not be equal to the strain. Now, when your weapons are dulled, your ardor damped, your strength exhausted and your treasure spent, other chieftains will spring up to take advantage of your extremity. Then no man, however wise, will be able to avert the consequences that must ensue. Thus, though we have heard of stupid haste in war, cleverness has never been seen associated with long delays. . . . It is the rule in war, if our forces are ten to the enemy's one, to surround him; if five to one, to attack him; if twice as numerous, to divide our army into two. If equally matched, we can offer battle; if slightly inferior in numbers, we can avoid the enemy; if quite unequal in every way, we can flee from him. Hence, though an obstinate fight may be made by a small force, in the end it must be captured by the larger force.

—Sun Tzu, *The Art of War*

At last we have arrived at the very heart of the matter. We have worked our way around the periphery in an ever-decreasing spiral rather than charging at the target. We have done so under a cloak of anonymity and invisibility. Throughout we have learned our lessons well, gathering information about the target, analyzing the developing situation, and exerting subtle influence along the way. Unless all of this has simply been an idle pastime or an amusing parlor trick, then the gauntlet is thrown and the battle joined. Now is the time when the elements of the art converge and the faculty is assembled. Now is the time for action. But in the vernacular of the sweet science, it is of paramount importance to "box clever."

Strategy is defined as follows: "The science and art of using all the forces of a nation to execute approved plans as effectively as possible during peace or war." Derived from the ancient Greek word *strategos* meaning "general," this ability is vital to the enlightened commander and lies at the very heart of the art of the butterfly. Employed correctly, it can allow an objectively inferior force to prevail over a far more heavily equipped enemy and permit victory to be snatched from the jaws of what appears to be inevitable defeat.

Every strategy embraces a number of tactics, employed singly or in combination with one another. Each tactic in turn depends on the execution of specific techniques. Given the sheer quantity of possible approaches to almost any objective, the number of potential permutations and combinations is infinite. There is, of course, no single approach, no formulaic strategy that can guarantee victory at all times and in all places. There are, however, certain attributes common to the waging of a successful campaign that will prove valuable no matter what type of adversary the warrior encounters.

The first of these is strength. There are times when a show of massive force will serve to deter an attack or, at least, sap the resolve of the attacker. This objective is, of course, easier to achieve when the warrior has superior numbers at his disposal, but even when this is not the case, a show of strength is still an important and viable approach. In this latter circumstance, such a display may require the concentration of lesser forces so as to overwhelm one small part of a numerically superior adversary. It may also take the form of strength of resolve, a characteristic perhaps more commonly observed in the underdog. Finally, if the warrior has insufficient strength when acting alone, he may always consider the value of forging alliances to achieve this same effect.

Another powerful tool in the execution of strategy is speed. The

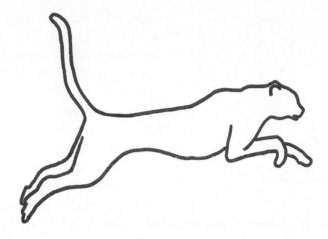

strongest attack is useless if the target has moved by the time the blow has landed. Being able to act with blinding speed provides a tremendous advantage in virtually any endeavor. It makes possible the elimination of threats of all sorts before significant damage has been done and generates a momentum that is hard to overcome. On the individual level, reaction time is largely a physiological matter determined by the so-called "fast-twitch" muscles, but a degree of additional speed can be achieved by rigorous training. When dealing with groups, however, speed is a function of organization and preparation; areas that can always be improved with a little effort.

As important to eventual victory as strength and speed is the ability to bring force to bear with precision. A diamond, the hardest naturally occurring substance known to mankind, can be cracked with the tap of the jeweler's hammer. And a gymnasium full of dominoes or a house of cards can be toppled by the slightest breath of air. Because tremendous resources are available to combat an attack does not necessarily mean that they should be deployed automatically. Better and more expeditious routes to the same destination can often be found. Not only does this approach ensure that reserves remain plentiful, but it is also a far more elegant way in which to conduct one's business. The achievement of spectacular

results with minimal effort is, in fact, the hallmark of the practitioner of the art of the butterfly.

In such matters, it is vitally important to manage the interplay among competing objectives as well as to administer the resources with which they are to be achieved efficiently. This is a matter of balance. However powerful, rapid, and precise a single operation may be, it is rarely carried out in a vacuum. There are typically a variety of competing considerations to be accounted for, and the status quo can change between two heartbeats. The best strategy, therefore, involves the careful and creative allocation of assets among multiple objectives.

There is also a balance to be struck in determining the optimal number of initiatives to undertake at a given time. By waging a campaign on several fronts, the chances of victory can be increased significantly, but resources must be stretched accordingly. This attack can be broadened by increasing the size of the team or simply the scope of the enterprise. And if it is impossible or otherwise unworkable to bring multiple assets to bear on the target at the same time, a similar statistical improvement in results may be achieved by making repeated attempts over time.

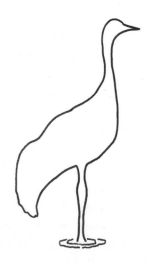

Paramount among the characteristics of a sound strategy is the acquisition and application of intelligence. The warrior must think. When commanding a group of people, whether it is a platoon, an office, or a group of volunteers, one should en-

sure that there is an intelligent division of labor and that
specific assignments are appropriate to individual skills.
Musashi likens the making of
such determinations to a master carpenter selecting pieces
of wood in the construction
of a building. Even when the
strategy in question is to be
implemented by a single person, the same organizational

imperatives apply, except that they relate to the management of the
practitioner's own time and abilities.

What particular strategy he ultimately selects depends on the
type of engagement, the character of the enemy, the nature of the
surroundings, and many other factors besides. These will of course
vary by profession and endeavor. For the law enforcement professional investigating corrupt organizations, for instance, there is an
ongoing, evaluative process intended to determine whether conditions are right and evidence sufficient for a judicially sanctioned
search and seizure or whether a more covert offensive supported by
electronic eavesdropping devices and surveillance equipment is required. The tactical imperatives of these differing strategies vary
greatly. Under the former approach, a show of force coupled with
the element of surprise may be necessary to guarantee officer safety.
The latter mission, by contrast, calls for the most discreet and low
key of operations.

In the world of the intelligence analyst, the nightmare scenario is
that weapons of mass destruction, including radiological, chemical,
biological, and nuclear materials will find their way into the hands
of terrorists. When such concerns arise within the jurisdiction of allied nations, the best approach has often been to report the matter
through diplomatic channels, secure in the knowledge that no re-

sponsible members of the international community would tolerate a threat of this nature on their own soil. When the materials are being stored on hostile ground, however, more drastic, unconventional, and unilateral measures may be required.

In courts of law around the world, strategic decisions are made and implemented on a daily basis. Some attorneys delay plea negotiations until the eleventh hour in the hope of securing the last, best offer. Others manufacture interminable delays, hoping that the prosecution will wither on the vine. In trial, elaborate measures are taken to distract the fact finder from the obvious weakness in a given version of events or line of argument or to minimize the impact of potentially harmful evidence. On rare occasions, even when confronted with no reasonable prospect of success, as in the defense of a strong death penalty case, sound strategy may require fighting to the bitter end.

For the psychologist, and indeed physicians of all kinds, the enemy is disease, in any of its mental or physical incarnations. Some conditions are well understood, and reliable treatments are taught in medical school and documented in the literature of the professional. Here, the doctor's course is clear. But the more difficult strategic decisions occur when the effects of treatment may be as bad as the symptoms of the disease itself. Should the psychiatrist force open doors that the mind has locked to defend itself? Should the surgeon operate when the possibility of complications is on par with the chances of success? In some cases at least, the best strategy for the patient may be to do nothing at all.

In the financial world, as recent scandals and recessions have made painfully clear, there are no sure things. The supposed security of managed mutual funds has been shattered by reckless and willful misconduct on the part of trusted fiduciaries. The business cycle has become ever more mercurial, and even the safety of such hitherto rock-solid investments as indexed portfolios, government bonds, and FDIC-insured accounts has come under fire. As a result, investment strategies have shifted toward a more conservative ap-

proach, both in terms of holdings
and promised results. And in an effort to guard against future misun-
derstandings, individual investors
are demanding to know more about
the strategies employed by their
brokers.

Of all the historical examples
available to the practitioner of the
butterfly arts, however, one emerges
as preeminent. This is so, because, more than any other single
event, it represents the fusion of virtually every aspect of this discipline. It was an operation of unprecedented strategic importance. It
involved combatants of vastly disproportionate strength as well as
diametrically opposed ideology. It required the cooperation of the
law enforcement professional, the covert operative, the analyst, the
strategist, and the warrior. It employed, and indeed, depended on,
the arts of invisibility, mind reading, prognostication, and behavior
control. And ultimately, it culminated in a victory that came as close
to a demonstration of invincibility as has ever been seen.

The year was 1943. For four years, the armies of Nazi Germany
had swept across Europe like a plague, laying waste to everything in
their path. Great Britain alone remained. The Axis powers had tried
to reach out across the English Channel several times in order to
capture this last Allied stronghold in Europe. Each attempt had
failed, but at significant cost to the defenders. England's closest allies, the United States and Canada, were three thousand miles away
across the dangerous waters of the Atlantic. Yet for an Allied victory
to occur, not only would the tiny island have to hold fast against the
combined might of the enemy forces in Europe, but she would have
to recapture that lost territory.

The most direct approach to the European mainland led to the
coastline of France. At that time, the Nazis had sixty divisions of
troops stationed in this country as well as six divisions of Panzer

tanks. Estimates place the number of available German soldiers somewhere between six and nine hundred thousand. Furthermore, under the command of famed German field marshall Erwin Rommel, the French coastline had been heavily fortified with concrete bunkers, obstacles, gun turrets, and over six million mines. Launching any direct attack against such a formidable adversary seemed suicidal.

Faced with these seemingly insurmountable odds, Prime Minister Winston Churchill devised a policy that was to guide virtually every aspect of the yearlong preparations for the inevitable invasion of France that was code-named Operation *Overlord*. "In wartime, truth is so precious," he said, "that she should always be attended by a bodyguard of lies." Thus, Operation *Bodyguard*, arguably the greatest deception and manipulation in the history of armed conflict, was conceived.

Bodyguard was composed of six major initiatives, and thirty-six suboperations. The first step for Allied strategists was to study past invasions, including the successes of Operation *Torch* in North Africa and Operation *Husky* in Sicily; the problems encountered at Anzio and Salerno; and the disastrous landing in Dieppe, in order to determine the best course of action. The forecasts of the analysts quickly confirmed that unless a substantial portion of the German defensive forces could be diverted from the beachhead, the landing force would not stand a chance.

The shortest distance between the two nations was the twenty-two-mile stretch of water that separated Dover from the highly accessible beaches of the Pas de Calais. By employing both their powers of deduction and intercepted enemy intelligence reports, Allied Command was able to look into the minds of the adversary and determine that this is precisely where the attack was expected to take place. With this in mind, the somewhat less obvious target of Normandy was chosen as *Overlord*'s true objective.

Fortunately for the British, in the early years of the war, domestic law enforcement had been extremely successful at identifying and turning agents of the Axis powers residing in England. Under threat of prosecution or exposure, this network of double agents embarked on a massive campaign of disinformation, confirming in the minds of their German masters the false location of the invasion forces. In so doing, they divided the story up into pieces so as to compartmentalize the process as well as to ensure that the intelligence did not appear to have been procured too easily. One particular double agent, code-named *Garbo*, even received the Iron Cross from Hitler for his services in this regard.

It was critical to Allied strategists that German attention should be drawn away from the intended target and that no hint of the actual destination should be revealed. They therefore had to make thousands of landing craft and hundreds of thousands of troops massing in southern England simply vanish. In order to achieve this effect, two major and complementary operations were commenced. By employing elaborate camouflage, concealment and deception (CCD) measures and maintaining strict operational discipline at the invasion force's true location as well as duplicating the lighting schemes of entire ports and portions of coastline at other locations, the British made entire divisions disappear.

Meanwhile, Operation *Fortitude* was intended to distract enemy attention from the real base of operations by creating "phantom forces" in Scotland, Kent, and elsewhere. So as to economize, fake tanks and watercraft were constructed of canvas and rubber, and sophisticated techniques were used to allow a small number of operatives to simulate the radio traffic and other signs of massive troop deployments. The Firth of Forth was filled with mock vessels, and deliberately readable signals intelligence was broadcast regarding an imminent invasion of Norway. Likewise Operation *Zeppelin* created the impression that a similar attack on the Balkans was imminent. Finally, an entire fake invasion army, known as "FUSAG," was placed under the command of American general George Patton. The use of Patton in this capacity was a particularly effective psychological component of the operation because Hitler and the High Command believed him to be the most "German" and, therefore, most valuable Allied commander.

As D-Day grew closer, intelligence reports from operatives in occupied Europe continued to confirm that the Nazis were expecting invasions at locations other than Normandy. More directed preparations began in earnest. Advanced reconnaissance forces crept ashore at Normandy to verify conditions and rehearse the landing. Research on this location was stepped up and even involved the solicitation of postcards and holiday pictures from any in the general public who might have vacationed there before the war. Special, purpose-built machines, such as flail tanks intended to clear minefields, were developed by Allied scientists and mechanics.

Bodyguard operations were executed in minute detail. Such collateral deceptions as false newspaper reports, artificial control over stock market levels, and staged diplomatic negotiations contributed to the illusion. The effect on the behavior of the German commanders was tremendous. Nineteen divisions were ordered to the Pas de Calais. Eighteen were stationed in Scandinavia to meet the anticipated attack on Norway. Only half of the available Panzers were placed under Rommel's command, with the rest held in reserve and their commanders ordered not to move without Hitler's express approval. The stage was set.

Notwithstanding the might of the combatants, the engagement was still subject to the vagaries of the weather. Initially slated for May 1944, the invasion had to be postponed because of bad weather. When June arrived, conditions had not improved significantly. Then, analysts spotted a potential break in the weather on June 5, a time when tides would also be low, exposing German landing obstacles, and when the long nights would assist the paratroopers in making their aerial landings. More bad weather on the fifth delayed departure again. Even at this late date, records reveal that the German High Command remained oblivious to the threat. At 4 A.M. on June 6, the word was given.

In order to maintain the illusion, the famous "Dambuster" squadron of Lancaster bombers flew away from Normandy toward the Pas de Calais, dropping window[2] in complex patterns so as to fool German radar installations into believing that a fleet was sailing north toward the expected target. Meanwhile, the Royal Navy sailed to Normandy towing radar-reflected balloons that rendered them virtually invisible. Dummy paratroops were also dropped at locations far removed from the landing zones. Together with a small contingent of Special Air Service (SAS) soldiers equipped with sound-making devices, this ruse served to spread German defensive forces even thinner.

So successful was this grand strategy that 176,000 Allied soldiers were able to establish the now celebrated beachheads code-named: *Utah, Omaha, Gold, Juno,* and *Sword.* Even during the attack, the deception remained intact, and Hitler refused to divert reinforcements to Normandy, secure in the knowledge that the phantom armies would soon be arriving elsewhere. Amazingly, a communiqué intercepted five weeks after the invasion indicated that the German High Command still had not realized that it had been duped. Such is the power of the butterfly.

Had the Master misjudged and the student actually struck, could he have countered, even with his guard down? Probably. Experience had shown him to be the wisest of strategists, a magician who always had something up his sleeve.

---

2. As discussed in section 1, window refers to tiny pieces of tinfoil dropped from aircraft so as to create the appearance of a cluster of secondary targets on radar screens or to swamp the screen with multiple returns.

BE RIGHT

Coming now to the other qualities mentioned above, I say
that every prince ought to desire to be considered clement
and not cruel. [H]e ought to take care not to misuse
this clemency . . . with a few examples he will be more
merciful than those who, through too much mercy,
allow disorders to arise, from which follow murders or
robberies . . . Nevertheless he ought to be slow to believe
and to act, nor should he himself show fear, but proceed
in a temperate manner with prudence and humanity, so
that too much confidence may not make him incautious
and too much distrust render him intolerable.

—Niccolò Machiavelli, *The Prince*

From equal parts legend and philosophy comes the story of three
brothers trained in the art of healing. So great was the skill of the
youngest that he could be summoned at the last possible moment
and wrest terminally ill patients from the grip of death. As a result,
he was celebrated throughout the world as one of the foremost
physicians of the age. The middle brother was adept at consistently
reversing the course of a potentially fatal disease before it had truly
taken hold of the victim. His name was therefore spoken in the
highest circles, and his treatments sought by ailing people throughout the land.

The eldest, by contrast, had a revolutionary approach to medicine. He lived and worked in a small community in which he had
the opportunity to see those under his care on a daily basis. He was
thus able to detect the onset of disease before it was even apparent
to the patient and to take steps to ensure that the illness was cured
before the symptoms manifested in any obvious fashion. In this
way, he cared for his friends and neighbors for many years, and they
all lived well into a healthy old age. His reputation, therefore, was
known only within the village itself.

The progression presented in this tale illustrates the principle of refinement, the evolutionary process through which an art or science becomes more sophisticated. The instruments and methods of warfare have also been undergoing a process of refinement for thousands of years. From the first copper blade, forged over four millennia ago, to the modern sniper rifle and from the medieval catapult to the smart bomb, the goal has been to increase power, speed, and accuracy, and in this regard, tremendous progress has been made. Likewise, in the evolution of the arts of unarmed combat, mankind has progressed from merely exchanging heavy blows with clenched fists to exploring ever more sophisticated ways of inflicting damage.

Over time, Chinese masters of Kung Fu developed fighting methods that employed sophisticated angles and methods of delivering strikes with hand and foot to defeat larger opponents. Japanese warriors devised systems of combat that exploited principles of balance and points of natural vulnerability to throw and lock their opponents. Okinawan farmers found ways to adapt agricultural tools and indeed their own bodies to combat purposes through intensive training.

As these arts blended and matured over time, the process of refinement continued. The monks at Shaolin developed the ability to harden their bodies and spirits, making themselves much more resistant to attack. The samurai learned to project his opponent's momentum, blending with his attack rather than having to haul him over the shoulder like a sack of potatoes. The farmer conditioned his arms, fists, and mind to the point that he could shatter thick piles of wood or brick with a single blow.

Eventually, perhaps even as a result of some sort of martial cross-pollination, masters in each of these disciplines found ways to wreak havoc on their opponents with the lightest of touches. In China this ability was called *din mak*—the death touch. In Japan and Okinawa, it became known as *kyushojutsu*, a reference to one of the principle places in which this particular skill was developed.

For those who have witnessed or experienced the application of these techniques, their power is as impressive as it is undeniable. But to the strategist, the ability to cause such significant injury with minimal force is only the penultimate evolutionary step. There is another level to be considered. In the progression from much force to moderate to little, the next step must, of course, be none at all. By extrapolation, therefore, the ultimate ability must be to defeat the opponent without direct engagement of any kind.

This idea is hardly a new one. As Sun Tzu counseled almost 2,500 years ago:

> In the practical art of war, the best thing of all is to take the enemy's country whole and intact; to shatter and destroy it is not so good. So, too, it is better to recapture an army entire than to destroy it, to capture a regiment, a detachment or a company entire than to destroy them. Hence to fight and conquer in all your battles is not supreme excellence; supreme excellence consists in breaking the enemy's resistance without fighting.

The master strategist, therefore, is the one who can achieve his goal while avoiding direct confrontation altogether. In so doing, he conceals his intentions, conserves his resources, and maintains his relationships. By employing wise strategy, he stands to gain everything and lose nothing. For these good and sound tactical reasons alone, this is an avenue worth exploring.

But there is another reason that this restrained approach should be given due consideration, especially by any who study or practice the butterfly art. As humanity's technological and tactical abilities grow, it is becoming increasingly clear that our knowledge in the realm of weaponry and warfare threatens to surpass the wisdom with which we govern their employment. In this regard, it is instructive to note that the deadly abilities just described evolved in large part from ancient Eastern healing practices and the philosophy of balance among the elements.

In order for there to be harmony in a system, strength must be tempered by mercy and aggression blended with forbearance. It is

said that the progress of the student through an art will often parallel the evolution of the art itself.
As the practitioner develops newfound abilities and hones them to
an extraordinary level, he should
take care not to employ them
simply because he can. The right
way, on occasion, may be not to
fight at all; the most appropriate
solution: to withdraw. Or in the
words of the Master, "sometimes
the best block is not to be there."

In addition to the positive effect
that balance has on the system as
a whole, be it a courtroom, a community, or a league of nations, this
philosophy of harmony will benefit the practitioner as well. The
person who governs himself with
moderation, refinement, and restraint at all times enjoys a state of
equilibrium that is difficult to upset. Secure in the knowledge that his
cause is just and his judgment wise, he will have an attitude that is
both optimistic and contagious; he will become accomplished at
and accustomed to success; and he will be able to defend his position, when challenged from the moral and ethical high ground. According to some commentators, it is perhaps this last consideration
that contributed most to the invincibility of the Allied forces in the
dark days of World War II.

The soldier who can make his way across hostile territory or the
agent who can accomplish an exfiltration without ever firing a shot;
the police officer whose mere presence in the community prevents
crime; and the attorneys who negotiate a plea that does substantial
justice to all parties—these are the *master strategists*. The financier

who invests wisely and avoids becoming greedy; the psychiatrist whose work with a patient prevents the emergence of acute symptoms, and the parent whose children grow to be good and strong without the need for excessive interference—these are the *true masters of the art of the butterfly.*

He was a remarkable man. Born to a bygone era and forged in the fires of a thousand battles. The world will not see his likes again. Part warrior, part magician, he performed miraculous feats as though they were nothing more than idle curiosities. Perhaps to him they were. But in retrospect, it was not the man's ability so much as his character that had the most profound effect. He shared his art with those he deemed deserving, he lived life by his own code, and he was a servant to no one and no thing. He had right on his side. Before we left, he told us:

> There is another world—a shadow world—that lies just beneath the surface of our own. Men are often not what they seem, nor events as they appear. Believing this is the first step to enlightenment. Learning to peer beneath the surface and to make use of what you find is the next. This is the fifth teaching in the Art of the Butterfly.

Epilogue

Returning to that fateful winter night in 1931, where our inquiry began, Sir Winston Churchill, Britain's prime minister during World War II, did survive the inevitable automobile accident, as one might expect of a man of such cast iron temperament, but he did not do so altogether unscathed. The car that struck him was traveling a little more than thirty miles per hour, and he was dragged for a few yards before being thrown free. He sustained cracked ribs as well as a number of deep lacerations and bruises. Fortunately, his wounds began healing quickly, but as we have come to understand is often the case, the effects of the incident extended well beyond its initial parameters.

Immediately after the accident, Churchill was taken to Lenox Hill Hospital. While there, he contracted pleurisy, which prolonged his convalescence considerably. In time, of course, he recovered from this additional complication as well. Deeper than any of the physical scars he sustained, however, were the psychological effects of the trauma. He experienced severe aftershocks and bouts of depression—dark days visited by what he referred to as "the Black Dog"—long after his bodily symptoms had disappeared. For the first time in many years, he showed no interest in painting. He had difficulty sleeping through the night. Later, he wrote to his doctor about "a great and sudden lack of power of concentration, and a strong sense of being unequal to the task which lay so soon ahead of me."

According to Churchill's wife Clementine, the accident of 1931 was the third in a series of misfortunes from which she feared her husband might never recover, the first of which was the ousting of his party from power in the general election of 1929, and the second of which was the crash of the markets in the same year. Such a triumvirate of troubles might have beaten a lesser man into submission. In the case of Churchill, these blows or, more accurately, the overcoming of them helped to hammer out the heart of a lion.

Perhaps in an effort to cull opportunity from this veritable stampede of adversity, Churchill wrote about the experience for the American papers. His article begins with a reference to a production he had seen some time before in a Paris theater, entitled *At the Telephone*. Knowing full well that his words would be published on front pages across the country, Churchill took the time to describe in paragraph after paragraph the plot of the play in which a hus-

band is called away on business and takes many elaborate measures to protect his wife's safety in his absence. One by one, these precautions collapse, each minor incident affecting another, until at last a complex series of coincidences has rendered the wife utterly defenseless. Clearly, even in 1931, the strange way in which seemingly minor and unrelated occurrences can build momentum until a critical, collective, and decisive velocity is reached was not lost on the great statesman.

The courage, determination, and ingenuity with which Churchill guided Britain through her darkest hours are a matter of record. The question, then, is whether the same result could have been achieved without his leadership. The answer, of course, is a matter of opinion. As previously discussed, some argue that history is driven not by individual personalities but by political and economic forces. Others maintain that one man can make a difference. At least one thing in this regard is clear: in the political climate of 1940s Britain, it was Lord Halifax, and not Winston Churchill, who appeared to be the likely choice to succeed Neville Chamberlain.

Halifax was opposed to the idea of war with Germany, and documentary evidence has subsequently revealed that he had already begun the process of negotiating terms with Hitler in May 1940. Some historians contend that the political tide was turned at the last moment almost entirely by a single, powerful speech delivered by Churchill on May 28, in which he challenged the cabinet, and said "If this long island story of ours is to end at last, let it end only when each of us lies choking in his own blood upon the ground."

Writing many years later about Churchill's role in World War II, Charles Krauthammer remarked, "Churchill was, of course, not sufficient in bringing victory, but he was uniquely necessary." Whether or not this view carries the day, it is a hard heart and a narrow mind indeed that would refuse to acknowledge that things *might* have turned out very differently had the car been going a little faster on that chilly New York night in 1931. And for our purposes, a "maybe" is enough, for we now operate in the realm of the butterfly.[3]

3. Churchill was himself extremely fond of butterflies. It is said that his fascination with the noble insects began while he was a prisoner in South Africa during the Boer War. In 1946, he had a Butterfly House constructed at Chartwell so as to allow the creatures to "liberate" in his garden. Juxtaposed with a portion of his autobiography discussing the effects of great personalities on the course of history, Churchill writes:

> I have always loved butterflies. . . . The butterfly is the Fact—gleaming, fluttering, settling for an instant with wings fully spread to the sun, then vanishing in the shades of the forest. Whether you believe in Free Will or Predestination, all depends on the slanting glimpse you had of the colour of his wings—which are in fact at least two colours at the same time. But I have not quitted and renounced the Mathematik to fall into the Metaphysick. Let us return to the pathway of narrative.